The Harrowing of Hell
DACHAU

The Harrowing of Hell
DACHAU

Marcus J. Smith

State University of New York Press

Originally published as *The Harrowing of Hell: Dachau* © 1972,
The University of New Mexico Press

Published by
State University of New York Press, Albany

© 1995 State University of New York

For information, address State University of New York Press,
State University Plaza, Albany, N.Y., 12246

Production by Marilyn P. Semerad
Marketing by Fran Keneston

Library of Congress Cataloging-in-Publication Data

Smith, Marcus J.
    [Harrowing of hell]
    Dachau : the harrowing of hell / Marcus J. Smith. — [New ed.]
      p.   cm.
    ISBN 0-7914-2525-8. — ISBN 0-7914-2526-6 (pbk.)
      1. Dachau (Germany : Concentration camp)   2. Holocaust, Jewish
  (1939–1945)—Germany.   3. Holocaust survivors—Germany.   4. World
  War, 1939–1945—Health aspects—Germany.   5. World War, 1939–1945—
  Refugees.   6. World War, 1939–1945—Personal narratives, American.
  7. Smith, Marcus J.   I. Title.   II. Title: Harrowing of hell.
  D805.G3S596   1994
  940.53'18'094336—dc20   94-35252
                                                                        CIP

10 9 8 7 6 5 4 3

For Patricia, Frederick, Peter, Andrew, and others of the post-World War II generation in the hope that their knowledge of a police state is gained only from reading.

We lived in this place as prisoners and dead shadows for long years. We had the courage and patience to endure the greatest suffering that human history has ever known. We were submitted to the most cruel tyranny of the world.

But now we are free.

Dr. Ali Kuci, Communiqué No. 20, Dachau, 1945

CONTENTS

Illustrations by Zoran Music, when a prisoner at Dachau, follow page 81

FOREWORD

At the end of April 1944, in Germany, Marcus Smith (then 26 years old) underwent one of the formative experiences of his life. A Lieutenant who had completed medical school and a one-year internship before joining the U.S. Army, Marcus was the sole medical officer attached to a small displaced person (DP) team that was sent to the Dachau concentration camp the day after it was liberated by Allied troops and several days before the shocking conditions of the camp were publicized throughout the world. Until additional Allied units and Red Cross personnel arrived at Dachau a few days later to assist with repatriation, the ten members of the team, with Marcus as the only doctor, were on their own to do what they could for nearly 32,000 starved and seriously ill camp survivors.

In a notebook and in detailed daily letters to his wife, Carol, Marcus recorded what he witnessed, his activities and those of his colleagues, the progress and setbacks in the rehabilitation process, the troubles and joys of the survivors, and his own reactions.

In May 1945, Marcus was awarded the Bronze Star for his work at Dachau; a month later, he was promoted to Captain. His final European assignment was to work with a Russian repatriation center. Marcus then returned to the U.S., completed a residency in radiology, and in 1948 settled in Santa Fe, New Mexico, where he practiced medicine and raised a family. He also served on the editorial board of the *Rocky Mountain Medical Journal* (1959–1981) and its successor, the *Western Journal of Medicine* (1981–1984); wrote *Error and Variation in Diagnostic Radiology* (published by Charles C. Thomas in 1967), researched and wrote about the history of medicine in New Mexico, and participated in arts and other community organizations.

Twenty-five years after his experiences at Dachau, Marcus unearthed his Dachau notes and letters and used them as source materials for this book, which was first published by the University of New Mexico Press in 1972 under the title *The Harrowing of Hell: Dachau*. From the perspective of a young physician, Marcus describes his experiences, shedding light on the immense difficulties and complexities of the large–scale tasks DP Team 115 completed, against great odds, to combat epidemic diseases and starvation and to repatriate the former prisoners. Marcus also describes some of the people the team tried to help—men, women, and children from all walks of life, of many nationalities and religions. Believing that we must never forget what happened, Marcus tells his moving story with simplicity and grace. In a letter written in 1972, Marcus explained, "I have written the book for the post–World War II generation; it is dedicated to my children with the hope that they will remember the events that have shown how thin the veneer of civilization really is."

Just before he was transferred out of Dachau, some survivors gave Marcus several drawings that bore the signature "Music." Only after *The Harrowing of Hell: Dachau* was published in 1972 did Marcus learn the identity of the artist—Zoran Music, an acclaimed artist who maintained studios in Venice and Paris and whose paintings, drawings, and other works had been exhibited in galleries and museums throughout Europe. Marcus learned Music was born in 1909 in Gorizia, an Austrian-dominated town in Slovenia that became part of Italy after World War I. In the 1930s, Music studied at the art academy in Zagreb and traveled to Spain, where he copied the works of Goya and El Greco. In 1943, he settled in Venice; in 1944, he was arrested by the Gestapo. Accused of complicity with anti–Nazi factions, he was deported to Dachau.*

Memories of Dachau continued to haunt both Marcus Smith and Zoran Music over the ensuing decades. While Marcus wrote about his experiences, Music incorporated images of Dachau in many of his later works.

* Giuseppe Mazzariol, *Music* (Milano, Gruppo Editoriale Electa, 1980)

Centre Georges Pompidou, *Music, L'oeuvre Graphique* (Paris, Editions de Centre Georges Pompidou, 1988)

From the late–seventies until his death in 1986, Marcus enjoyed a warm correspondence with Music; he particularly treasured some additional works of art and books about Music that the artist sent him.

We are very grateful to the State University of New York Press for recognizing the importance of *The Harrowing of Hell: Dachau.* We feel this touching story of the efforts of DP Team 115 to accomplish its mission in the aftermath of a horrific tragedy provides a unique view of post-liberation concentration-camp rehabilitation as well as a meaningful lesson for today.

PATRICIA A. SMITH
FREDERICK M. SMITH, PH.D.

PREFACE

For twenty-five years I was unable to think about my experiences in Dachau, about the spring of 1945, when Allied forces were fighting their way into Germany, and I was medical officer of the small team sent into the concentration camp the day after its liberation from the Nazis. Our assignment: to reclaim the lives of the more than 32,000 prisoners still there.

Recently my nightmare began to recur, exhumed by violence in our troubled country. I wondered: Is the malignancy of Nazi Germany, which we thought we eradicated a quarter of a century ago, growing in America?

At last I tried to remember details. I opened a frayed box and took out the souvenirs of Dachau. Letters I had written home. A map. A blue-and-white album of photographs, made of convict's cloth, a gift to me from inmates. A Death's Head insignia. A blue notebook with mortality figures and faintly remembered names and places.

This book is about the world of displaced persons, their struggle to stay alive, the strange situations that arose as they rediscovered their identities and nationalities—those who could, that is. Many were beyond help—the thousands who died of starvation and disease in the days following our arrival. Those who lived taught us that in a police state human rights and freedoms do not exist, and individuals are not protected by law; that a concentration camp is the ultimate achievement of a police state, a place of darkness in which a human being's life counts for nothing. We learned these truths from a Frenchman who said he willed himself to live so that he could tell the world what had happened . . . from a Catholic priest who sent us each a copy of his autobiography, *The Church in the Bonds of Dachau* ... from a Pole who whispered as he died, "Remember us" ... from a Jew (few survived; only 8 percent of the prisoners we found in Dachau were Jews) who asked if we were Jews or Germans.

This is also the story of DP—Displaced Persons—Team 115: ten U.S. infantrymen hastily trained to feed, clothe, treat, and repatriate some of the millions of displaced persons in Germany at the close of the war. As civilians imbued with a spirit of fair play, tolerance, equality, and sympathy for the underdog (although those attributes were not always evident), our soldiers—and the team was only a small example—fought as earnestly to save the lives of Germany's slaves as they did to crush the troops of the SS. I became convinced that our forefathers had excellent judgment when they stressed the importance of a civilian army.

When I showed the manuscript to another doctor, one of my colleagues, he commented that I wrote about the experience clinically, as though I were observing a patient. Yes, I said, that is the way it was: I could not have kept going without trying to be impersonal, even detached. But your remoteness was only skin deep, he continued; you were shattered by the visible evidence of genocide; your mind was unable to function, and you banished the experience from consciousness. Perhaps you wrote the book to rid yourself of the stench in your subconscious. Now it is out of your system.

I denied it at the time, but perhaps he was right.

Now, when charges of censorship of the press, civilian surveillance, and police brutality fill the air, when people rally around slogans rather than reason, when bigotry, intolerance, and religious wars are common through the world, when fires of racism, ultranationalism, and totalitarianism still burn, consuming the minds and souls of men because they have forgotten—or never knew—it seems useful to permit this repressed material to surface, to publish this account of the aftermath of fascism.

"Those who do not remember the past are condemned to relive it," said Santayana. Other philosophers say that a knowledge of the past has no saving power.

But it is our only hope.

I would like to thank my wife, Carol, for keeping my letters, and for her innumerable helpful suggestions. I am grateful to the archivists of the United States Army, the General Services Administration, the American Red Cross, the International Red Cross, the International Tracing Service, and the Dachau Concentration Camp for their assistance, to Doctors Richard M. Angle and Rudolph Kieve for their invaluable comments and criticisms, and to Mrs. Ruth Jackusch, Mrs. Luri Guldbeck, Mrs. Vivian Kerr, Mrs. Hortense Goldstone, Colonel Leo Cawthron, and Senator Joseph M. Montoya for technical assistance.

Theodore N. Ferris, Jr., was the only member of the team whom I was able to trace. Now living in Lakewood, Ohio, he is an editor for the Educational Research Council of America. I sent him one of the revisions of the manuscript; his detailed comments were of inestimable value. Without his enthusiastic and generous support, I would have dropped the project. He has also permitted the reprinting of his poem, "Dachau, Germany," from his book of verse, *Cloudview.*

I am indebted to Jack Potter for his scholarly criticism of the manuscript, for his many suggestions, and for his time-consuming, always constructive efforts.

Drawings in this book are the work of a prisoner of the concentration camp, presumed dead. I have been unable to trace him. They were given to me by other former prisoners upon my departure.

I am grateful for permission to quote from the following:

Kurt von Schuschnigg, *Austrian Requiem,* copyright © 1946 by G. P. Putnam's Sons.

Dietrich Bonhoeffer, *Letters and Papers from Prison,* copyright © 1953, 1967, 1971 by SCM Press, Ltd.

Whitney Harris, *Tyranny on Trial,* copyright © 1958 by Southern Methodist Press.

INTRODUCTION

At the end of April 1945, American troops of the 42nd and 45th Divisions entered the concentration camp at Dachau, near Munich, liberating its 30,000 inmates and the some 40,000 other prisoners at nearby *Nebenlager*, or auxiliary camps, who had been working at forced labor in German war–related industries.

In operation since March 1933, Dachau was the oldest of the camps the Nazis had established for the concentration and extermination of those the Reich considered undesirable politically, socially, or racially. Designed to hold 5,000 prisoners, Dachau had become hideously overcrowded. By early 1945, hundreds of inmates were dying every day of starvation and disease, particularly typhus. And the places of the dying were being quickly filled by contingents arriving from other camps, including Auschwitz, Buchenwald, and Flossenburg. The Nazis were struggling to obliterate evidence of the genocidal purposes of the camps as the Allies advanced from the west and the east deep into German territory. The first soldiers who entered Dachau found some forty boxcars on the railway line just inside the camp gate, filled with the bodies of men, women, and children who had died of hunger, thirst, disease, and exposure during a death trip, most likely from Buchenwald or Birkenau.

Not every camp was liberated. The Nazis had liquidated several of the extermination centers, including Treblinka and Sobibor, in late 1943; in the winter of 1944–45, Soviet troops entered several of the remaining death camps in eastern Poland, including Majdanek and Auschwitz, but nearly all the inmates had already been exterminated or sent on forced marches toward camps in the west. The images of liberation familiar to the western world—piles of emaciated corpses, mass burials in vast pits, soldiers handing out their own rations to ragged inmates, survivors dressed in striped pajamas staring blankly out of dark, sunken eyes—have come through photographs taken in Bergen-Belsen, Buchenwald, Dachau, and other camps in Germany.

Yet, there is relatively little scholarship about the liberation of the camps located in Germany in the major Holocaust histories, war crimes transcripts, and military histories, and even in studies of individual camps. The record of the endings of the concentration and extermination camps between 1943 and the close of the war, particularly of the liberations by the Allies, has been less well documented by historians than many other aspects of the Holocaust.

More documentary evidence and historical record, especially of its liberation, exist for Dachau than for perhaps any of the other camps. Dachau has the dual distinction of being the first of the Nazi camps, established the year Hitler came to power, and of being the camp liberated within hours of the Führer's suicide in Berlin twelve years later. It was at Dachau that the system of torture, terror, and ultimately extermination that became the "univers concentrationnaire" was tested and refined.

But even for Dachau, many details remain sketchy. According to Barbara Distel, who is director of the concentration camp memorial site at Dachau and keeper of its archive, although the Nazis maintained meticulous records almost until the end of April 1945, many important documents were hastily destroyed as the Allied forces approached. She is convinced that the most important source of information is to be found in the reports of surviving prisoners, written largely in the initial years after their liberation. Unfortunately, many have not been published or are now out of print.

Some accounts of personal experiences in Dachau are available; for example, *The Beasts of the Earth* by George Karst (a pseudonym), published during the war, is a minor classic about the experiences of a political prisoner who spent a little over a year in the camp in the late 1930s. And there are some highly personal memoirs of the time of liberation, such as Nerin Gun's *The Day of the Americans*. Michael Selzer's popular account, *Deliverance Day: The Last Hours at Dachau*, is based on interviews and personal narratives collected long after liberation. While rich in its details and its immediacy, the book was not intended to be viewed as a scholarly/historical account. Instead, it is almost collage–like, providing a somewhat impressionistic sense of the days of liberation.

In the only recent general study of liberation, *The End of the Holocaust: The Liberation of the Camps*, a work that offers a very useful synthesis of basic facts about the end of each camp plus an annotated bibliography and recommendations for filling certain gaps in information and scholarship, Jon Bridgman concludes that "the drama of liberation . . . is somewhat more interesting historically if one considers not simply that brief shining moment when the liberators burst into the camps and declared the inmates free, but rather that period of time extending from some weeks before the arrival of the liberators to a like period after" (pp. 9-10).

Dachau: The Harrowing of Hell presents a detailed rendition of just such a time—the period immediately following liberation at Dachau. Only hours after the Americans entered the camp, after a day filled with jubilation and intense emotion, twenty-six-year-old Army doctor and First Lieutenant Marcus J. Smith and the nine other members of Displaced Persons Team 115, who had been assigned to Dachau, found themselves facing the gritty realities and unimaginable challenges of dealing with the needs of thousands of ethnically diverse, sick, starving, psychologically stressed former prisoners.

For several days, Smith was the only medical officer in the newly liberated camp. Though trained as a radiologist, he rapidly became a "battlefield expert" in public health. Working with a French transportation group and other military and civilian agencies of the Allies and with members of Dachau's International Prisoners Committee (IPC), which had been formed before liberation as the official system of camp control began to break down, Smith and his team were responsible for feeding the prisoners, for treating the vast number of starving, sick, and dying, for sanitation, fuel, water, and disinfection, even for burial of the dead—all the elements of a large public health establishment.

Because the newly liberated inmates represented nearly forty different nationalities, Smith had also to cope with "traditional" intercultural conflicts that intensified inexorably as basic conditions began to improve. With liberation and improving physical conditions, the former prisoners began to think about the future and grew eager to get out of the camp and start the return to "normal" life. Smith and DP Team 115 dealt endlessly with dissatisfactions that seemed especially trivial in light of the inmates' recent past—complaints related to food, petty thefts, perceived favoritism, goldbricking, the resurfacing of national frictions and prejudices.

After six weeks at Dachau, when conditions had begun to stabilize and rehabilitation and repatriation were under way, Smith received a new assignment at a Russian repatriation center. He was awarded the bronze star for his work at Dachau and was susbsequently promoted to captain.

The reissue of this book is very timely. In the early 1970s, nearly a quarter-century after his pivotal months in post-liberation Dachau, Smith returned to the memories of his experiences, reexamining his notes, his letters to his wife, his mementos—a map, some drawings by a then unknown inmate, a photo album bound in inmate cloth that had been presented to him by former prisoners—to reconstruct his unique experiences as doctor to the newly liberated inmates of Dachau.

The book remains most valuable to modern readers for its contribution to the history of the Holocaust, providing richly detailed information on an aspect of that history about which relatively little is known. But it also has a subtler value, as a meticulously detailed account of how a sensitive human being confronted and dealt with an essentially unimaginable experience. The book presents glimpses of how a young man's own "callous, death hardened county hospital exterior began to crack," of how he moved rapidly from being a doctor accustomed to treating one person at a time to being capable of addressing on a mass scale unprecedented human needs produced by unthinkable cruelty and suffering.

In the preface to the first edition of the book, Smith explained his motivation for writing it so long after the events it recalls:

> *Now, when charges of censorship of the press, civilian surveillance, and police brutality fill the air, when people rally around slogans rather than reason, when bigotry, intolerance,*

and religious wars are common through the world, when fires of racism, ultranationalism, and totalitarianism still burn, consuming the minds and souls of men because they have forgotten—or never knew—it seems useful to permit this repressed material to surface, to publish this account of the aftermath of fascism.

"Those who do not remember the past are condemned to relive it," said Santayana. Other philosophers say that a knowledge of the past has no saving power.

But it is our only hope.

Like countless others who endured the Holocaust or who were in some way observers of it, Smith was driven to be a witness, to say "no" to it by refusing to permit his experience of it be unrecorded. In the quarter-century since the first publication of this book and the half-century since the liberation of Dachau, it would seem reasonable to hope that enough time has passed, enough witness has been borne, enough has finally been learned of the lessons of the Holocaust. But recent events lead us to divergent conclusions. Holocaust denial has proliferated again in the past decade, especially on college campuses. The World Jewish Congress is now monitoring the resurgence of anti-Semitism worldwide. Membership in racist organizations is on the rise in the United States. Right-leaning and fascist-tinged candidates are winning elections in major European nations and in former Soviet republics. Ethnic cleansing is a reality in the former Yugoslavia, in Rwanda, in Tibet. A reunified Germany still struggles with *Vergangenheitsbewältigung,* with coming to terms with the past: although the film *Schindler's List* played to packed houses when it premiered in Berlin in March 1994, claims were also circulating that it was part of a plot to perpetuate the "Auschwitz myth."

The number of visitors to the Dachau memorial now exceeds one million people each year. Yet, in the city of Dachau, there is continuing resistance to the suggestion that there be added to the memorial site and archive a *Jugendbegegnungsstätte* or "place of encounter" like that in the town of Oswiecim—a place where groups of young people would come to explore and discuss a whole range of issues inspired by the history and reality of the camps.

Most Dachauers would prefer that the link between the camp and their city, the camp and their lives be severed forever.*

PATRICIA A. FARRANT, PHD
Iowa City, Iowa
July 1994

*Timothy J. Ryback discusses this controversy at length in "Report from Dachau," in the August 3, 1992 issue of *The New Yorker*, pp. 43-61.

Full citations to books/sources mentioned in this introduction:

Bridgman, Jon. *The End of the Holocaust: The Liberation of the Camps*. Portland, Oregon: Areopagitica Press, 1990.

Distel, Barbara. "The Liberation of the Concentration Camp at Dachau," *Dachau Review* (English translation of *Dachauer Hefte* , Number 1, (no date), pp. 3-11.

Gun, Nerin. *The Day of the Americans*. New York: Fleet Publishing, 1966.

Karst, Geroge M. (pseud). *The Beasts of the Earth*. Translated by Emil Lengyel. New York: Albert Unger, 1942.

Selzer, Michael. *Deliverance Day: The Last Hours at Dachau*. Philadelphia and New York: J. B. Lippincott, 1978.

The Beginning   1

BACK TO SCHOOL

Our appearance is hardly likely to inspire confidence, embraced as we are by dust, dirt, and mud, our inseparable companions. The habit of cleanliness, only a recent development in human history, is quickly lost in the combat zone because it is dependent on the availability of water. Here water is a precious substance we keep under guard, transport in our olive drab truck, purify, and use almost entirely for cooking and drinking. There is not enough for showering or bathing.

One of the first truths I learned in the Army was that survival was not contingent on washing more than once a day. Here, each morning, we transform our helmets into washbasins—the "baths." Shaving is a hardship to be postponed whenever possible. But my addiction to concepts of antisepsis still compels me to rub a few drops of heavily chlorinated water over my hands whenever they become unbearably sticky.

Sometimes weeks or months would pass before someone would chance upon laundering or bathing facilities and it was expedient to make use of them. Last week, in an almost completely deserted French village close to the German border, one of our enterprising men negotiated an agreement with a withered widow who gratefully scrubbed everyone's clothes in return for several bars of soap and boxes of C rations. We carefully packed the clothes into our musette bags.

Then two days ago, we heard of a shower room in a power plant converted into a commercial venture by a resourceful elderly German couple. We took turns, gamboling noisily beneath the beautiful hot water, then luxuriated in our still-fragrant clean clothes. As we were leaving, four gaunt, bedraggled, weary, menacing-looking men—displaced persons—entered the grounds.

The obese German lady waddled over to us.

"Please," she whispered. "Please. Stay a little longer. They are Russians and will take everything."

We paid for the showers. I climbed into a jeep with the company CO and two of the men. The CO ordered the driver to leave.

No one turned to watch.

As the war continues, more of these homeless wanderers abandon their hiding places in desolate hills, dismal caves, and gutted cities. Going somewhere, trudging slowly, they carry packs and bundles, or push small carts and baby carriages. They roam nervously through the countryside like suspicious dogs alert to the presence of enemies, sniffing for food smells, evaluating the terrain for potential shelter. There is a sameness to their appearance: I can guess their nationalities only from their languages, not from their facial features or clothing. They are thin, pale, hungry, tired, and dirty, probably as dirty as we are, and for the same reasons. They ask for food and cigarettes. Unhappy, morose people.

I find it difficult to realize that they were once loved, indispensable to their families; that our parents, wives, and friends would look and behave the same way if they had been the dispossessed, if they had just emerged from years of drudgery in slave labor camps.

Sometimes German civilians ask us to protect them from the wanderers, but we cannot help them, and the enlisted men make the routine response:

"They are your problem. You brought them here."

Tonight I am sitting in a blacked-out room illuminated by a Coleman lamp. I am again dust covered and mud splattered, but unaware of my appearance. Nor am I thinking about the plight of civilians. My attention is on stud poker, a game that is almost always in progress when business slackens in the "Station," as it has today.

The Station, the treatment room for the sick and wounded, is the heart of the medical collecting company, open twenty-four hours a day—except when we pack and move to a new location. A medical officer and a cadre of medical corpsmen are on constant duty. I am the medical officer of the day.

The room is jammed with medical and surgical equipment. I

am so used to the stench that I do not notice the sweet winter-green scent of methyl salicylate that the sergeant has recently used to rub down a soldier's aching back, nor the extramedical smell of French fries floating in from the adjacent kitchen, nor the chronic locker-room odor of unwashed soldiers.

Only three patients since noon. The first soldier was dead on arrival; he had been playing with a German bazooka, and his legs and half his face were blown off. Everyone was upset; his body should have been sent directly to a burial registration unit. The second needed a hernia repair and was evacuated to a rear echelon hospital. I was able to return the third patient to duty after deciding that his trench foot was mild and would respond to treatment.

Now another patient, I think, as I hear the sound of a jeep; but he cannot be in serious condition, otherwise I would hear the roar of one of our ambulances.

The soldier who enters is not a patient; he is a courier from Battalion Headquarters with a message for me. This is a surprise. I am a quiet, undistinguished first lieutenant; I cannot imagine why anyone would send me a message.

But my astonishment is not overpowering. As I temporarily withdraw from the poker game, I retain enough presence of mind to count the number of matches in front of me; each match is worth one franc. I acquired this savoir faire as an intern, at the poker games at Kings County Hospital, where I had to leave at a moment's notice to take care of patients who overfilled the Emergency Ward of that gigantic hospital. That was three years ago, but the habit persists.

I sign for the message. It is very brief. I am to report to Division Headquarters at 1100 hours, 15/3/45, taking along only my mess gear and sleeping bag, which means I won't be there long. The runner, now happily warming himself in front of our prized potbellied stove, informs me that 15/3/45 is tomorrow.

These special numerical symbols are used by the military to indicate a moment of time, and after all my years of service I still have to resort to laborious digital translations to understand whether they represent A.M. or P.M., or month-day or day-month. In this case, the 15/3/45 figure is easy: I know it is the fifteenth day of March, 1945. It cannot be the third day of the fifteenth month unless somebody has changed things.

Of course, I question the runner, who tells me that his sergeant-who-knows-everything (modern computers evolved from top sergeants) says that I am being sent to school, but that is all I can extract except for the location of the administrative center back in France, top secret, naturally. Then the messenger, like the moving finger, moves on.

Unimaginative witticisms and mundane platitudes are aimed at me by my comrades, and then wearied by the dullness of the day, I think about retiring for the night.

There has been no action near here today. I hear only the mean, cold winter wind whistling through the hills, the occasional boom-whistle of one of the big guns, and the reassuring, intermittent rumble of planes: reassuring because they are ours.

One of the corpsmen carefully puts away the greasy, overly fingered deck of cards, the candy bars and liquid refreshments. I look at one wall where a crucifix hangs and at another where a sign is posted asking the former German military patients, *Hast du nach Hause geschrieben?*

Nein, I answer. I have not written home today. Not yet. The only positive value of war is its revival of the craft of letter writing, and in this outfit almost everyone writes daily or two or three times a week. I know because I have to take my turn censoring the letters, but the censorship is purely one of names of cities and unit numbers. We cannot tell anyone at home where we have been until two weeks have passed.

So I write the heading, "Somewhere in Germany"; this is still refreshing because it has been "Somewhere in France" for months and months until five days ago. But the company has not advanced very far. The Station is in a former German convalescent hospital operated by a Catholic order, in the tiny town of Kleinsblittersdorf. In the daytime I can still see the Saar River, and on its French side the big sister city, Grossblittersdorf. Patches of green forest and pine trees are visible and every inch of land seems to be under cultivation. It would be pleasant to go sightseeing, but this impulse is throttled by the knowledge of surrounding mine fields and the fear of booby traps and nervous sentries.

In my letter I describe the terrain. I doubt whether the information will be appreciated, but I mention that on the French side there are unending piles of manure on the ground, and here, on the German side, I do not see any manure piles. Perhaps a difference in farming techniques. I mention the quietness, the lack of action, and the volleyball game that everyone participated in this morning in front of the damaged chapel. I write about the Germans who have stayed here, the caretakers, and the nuns, and describe their fleeting black shadows.

No one has initiated conversation with them because our version of the nonfraternization policy is to grunt and bark our orders and questions.

"We stay here." "Where is the water?" "Does the electricity work?" This is the extent of the dialogue, and none of us realizes that our interpretation of the policy makes us sound rude and authoritarian.

I also tell my wife that I was able to send her $81 by the PTA (personal transfer of accounts) method, after giving the finance clerk 4,015 francs. French currency is still in use. When the order comes to exchange francs for marks, I will know that the Division brass feels secure on this new soil.

I reassure my wife that there is little danger here, largely true. Then I end the letter by saying that I am going back to school, I know not why or for what, and I retire into my sleeping bag, a little boat in a little bottle.

The earsplitting noise begins at 0100 hours (let's see, that is 1:00 A.M.) when the 7th Army opens its attack on the mighty Siegfried Line, the supposedly impenetrable barrier to Germany because of its innumerable concrete pillboxes and wedge-shaped antitank obstacles, the dragon's teeth. All the artillery in the world seem to be on our backyard; the 155s and 105s roar themselves hoarse. For miles around, the earth is illuminated by the artificial moonlight of immense, dazzling searchlights. The gunners must be proud. They make the earth tremble and shudder and further humiliate our few remaining windowpanes.

I listen to the challenge of the guns. I watch the blazing lights. Armageddon? It takes more than this to keep an experienced soldier awake.

The usually considerate mess sergeant has concocted an unfriendly batch of powdered eggs for breakfast, but this is better than C rations, and his coffee is acceptable. So I have little to complain about as I depart by jeep for the new school—except the cold weather, the early hour, and the rotten roads.

At Division Headquarters, I am directed to a nearby displaced persons—DP—camp, a cluster of run-down buildings. I enter a makeshift classroom where other officers, lieutenants and captains, are waiting. Most of them wear infantry and cavalry insignia; a few are from the Medical Corps. I recognize no one.

A small table and a faded blackboard are at the front of the room; a large four-color map of Germany is tacked to a wall. Through the window I see DPs walking back and forth, waiting for breakfast.

We come to attention as a colonel with a no-nonsense demeanor strides in, introduces himself, points to the map, and announces, "This is Germany!"

"In Germany," he continues, "there are ten million displaced persons—DPs. YOU will take care of them!"

The officer sitting next to me is busy counting heads. He whispers that each of us in the room will have to take care of a half-million DPs—if the speaker's figures are correct. (In fact, they were incorrect. Historians later showed that a total of 13.5 million DPs were handled, half by the Americans, English, and French in their sectors of Germany, and half by the Russians in their sector.[1])

We learn the difference between refugees and displaced persons. Refugees are civilians in their own country who want to return to their homes but, because of the chaotic conditions created by the war, need help to do so. Obviously, homeless Germans in Germany are refugees, but not our responsibility unless they are concentration camp survivors. DPs are people outside the boundaries of their own countries who, because of the war, need help to survive and later to go home or to some other country. There are many categories of DPs, such as stateless persons, political prisoners, fugitives, enemy and ex-enemy nationals, and ex-prisoners of war. However, most of the DPs will be the people driven into Germany by the Nazis and used by them as laborers.

When the need arises, small "combat DP teams" will be formed and we will be placed on detached service with them for an indefinite time. We will take orders from G-5, the new section of the Army that handles civilian affairs. The term "G-5" stirs my long-dormant imagination. Intrigue? Romance?

As the Allied troops advance and German military and civil controls deteriorate, DPs and refugees will be forced to search for food and shelter, thus blocking the highways. This cannot be allowed. These channels must be kept open to permit the Allies to continue their pursuit and destruction of the enemy.

Initially, orders will be transmitted to DPs in a newly liberated area to remain where they are. Military police will then route them to collecting points and temporary camps. DP teams might take over at these locations, but more likely at larger "assembly centers" where DPs will be housed until they are repatriated.

A ten-minute break. I think back to the last Army school I attended. Shortly before going overseas, I was assigned to a camp in Texas where I helped train black medical corpsmen in battalion aid station duties and first aid principles. For seemingly endless days, as we camped on dusty and wind-swept plains ("maneuvers"), the men packed and unpacked medical chests and bandaged each other. Between drills everyone played poker, and in the evenings, under the dim light of a lantern, I read and reread my Army training manual.

Be forceful, it said. Avoid lecturing. Use action, visual aids, demonstration, participation, and repetition. Little was left to the teacher's imagination. In practice, this method seemed to work well because the poor teachers achieved results by using the recommended tactics, while the competent teachers were not shackled.

The instructors here must have been exposed to the same manuals. They use all the accepted techniques, except repetition, but only because there is insufficient time to present the material twice.

The recess is over. As the hours pass, it becomes more difficult to concentrate because the classroom is next door to a kitchen in which dinner is being prepared. Shrieks, murmurs, and gurgles penetrate the walls, distracting but pleasant, the long-forgotten sweet sounds of domesticity. I can see a young girl hurrying toward the kitchen carrying a handful of trays, and I have to wrench my mind back to the subject under consideration.

The information we receive falls into several categories.

Characteristics of assembly centers. We should select clusters of buildings located at outskirts of cities or towns, close to highways, large enough to accommodate at least 2,000 men, women, and children. If the rooms are overcrowded, epidemic diseases may spread rapidly—I think back to the contagion units, distant memories of smallpox, typhoid fever, and other communicable diseases.

Washrooms, a laundry, kitchens, warehouses, offices, examining rooms, a dispensary, and a hospital are essential. We should consider the adequacy and safety of the water supply, waste disposal system, and electrical circuits.

Care in assembly center. Violently uprooted from their homes, forced to labor under appalling conditions, grudgingly given a minimum of food and a token of medical care, the DPs deserve our consideration. They may be helpless or sick; we will need to provide care for them. Food is vital—everyone is to receive a minimum of 2,000 calories a day; we listen to a discussion of dietetics.

We must provide many community services as well as opportunities for counseling, education, recreation, and religious activities, all denied by their former masters. Red Cross workers should be permitted to work with the DPs; they will be particularly welcome because of their lines of communication to most European countries, permitting many DPs to contact their families.

Supplies. We will need to requisition the hundreds of items needed to support a modest existence. Foods, medications, clothes, bedding, dishes—the lists will be lengthy. Also, the little things that make life pleasant, such as soap, toothpaste, stationery, candy, and cigarettes. (The last two were highly regarded.)

No warning. The instructor drops his bomb.

Our mother and father, the United States Army, will not provide supplies. All materials and services for the care of DPs are to come from German sources only—"existing local resources."

Everyone in the room is now listening carefully.

We will request. They will supply. The policy is simple. We are the occupiers: the occupied do as we say. There will be no problems.

The lecturer pauses. It may be, he says, that the supplies requested may not be available or the facilities selected may be inadequate. If so, IMPROVISE.

How does one improvise? I wonder. For the last few years, everything I have ever needed for my patients has been furnished by the United States Army. On the spur of the moment, will I be able to provide life-sustaining services and material for thousands of deprived people from a war-ravaged country depleted of its resources and manpower? Do the other students feel as uncomfortable as I do?

Self-help. We are to involve the DPs to "a maximal extent" in community activities. Many DPs will be mentally and physically ill, the inevitable consequence of years of slavery. Full- or part-time participation in the operation of the center will speed their recovery and rehabilitation; they will realize that they are no longer working for the Germans, but for themselves.

There are other considerations. Our teams will be small, and we can use all the help we can get.

And mischief springs from idleness: we need to keep the DPs busy.

If the DPs cannot provide all the skills needed for the operation of the centers, existing Army labor policies allow for employment of civilians with these abilities.

Military control. Civilian employees of the United Nations Relief and Rehabilitation Administration may be working with us when the fighting abates; eventually they may replace us. Regardless, the Army remains in charge.

Although DPs are under the jurisdiction of American Military Government (MG), they must also obey the laws of their host country and the rules we establish for assembly centers. We will find that if we share the responsibility for maintaining law and order with the DPs by permitting their leaders to enforce regulations and administer justice, life will be much easier for us.

We are in favor of the easy life.

Late in the afternoon, I walk to the transient officers' quarters with two classmates, one a tall, quiet Iowan, the other a short, garrulous Puerto Rican who can bellyache more than anyone I know.

In the service, a certain amount of grousing is normal; an uncomplaining soldier is in danger of being referred for psychiatric evaluation. The expressions of discontent touch all aspects of military life: foul-ups, food, roads, weather, mail deliveries, pay, sleeping facilities, equipment, lack of equipment, discipline, lack of discipline, filth, latrines, rank-pulling, slowness of promotion, incompetence of replacements, delay or injustice in the granting of furloughs, absence of women, and ingratitude of civilians. My complaints usually skim lightly over the outdoor life, cold coffee, C rations, Spam, and the fig bars in K rations.

Nothing is achieved, of course, except a reduction of inner tensions.

My Puerto Rican acquaintance loses my good will when he informs me that not only does he dislike DPs but, furthermore, he intends to return to his native land after the war so that he can never again be drafted into the United States Army. The Iowan, about twice as large as the Puerto Rican, lets us know that he too does not like DPs, nor for that matter does he have any use for "spiks." Nothing personal, he adds; they are all lousy foreigners. The Puerto Rican bristles, then explodes in Spanish. I think he is contemplating homicide.

I avoid them at supper. Afterward, I try to read a few pages of a mystery story by Dorothy Hughes, *The Fallen Sparrow*, but do not succeed. My mind wanders to the residents of the DP camp and I wonder if they are like the men and women I knew in New York City. I grew up in a brownstone section swarming with noisy, excitable, bargain-hunting, price-haggling, bundle-carrying people. Across the street lived a fat Italian lady who often sat in her living room in front of an open window, drying her hair, her ample breasts inadequately supported by the windowsill. I remember the Polish iceman, the Irish policeman, the wandering Gypsies, the German marching band, and the Sicilian organ grinder and his gaily dressed monkey. There were ethnic social clubs and lodges, crowded one-owner shops, holy days and processions, and picturesque parades in which the marchers sported decorative old-world costumes. Food was everywhere, possibly because memories of hunger or starvation were still strong. I recall pushcarts bulging with freshly watered vegetables and fruits, propelled by burly, sweating Italians. Every block had restaurants and delicatessens, their Hungarian, Jewish, Romanian, and Italian owners proud of their mouth-watering specialties. Then there were the bakeries, their shelves filled with the artistic and exotic pastries of German and French bakers.

My school friends and I played stoopball and stickball on the bustling streets. Sometimes I visited their homes, heard their parents lapse into foreign tongues, and became aware of their anxieties and fears: starvation, persecution, Hell, unemployment, eviction, an unmarried daughter, loss of funeral benefits, inadequate education for their children. For some, sickness was an evil invoked for a misdeed, a curse; hospitals were death traps. As an intern, I discovered that often their credulity and superstitions interfered with the medical care that could have helped them. They were overwhelmed by death, their weeping in the hospital corridors and streets was loud, unrestrained, unnerving. I learned to like these people with their quaint customs, to savor their inexpensive gifts when I helped one of them get well: homemade bread, tortes, or wine—life symbols, I suppose.

Perhaps I should tell my classmate from Iowa about them, that they were neither better nor worse than his mother or father, but I do not think he will believe me. I hope I do not have to work with him, or with others like him: people concerned only with their own problems. I prefer my comrades at the collecting company, who, despite their griping, feel as I do, that there is an important job to be done. I reflect that I was one of those on the long, cold line that gray December day following the bombing of Pearl Harbor, but orders did not arrive until 1943, after I completed an internship. Then, after a succession of posts at general hospitals in Hot Springs, Arkansas and Santa Fe, New Mexico, a training session in Memphis at the University of Tennessee, and a fortunately brief stay at an unsympathetic camp in central Texas where recreational opportunities were limited to revival meetings and whorehouses, I left for the European Theater of Operations.

It has been a long time, but perhaps soon I will be taking care of the distant cousins of the people I used to know in New York.

The next morning all the students return, including the Iowan and the Puerto Rican; no knife wounds are evident. Another important subject is to be discussed—*Records*.

"Of course," says the new speaker, "there will be a few forms to fill out, but these will be rather simple and kept to a minimum."

I have heard this before.

Personal information about each DP is to be listed on index cards and registration sheets: name, date of birth, marital status, names and ages of children, nationality, previous address and employment, and destination. Records are to be kept of supplies obtained and disbursed, relief payments, requisitions, vouchers, inventories, loaned equipment, and lost, damaged, or destroyed material. Other printed forms are demonstrated, such as the AEF DP Meal Record Card, Assembly Center Weekly and Daily Reports (census, national characteristics, and camp problems), DP Free Issue Voucher, and Memorandum Receipts. We will also be making regular reports of our activities and recommendations, and special reports when repatriation begins.

As a medical officer, I doze through these bookkeeping minutiae, hoping that my time will be devoted to professional activities. But I do listen attentively to information about monthly narrative medical records, medical clearance records, and reports of treatments, immunizations, disinfections, food handler examinations, and inspections of facilities for sewage disposal and water supply.

Reams of paper to fill out, undoubtedly in duplicate or triplicate. My mind wanders, and I tell myself that if I ever get to a post exchange, I must remember to buy another fountain pen and more ink. I carry two pens at all times, but one of them leaks slightly, and after studying others I have concluded that it needs to have a tiny hole drilled in its cap. Probably body heat causes the air column in the cap to expand and suck up the ink. I am going to contact a dentist for this operation but only after I write to my wife and present my hypothesis to her. My weakness in college was in physics; particularly puzzling were the relations between pressure, temperature, and volume of gases.

But my wife has a scientific mind. I am sure she can analyze my hypothesis. She will probably write back that I need a hole in my head. The situation is not simple. I have looked at other such pens and some do not have tiny holes in their caps and do not leak. I prefer to use this one; it was an anniversary present, but lately I have been using another with a thicker point, one that does not write as smoothly.

I am not the only one who worries about trifles like pens and ink. They present a problem under field conditions because sometimes they disappear, sometimes there is no ink. Perhaps a fountain pen is a link to the other, distant world. Perhaps writing letters is an act of catharsis.

I recall a friend in a tank repair and transport squadron who became very disturbed during the frenzied activities on the Normandy beachhead: because he had lost his pen, not because of the fierce enemy resistance. Unable to do anything useful, he spent the day calling battalion, regimental, and division headquarters on his frustrating, hand-cranked field telephone, hoping someone would hunt for his pen in the area where he had been the day before. No sleep that night, not from worry about the dangerous foe lurking close by, but from anxiety about his missing pen. The next day he asked for permission to look for his lost treasure and, as he was worthless to his company, his request was granted. He returned to the beach and found his pen where he had left it, still in good condition. His agitation vanished, and he was able to work again.

My daydreaming is over, and I focus on the speaker who is talking about repatriation, the ultimate goal of our efforts, to be achieved as rapidly as possible. To hasten the homeward movement we will have to keep the DPs in good health and out of jail. Discipline in the camps would be facilitated by housing the DPs according to their nationalities. Stateless people will have more problems than others—they will suffer because they have no legal protection, may not be able to live where they wish, and will be entirely dependent on such unpredictable governmental attitudes as generosity.

At all times, whether in assembly centers or repatriation camps, we should strive to improve the standard of living of the DPs, at the expense of the Germans. The DPs are to receive preferential treatment—this is official policy.

We are taken on an inspection of the camp and now I am not sure what preferential treatment means. The overcrowding of barracks and small and large bedrooms is apparent, and in these quarters Russian and Polish women, smelling of onions and sweat, sit and do nothing, or keep busy with minor jobs, or with games, particularly sexual. Despite primitive curtains strung about dilapidated beds, such activities are blatant. Neither the adult nor the young residents in the area seem interested, but the visiting students stare with embarrassment.

The DPs chatter, gossip, laugh, squabble, grumble, wail over the past, watch each other, but they seem detached—they are not interested in what we are doing. Their bathrooms and washrooms are inadequate, the storerooms, nursery, and clerical and administrative sections cramped, but the kitchen is clean and busy, tantalizing with its fragrance of fresh baking bread. I pay special attention to the rooms and equipment used for medical examinations, immunizations, and disinfection.

It is a real camp and the men and women here are protoplasmic truths; they breathe and walk and eat, but everything here seems remote to me, cloudy and blurred, a strange, alien world not relevant to my recent existence in a collecting company where I was immersed in the excitement—or dullness —of battalion activities. Still, part of my mind recognizes that the latter is unreal, and the former a truer representation of humanity, albeit under stress.

We return to the classroom. Part of the teaching ritual is to review all of the material that has been presented before the students rush away and forget everything, in the hope that something will be retained, and a major attempts a short summary.

For a few minutes he emphasizes the basic policies, stressing the need for an effective organization. Then he excites everyone's curiosity. The teams will expand in size as additional personnel are assigned—Allied liaison officers, French nurses.

Très intéressant, I think as I reach back many years for my high school French. What was that proverb that hung on the wall? *Honi soit qui mal y pense?*

I must obtain a French-English dictionary *tout de suite*.

A liaison officer is an accredited Allied officer who will work directly with his nationals and with us. Perhaps relations will not always be simple and tranquil, but it is our job to get along with him, and his to speed our operation and prepare his countrymen for repatriation.

Then our instructor asks for questions, another part of the Army teaching ritual, and I know that we are almost through.

"Suppose you can't obtain one-half ounce of sugar daily. What should you do?"

"Use a substitute. Jam. Improvise."

The magic word again. The stress on principles, not particulars, the reiteration of the need for flexibility in administration and organization.

"Can I have a DP shot if he tries to escape from the camp?"

"You are not running a prison. DPs should have freedom, but they have to obey military rule. Remember that most of them have been brought into Germany forcibly as slave laborers."

"Why won't the Army furnish us supplies?"

"The DPs were brought here by the Germans. Therefore it is the Germans' responsibility to provide for them. They must furnish all the supplies, materials, services, and facilities that you consider necessary for the proper care of the DPs."

There are other similar questions, then the instructor distributes two booklets. One is a *Guide* for the administration of assembly centers, containing organizational and operational policies and valuable, occasionally exciting, medical, sanitation, and nutritional data. For example, one way to convert a diet from 2,000 to 3,000 calories is to add 5 ounces of wine to the basic diet, increase the sugar from ½ to 1½ ounces, and increase the bread from 11 to 24 ounces. Five gallons of rice pudding will feed 100 people in an "eating center." "Underknickers" is synonymous with "underpants." [2]

I make up my mind to read this pamphlet in detail—it is more interesting than the first aid pamphlets I used in Texas.

The second booklet contains instructions in about twenty European languages for obtaining registration information from DPs.

Then a parting word.

This is the last time we will be together, the last time we will see our instructors. When the teams are activated, life will be different for us because we will have added responsibilities and no detailed protocol for guidance. We must expect internal conditions and problems to vary from place to place and we must adapt to these environmental changes. But one thing is definitely forbidden—regardless of circumstances, we are not to permit our camps to be converted into whorehouses.

School is over and we are dismissed, to return to our regular units.

As I leave the school I wonder about the information given to us. How do the military authorities know that there are ten million DPs in Germany? I am troubled by the thought that at this late time, March 1945, the Army has just begun to form units to handle civilian problems. And I have other misgivings, brought on by the questions asked in the classroom, which revealed our lack of understanding of the problems of homeless and persecuted people, and our astonishment at the emphasis on improvisation. But the instructors were undisturbed. Our naïveté, ignorance, lack of sympathy, and, in some cases, intolerance did not seem to bother them.[3]

Perhaps I would never be called to become a shepherd for the uprooted sheep—one does not always use the abilities and knowledge acquired in Army schools. Even so, the time had not been wasted. A portable shower unit was situated next to our quarters, and, happily, I washed away the accumulated grime and dust of many waterless days. The Army thinks—or tries to think—of everything.

2

THE DRAGON'S TEETH

I reach my collecting company by suppertime.

At first I am on the receiving end of gross sallies about my future role in the Army, remarks that emphasize fundamental instincts. I will be bedecked with garlands of flowers, surrounded by dancing natives, the liberator in the midst of frustrated, grateful Cinderellas. My camp will be a harum-scarum harem. My assigned C rations will be donated to the unenlightened, and I will dine elegantly and sumptuously in Continental style, bathed by Gypsy violin music. One of the enlisted men whispers to me that he can be very useful in my new unit because he grew up in the Polish section of Chicago. Can I arrange a transfer for him?

My homecoming is celebrated with wine and champagne, both in great abundance here. However, I soon fall into the old routine, characterized by occasional bursts of hyperactivity interspersed with the more usual long periods of dullness and tedium. At night, card games by candlelight or lantern and then to sleep. During the day, if there is no work to be done, I sleep late, skip breakfast (thereby losing 25 cents), write letters, read old magazines and books shipped from home. At the moment I am reading *The Late George Apley* and *War and Peace*. The Army newspaper, *Stars and Stripes* (Nancy edition), is free, but usually two to five days old when received. Then games, usually poker or casino, or volleyball if possible. Letters from home are read and reread but the intervals between mail deliveries are too long. Radios are rarely useful because of the lack of electricity.

Anything is acceptable if it relieves the boredom. One of the men blasts away with his cornet. No one complains. My recorder is tolerated. This was not true when I was stationed at a general hospital in Arkansas, where my fellow officers found the soft, soothing (to me) sounds of my recorder irksome. But not here.

At one of our installations we find an ornate piano that has two gold-colored candleholders protruding above both sides of the keyboard. An old German—we have permitted him and his wife to remain in the building—hesitatingly opens the piano for us. He tells us that he locked it three years ago, the day his son died. He rushes away before the music starts.

Suddenly we have a quartet: two violins—one bought, one borrowed—a guitar, and the piano. Later a corpsman unwraps his saxaphone, another discovers a drum, and a battalion soldier arrives with his trumpet. We have music and dancing.

There is no great distinction here between officers and enlisted men; a sense of togetherness exists different from rear echelon or stateside units. I can see a medical administrative officer playing cards with the mail clerk, a corporal, and this would be impossible except in the combat zone.

Every day free cigarettes, canned beer, peanuts, and candy are distributed. No one has a choice, and I usually wind up with peppermint patties, which I despise. Twice a month copies of *Life*, *Time*, *Newsweek*, *Ellery Queen's Mystery Magazine*, *Western Stories*, and *Omnibook* are distributed, and these circulate through the company.

But escape from boredom demands more than this, and the card games become noisy, violent sessions. Some of the men parade around in unusual attire. One carries a gaily colored parasol, another wears a dignified silk high hat, a third dons a striped black and white jacket; he calls it his new "fraternity jacket." A corpsman wraps a blue silk bandanna around his head. Forever afterward he is known as Long John Silver.

Souvenir hunting also breaks the monotony, and most everyone has a German bayonet, gun, helmet, camera, or binoculars.

Our men are litter bearers, ambulance drivers, and treatment personnel, and in administration and maintenance. They have varied backgrounds. One worked in a shoe shop in New Hampshire. Another was a drug salesman for Lederle Laboratories in the New England area, and even now launches into a talk describing the benefits of refined liver extract and globulins for measles. Unconsciously, he seems to reach for his sample and brochure case. A top NCO managed a milk farm in New Jersey; he speaks German fluently. Another is a former chiropractor from Ohio, and occasionally we discuss the intricacies of the sacroiliac joint. After the war he is going to move to Long Island, "where the money is."

One of the men practiced law before he was inducted. Here he is called the Shyster, which amuses everyone and does not offend him. Sometimes he is accused of ambulance chasing, his real function now, and the smiles break through.

Laughter is a rare flower, which we all cherish when it blooms.

A letter arrives from my wife, who is a resident physician in pediatrics at Children's Memorial Hospital in Chicago. Sometimes she writes about her patients, and I am delighted to read about a two-year-old who stuffed raw meat up her nose and was brought to the hospital by her inebriated father, lamenting the loss of good "red points." (Food was rationed during the War; meat could be procured only with these points—red food stamps, a certain number given to each person by the Ration Board for a one- or three-month period.)

The letter also mentions Frank Sinatra's classification by the Draft Board—2F: deferred as necessary to the war effort? I read parts of the letter to my comrades. We share our treasures with each other.

A collecting company collects wounded and sick patients from frontline battalion aid stations, and transports most of them to clearing companies in the rear. We are usually located from one-half mile to five miles from the front. The medical and surgical care we dispense is uncomplicated. We examine, change, or reinforce splints, dressings, and tourniquets, administer morphine, plasma, and antitetanus agents, and only in life-endangering conditons attempt emergency operations. Those patients with minor problems are returned to duty.

I am glad to be back, not only because my friends are here, but because I can find out about the attack on the Siegfried Line. The Division has been blasting through part of the West Wall of this formidable barrier, the last obstacle to the Rhine. Endless lines of jeeps, tanks, half-tracks, and trucks have been rumbling through devastated villages, spewing clouds of yellow dust. By March 21, our armored columns are loose in Germany.

We realize that something different is happening because we are asked to ship our personal luggage to the rear, dump all unessential liberated luxuries, such as a generator, sofa, mattresses, stoves, and a motorcycle, and resume a spartan musette-bag existence. The medical chests are rushed into our trucks and we make a long jump through a low mountain range, past brooks, valleys, patchwork fields, carefully plowed farms, a wrecked German gun, sheep, lambs, a shepherd and his collie —both out of a different age—and everywhere are pillboxes that blend into nearby pine trees and moss-covered walls.

Dead horses and cattle, and live ones. Now some of our men stop to milk the cows, although, with my usual pessimism, I counsel against this because of the possibility of acquiring tuberculosis or brucellosis. A dead German soldier lying under a dead horse. No one investigates—the body may be booby trapped. Piles of abandoned army equipment, shattered armor, and ruined vehicles. Untouched villages and intact houses. Sometimes as many as three white flags hang from one home.

In a small, battered town we stop momentarily to look at the words on a stone plaque that has been split in half; here Bismarck stayed in 1870 on such and such days. No one can identify the house: less remains of the nearby buildings than of the plaque.

Then past a roadblock made of huge logs, several feet thick, on which Russian names and words have been carved by the slave laborers who built this and other fortifications.

Wine with supper. One of the administrative officers has a mug he has been saving for this occasion, made of white porcelain and embossed with a picture of the imperial German eagle, its wings outstretched, gazing fixedly at powerful dragon's teeth. The inscription reads, "The West Wall Stands." We pass the mug around and toast the crumbling wall.

March 28 is a dismal, cloudy day as the company crosses the Rhine on a pontoon bridge near Mannheim. This badly demolished city consists only of barren, crumbling walls and littered foundations, a depressing sight. I seem to be able to adapt to anything except ruined cities. There are too many sights like this in France and England.

In Mannheim and some of the other battered cities we had noticed hastily painted, repetitious phrases on the walls of buildings, stating the philosophy of the divide-and-conquer school: "We believe in the Fuehrer," "One Faith, One Victory," "Onward, Slaves of Moscow," and "Americans Die, Tommies Live." A slogan that we discussed but did not understand was "Remember November 9, 1918." [1]

We measure time by the intervals between rivers, the major obstacles to progress. The next important period is between the Rhine and the Neckar, and then the jump to the Jagst. By this time I have forgotten all about the DP school. I concentrate on our problems from day to day.

Such as the soldier who reports to the Station one day late in March with a penile lesion that looks syphilitic. He says that his contact was in Marseilles in December, an absurd statement because the incubation of this unpleasant disease is usually about three weeks.

Venereal disease is considered by the Army as a line-of-duty ailment; soldiers are no longer punished for contracting the disease, as they were before 1944. Still, the situation is not clear in the case of our soldier. If he acquired his disease from a *mademoiselle*, he will not be disciplined, but if he acquired it from a *fräulein*, he may be in trouble because he will have violated the nonfraternizing policy. Would this be a court-martial offense? We now have something different to discuss. After exhausting our primitive knowledge of military law, we send the patient to a rear echelon hospital for confirmatory tests, and, of course, never hear the end of the story.

I reread my copy of the official *Special Orders for American-German Relations*. This order, neatly printed on a folded pocket-size card, is supposed to be carried by every soldier in Europe:

> American soldiers must not associate with Germans. Specifically it is not permissible to shake hands with them, to visit their homes, to exchange gifts with them, to engage in games or sports with them, to attend their dances or social events, to accompany them on the streets or elsewhere. . . .

Reasons were given:

> These [orders] are restrictive. They are definite. They are necessary, for we must prove positively to the German people . . . that Nazism has led them to the brink of de-

struction and has earned them our distrust and that of the world. Until they have proved themselves entitled to respect as a people and as a nation, we cannot afford them comradeship, faith or honor. . . .

The orders were not intended as a VD deterrent, nor did they serve as such.

3

INCREASED RESISTANCE

Heidelberg, which we pass through on the last day of March, is not an archeological remnant; its buildings are not tortured, twisted skeletons. But its bridges, including the one built in the eighteenth century, have been destroyed by retreating German troops. Otherwise, the city is virtually undamaged. Even the store windows are intact. It has been a long time since I have looked at colorful displays.

Because it is a vast hospital center, the city was not subjected to Allied attack, and for this reason also it was surrendered to the 7th Army without a fight. We hear that the capitulation provoked Hitler into a rage—he believed that all Germans should resist to the end, and he has sworn to recapture the city by April 20, his birthday.

A few well-dressed Germans on the streets, apparently unaware of Hitler's threat, wave at us in a friendly manner. I am surprised to see them because in other freshly captured German cities there were very few people on the streets, and those I did see were unsmiling, their dejected spirits seeming to match the drooping white sheets that hung from windows above.

Another difference: here Nazi slogans are not painted on the walls.

We are told that seven American soldiers are supposed to be patients in one of the German hospitals in Heidelberg. We locate the hospital and are greeted by a German military physician, a colonel, who wears a handsome full uniform and shiny boots. He clicks his heels and welcomes us with an instinctive, smart Nazi salute—but the automatic "Heil Hitler!" is gone. The American soldiers were in his hospital, but are now gone; they were picked up earlier by another American unit. He tells us that the German Army is collapsing because it has no more shells for its guns and no more fuel for its airplanes.

A few German soldiers are wearing Red Cross brassards and carrying holstered guns, and the CO sends a messenger to Battalion Headquarters describing the situation. A quick reply says that their people are too busy to take care of the guns. We should collect and destroy them. So they are collected, and one of our men is assigned the task of destroying them. I am sure a few more souvenirs are now available.

The last day of March is the day of the false armistice, celebrated wildly in Chicago and New York. After hearing the news, we vicariously join in the festivities by gorging ourselves with cheese, salami, sardines, chocolate, and liquid refreshment. No hot food because we are moving again.

There is no sign of an armistice here during the next few days, and at least one German airplane has enough gasoline to strafe our troops. We celebrate by drinking more champagne and wine, all marked "for the *Wehrmacht* only, not to be sold." No one would think of selling these treasures.

Our antiaircraft gunners have recently become ineffective. Their reflexes seem slow, probably because they have imbibed too much. I wonder whether the enormous caches of the juice of the grape in this region were deliberately planted by Hitler for this purpose, and I speculate whether they are his rumored new secret weapon. In our unit there has been too much drinking and the CO has locked up the liquor. Later, one of the battalion aid stations is lost. The CO prepares to hunt for the station, and asks me to come along. We find the missing unit without too much difficulty, and talk with its overwrought ranking officer. We decide that his unsteadiness is not from the aftereffects of too much champagne or wine, but the result of too much cognac.

We are also unhappy because one of our aidmen has been shot three times, in the back and shoulders, despite the visibility of his Red Cross markings. Other aidmen and litter bearers have been wounded in the past. About a month ago we were shelled by the respected, effective German 88 millimeter guns, notwithstanding the bright red crosses on the building. Despite these infractions, everyone wearing the Red Cross emblem continues to be unarmed, as prescribed.

Now spring is arriving and the hills and valleys beckon, the magnolias and apple blossoms seem to wave at us. The end of the winter comes at a favorable time for the DPs. As we move deeper into Germany, we pass a field where hundreds of DPs are camping; it would have been too cold for them to live in the open a few weeks ago. Until recently, they have been hiding in caves. Now the field is dotted with small fires over which they cook whatever food they have been able to find. Their freshly washed clothes are spread on the ground, drying under the friendly afternoon sun.

We set up our kitchen nearby, and as we line up for dinner we see some of the wretched, emaciated DPs staring sadly at our food. We give them our extra Spam and C rations, and some of the delicacies sent to us from our families.

Packages from home are a source of delight. We share their contents with our comrades. Early in April, I receive a package from my wife, and my vulturelike companions quickly assemble. A pair of blue loafer pajamas stimulates many remarks, and a book, *The Lost Weekend*, is greeted with interest. (Someone skims through it and announces that the hero has an aquiline nose.) Then I put aside several cans of cheese, but two pounds of luscious chocolates are rapidly devoured. One of the vultures retrieves from the packing material a crumpled page from a two-month-old Chicago newspaper, and reads from it a prediction by Gabriel Heatter, a popular radio commentator, that the war will be over last week.

Despite our boisterous reaction, we know that the battle in Germany is being won. This is evident as more and more German soldiers surrender. We also feel the impending victory when we hear the plaintive cry of the conquered Germans, *alles kaputt*—all is lost. These words become part of our vocabulary, and they delight us as a change from the usual obscenities; they may replace the old picturesque noun and verb, "snafu": situation normal—all fouled up.

In Mosbach we share a five-story building with DPs and Germans. We hear many sad tales from the DPs—from a Frenchman with an ulcer of his thigh, from a Belgian with an infected left groin, and from members of a Russian family from Yalta. These men worked on a tunnel, fourteen hours a day, seven days a week.

The oldest Russian is a pale, thin, middle-aged man, an electrical engineer. His daughter, 28, is a doctor who has been performing minor surgery in industrial plants. For a period of six months she remained underground in a hidden factory, unable to emerge because of incessant Allied bombardments. Her younger brother, a pallid-looking boy, perhaps 20, also worked in the tunnel.

They are proud of the deeds of the Russian Army; they hear about them by word of mouth.

Another unrelated 16-year-old Russian boy lives with them. He tells us unemotionally that he was taken away from Stalino when he was 13 and has been working since. He watched the Germans shoot his mother, sister, and father; he is proud of his brother, an officer in a tank unit.

The following day we witness a group of DPs angrily shouting at a middle-aged woman here in the building, and she starts to run from them, out of the building, down the road, with the others pursuing.

Soon a jeep arrives with two American military government officers. Did we see the woman? What was she wearing? Which way did she go? They say she was a Gestapo agent; they have information about fifty deaths for which she was responsible. And they drive away quickly.

I imagine episodes like this are occurring throughout Germany.

Surprisingly, as time passes our casualties increase. Near Allfeld, instead of the regular *Wehrmacht*, we have encountered an SS division, part of Hitler's special army. We find the SS men to be fierce combatants who belive in fighting to the last man. Now I understand the newspaperman's phrase, "a pocket of increased resistance." For us it means a tremendous increase in hemorrhage and shock, the two great enemies; every kind of wound—head, neck, face, torso, extremities; a nightmare of unending plasma and morphine administration; the anxiety and ceaseless questions—"How's it going up there?" or "Things a little better now?" Then the irritation, the fatigue, the increase in four-letter words, the deaths and injuries to personal friends, the attempt to avoid thinking about the men who can't reach the Station.

I worry about them, and about our litter bearers, ambulance

drivers, the adequacy of our supplies, and the local and regional strategy.

Afterwards, the infantrymen talk—they believe in Luck, and can prove it. One lieutenant tells about hearing the whine of an approaching 88 millimeter shell. He hit the gound, the shell landed inches from his feet, covered him with dirt, but didn't explode. A corporal tells about being in a circle with two other men when a silent mortar shell landed between them, killing the two men but leaving him untouched. Both felt that the X factor—Providence—was on their side.

I also hear other kinds of stories.

One of our soldiers tells about his patrol, captured by some SS men. All his comrades were killed, and he was forced to strip and was machine-gunned as he ran.

On April 7, 8, and 9 the collecting company is overwhelmed by 124, 73, and 187 casualties, respectively. And this is the time when newspapers and current periodicals are saying that the fighting in Europe is "over"; or that it has been over since Runstedt's attack (the Ardennes campaign) was repulsed. Our infantrymen know better; they have learned about the fanatical fighting ability of the SS troops.

Surprisingly, three SS soldiers are captured and brought in for treatment.

They are 17 and 19 years old, although one looks about 15, and says he has been in the army for only three weeks. These are the youths who undoubtedly spied on their parents and reported disloyal conversations, who have carefully ascended the special Nazi ladder, and now have been promoted into the *Waffen-SS*, the militarized combat units of the SS, forty divisions in all.

They request nothing, give us no thanks for the medical care we are reluctant to give, but do, remembering the Hippocratic Oath. Our enlisted men do not understand our professional vows; they do not approve of the careful and thorough treatment we have given the savage enemy.

Our regiment is held up for ten days, and this at a time when other American units are exploding through German lines. Finally, the SS pocket is shattered by a combined artillery, air, and infantry attack.

But our troops have paid heavily.

Wounded soldiers from ordinary German units pass through

our hands: they are not as bloodthirsty. A boy of 17 with a gunshot wound in one arm comes in crying, pleading, "*Nicht schiessen!*"

"We are Americans. We don't shoot our prisoners," announces one of our men.

Some captured soldiers are glad to tell us that their supplies are inadequate and their defeat inevitable. Then they ask for *Zigaretten* and *narkosis* (morphine).

German civilians—men and women—occasionally come to the Station requesting medical care for themselves, for their children, or for a relative at home who cannot be moved. When we are not busy we treat their illnesses or war wounds, knowing that no German doctors are available. Some of our patients seem to resent having to ask us for anything. Some are indifferent; they accept our treatment and leave silently. Some are openly hostile. A few are friendly and grateful.

We can make friends with the children. But that does not stop them from crying from pain or from anticipating the pain of our treatment. An exception was a seven-year-old blind boy with grenade fragments in his left heel. He was curious about everything, and never cried for his absent mother.

She was dead, I was told. The victim of an air raid.

Everyone suffers in the combat zone.

4

DP TEAM 115

I can forget about treating soldiers for a while. The DP situation must be serious, because orders arrive to report to Division Headquarters on April 10. A bottle of '37 champagne is opened for the brief farewell party. I am truly sorry to leave the company, a congenial outfit.

I collect my souvenirs and luggage, don my oversized field coat with its bulging pockets, climb ungracefully into a jeep, and repeat the farewell cry of the training camps, "This is it, men! Give them hell!"

The driver grits his teeth and we bounce away.

A trip by open jeep along a war-beaten road is a detour-hugging, boulder-circling, mudhole-sliding ordeal. Dust covers my face and my clothes and fills my lungs. The shrieking wind jars my nerves. My back aches, my kidneys drop, my feet freeze, my eyes and ears burn, and my nose becomes numb.

This life is for the outdoor man, willing to pit his fragile protoplasm against the mighty forces of Nature. I am a disciple of the quiet, sedentary life, of the hotel, not the tent, of the bed, not the sleeping bag, of the electric light, not the candle. Oh, give me a car with springs, a steel-enclosed body, upholstered seats, a rug on the floor, windows that close, and, above all, a heater.

After a four-hour delay at Battalion Headquarters, I am routed to Division Headquarters in Mosbach, where I am informed that I am now a member of DP Team 115. I check into the transient officers' quarters to await further developments.

These quarters are in a private house in the outskirts of the city, commandeered by the Army. Requisitioning private and public buildings is standard practice by an advancing army. Nevertheless, it still bothers me to see people forced to leave their homes at short notice, carrying personal possessions hastily thrown into pillowcases, laundry bags, boxes, or valises, then transferred to small carts or wheelbarrows. The young women faint when they discover they are being dispossessed, and the babies cry, but the older men and women accept silently. I recall the days of the Great Depression when evictions were commonplace: people ejected from their houses or apartments onto the streets, where they would sit next to their shabby property, waiting for a Good Samaritan.

Even though I rationalize the necessity for the seizure of the building in which I am now quartered, the family pictures hanging on the walls, the old letters, books, clothing, even the remaining dishes, and little things like an embroidered pillow or an old pipe, cast a depressing cloud over the house.

The order establishing the Team is dated April 14, 1945, and is, of course, "RESTRICTED." Brevity being essential, the communication reads: "The fol named off and EM from units indicated are placed on TDY with Seventh A Displaced Persons Team and upon completion of TDY off and EM will ret to their proper orgns. . . . By command of Major General Hibbs. . . ."

I meet the man designated as the commanding officer (CO) of DP Team 115, Lieutenant Charles Rosenbloom, a stocky, dark-complexioned man with little to say. He has been in the service for three years, all in the infantry. Before that he worked with juvenile delinquents in New York, although his home is in Holyoke, Massachusetts.

Rosenbloom introduces me to the two other officers on the Team.

The supply-mess officer is Lieutenant William L. Howcroft of Steubenville, Ohio. Slender and blond, he wears fragile silver-rimmed eyeglasses over his light blue eyes. He, too, is naturally reticent, except when he displays his outstanding collection of four-letter words, an admirable asset for anyone responsible for military requisitions and vouchers. Howcroft has completed one year of engineering at Ohio University and believes that he is too old to return to school after the war—he is 21.

Our adjutant, also in his twenties, is Lieutenant Marion R. Williams of Kansas City, Kansas, a slim and poised handsome man who studied voice before his induction and knows many operatic arias in their original Italian. I think this talent might help us if we were to be stationed in Italy, but I cannot think of its value in Germany. Perhaps he can brush up on Wagner.

The new CO is all business. He has been studying the two assigned pamphlets, and asks us to do the same. We have little to talk about at first, except to agree that the new assignment should be more interesting than our recent ones. Besides, says Howcroft, he won't have to shiver in a muddy foxhole any more. Anything is better than that. We agree. Each of us wonders why we were picked for the Team. Such questions can never be satisfactorily answered—we have all learned to accept our assignments without question, the *c'est la guerre* attitude essential for peace of mind.

The TO (Table of Organization) calls for six enlisted men: operations sergeant, mess sergeant, cook, clerk-typist, and two drivers. First to report is Harris H. Morivant, the staff sergeant in charge of operations, a nine-year Army veteran. Rosenbloom fills him in on the new job, and tells me that he seems to know his business. The mess sergeant is Michael J. Aricer of New Orleans, Louisiana, short and tough looking. I learn that he is devoted to southern cooking. Corporal Theodore N. Ferris, Jr., of Cleveland, Ohio, is the clerk-typist. He has worked in radio and theater in the past, and also writes poetry. At the moment this seems a useless talent. He does speak French, which should be helpful. (Aricer has a heavy southern accent. I wonder if the DPs we will handle will understand his English.)

Assigned as drivers are Technician 5th grade Chester S. Hollis from Oklahoma, a tall, quiet, heavy young man, and Private Donald E. Mace from Wisconsin, who says that he has been in police work in civilian life. The youngest, tallest, and best-looking of the men is Private Charles H. Eastman, who is 19; he is to be the cook.

The TO is now filled—four officers and six enlisted men. All ten of us are from the 63rd Infantry Division ("Blood and Fire"). No one has any special knowledge of or desire to work with refugees or displaced persons, no unusual insight into European traditions or history, and no experience in organizing or caring for large numbers of people; none of us has been in the executive or administrative section of the Army. Our educations are varied. Perhaps the only thing we have in common is the traditional antipathy of the infantryman, the foot soldier, to unnecessary discipline—"chicken shit," as it was sometimes called.

Abbreviations not only save time in the Army, they also encourage witty conversation. So we make appropriate remarks when Rosenbloom says that he has the TE (Table of Equipment) which calls for a jeep and two Army trucks—or their equivalents. Naturally we obtain the latter, captured German vehicles, all moribund as judged from their exterior appearance and interior sounds. We also acquire a shovel, four lanterns, two stretchers, and office supplies, including an ancient olive drab typewriter. Sergeant Aricer is aghast at the lack of cooking equipment, which he will have to "promote." (He acquires some in Mosbach, from unidentified sources. When queried as to their origin, he precedes his detailed explanation with the phrase, "Lieutenant, this is the truth. . . ." We learn that he uses these words when he thinks something may be true. But when he is sure it is, he announces, "Lieutenant, this is the God's honest truth. . . .")

My only medical supplies are a personal bottle of aspirin and a tube of penicillin eye ointment.

With these we are to drive bravely eastward, and provide and sustain the health and happiness of our share of ten million displaced persons.

THE JOURNEY

The food improves at Mosbach. Genuine eggs and Swiss cheese enliven the inevitable Spam. But eight dull days pass, while I wander, read, fidget, and watch the clock. Gin rummy, using reichsmarks, now provides the evening excitement.

War is a peculiar institution and so is the Army. I do not doubt the importance of victory, but it is difficult to accept the necessity of discipline and obedience during a period of vacuum, even after years of service. Oliver Wendell Holmes called his war, the Civil War, "dull and horrible." So too is this one, and they must all be, except perhaps when knighthood flourished and fighting was a way of life.

I know what Holmes said because I have been reading *Yankee from Olympus*, a fascinating story, except that I think the central character must have been a difficult man to live with because of his endless loquacity.

I roam the peaceful, cobblestone streets of Mosbach, avoid the modern buildings, and study the colorful walls of old, possibly medieval buildings, which look as though they were made of garishly iced gingerbread, their sharply pointed roofs all acutely angled. A postcard I find says that the city is 1,200 years old, and that it is the city of old frame houses.

At a DP camp with as many as four families in one room, I observe delousing methods using the new miracle powder, DDT. Then I inspect a small French hospital which has some concentration camp survivors and am appalled by what I see. I have watched patients being destroyed by cancer, but now I learn what the term "skin and bones" really means. Their voices surprise me—croaking, indecipherable sounds. I hope that we are not to be assigned to camps with such remnants.

Mosbach also has the Division "Exhaustion Center." "Exhaustion" is now the preferred word for what had been called "combat fatigue," "shell shock," or "battle psychoneurosis." This condition develops in some soldiers, regardless of age or rank, who have been exposed to combat for periods of time ranging from one hour to many weeks. These soldiers become pale and incoherent, sweat continuously, are insensitive to suggestion, and react violently to noises with wild muscular spasms and crying spells. In the past I have occasionally handled such patients. After sedating them with large doses of barbiturates, I sent them back to an appropriate treatment center such as this one. Here an Army psychiatrist, using rest and psychotherapy, is able to return most of his patients to active duty after four to seven days of treatment. (Today tranquilizers are used, I presume.) These soldiers are not malingerers. The men with exhaustion are legitimately ill.

During combat, one of our young litter bearers developed pain in the region of his appendix, then began to chain smoke and tremble uncontrollably. For one period of three days he did not eat or talk to anyone. There were no objective findings to support a diagnosis of appendicitis. After several recurrences he was assigned to noncombat duty.

April 12. The electrifying news of the death of Franklin Delano Roosevelt is broadcast on Radio Luxembourg in various languages, each announcement followed by the opening bars of Beethoven's Fifth Symphony. Mosbach is a somber place. American soldiers are downcast. Everywhere, flags are at half-staff, including those at the DP camps. Apparently "Roosevelt" was a magic word for the DPs, one that inspired hope during the years when no hope seemed possible.

The still-functioning German radio stations continue to vilify Roosevelt, and now Truman.

April 18. Orders for our first assignment arrive. Everyone is tired of inactivity, so that packing and filling our vehicles take ten minutes. There are no farewells. Sergeant Morivant and the CO have worked out the route with Division transportation, and we depart immediately for a long drive.

Despite our use of portions of the great four-lane superhighway, the Autobahn, the inevitable time-consuming detours harass us and everyone becomes irascible. I overhear one of the enlisted men making unkind remarks because the CO and some of the other officers have insisted on driving the newly acquired vehicles. In the Army the person who drives a car maintains it, and driving is the job of the men listed as drivers on our orders. I have been guilty of this in the past; it is refreshing to take a vehicle out for a few hours, but I must remember not to do that anymore.

We stop briefly at Heidelberg and Mannheim. Both cities have 7:00 P.M. curfews—the only signs of life at night are the wandering chickens and horses, and smoke rising from chimneys.

On April 19 we pass through Wurzbach and Kitzingen. One of our trucks grinds to a stop and our maintenance people cannot repair it. We transfer its contents to our other truck, send back for a replacement, permit Howcroft to say a few choice words as we leave it on a shoulder, and continue our journey.

We drive through Erlangen on April 20. Today Hitler is 56. There is no evidence of a parade or other birthday celebration in this vanquished city.

What is the Fuehrer doing now? I know he did not keep his promise to reenter Heidelberg today.[1]

More destroyed cities. The big, strong buildings are *kaputt*, but the fragile lilacs and pansies bloom amidst the rubble.

We pass through Nuremberg. Twenty kilometers later we reach Schwabach, our destination.

The First Camp   2

6

THE INDIGENOUS AUTHORITY

In Schwabach, Rosenbloom's first act is to report to an American Military Government (MG) captain who has arrived only a few hours earlier and has not yet had time to familiarize himself with the DP situation. The captain has a mountain of work to do—collect firearms and cameras, clear suitable civilian personnel, notify German authorities of the occupation policies and curfew, take steps to control hostile German civilians, establish controls over captured enemy material, and send out scouts for preliminary surveys of the industrial and agricultural status of the area.

A very busy man, this MG officer, but he takes the time to introduce the CO to a Herr Schmauzer, who is to be our guide. Rosenbloom learns that Schmauzer has never been a member of the Nazi Party, and that he offered his services to MG because of his sense of civic responsibility.

Rosenbloom brings Schmauzer to our vehicles and introduces him to everyone. Our guide is a thin, nervous, middle-aged man who possesses a sense of humor. When he laughs, his small Vandyke beard bounces. Like that of many Germans we are to meet, his English is excellent; he has lived in the United States in the late twenties.

This is my first nonmedical contact with a German citizen, and I observe Schmauzer critically. After a while, I decide that he is neither irritatingly conceited nor arrogant, but perhaps such attitudes disappear quickly in the people of a conquered nation.

Before the war, Schmauzer owned a factory in which phonograph and sewing machine needles were manufactured, but during the war, of course, he converted to more important things. He employed foreign laborers in his factory—Russian women—but he says he treated all the girls well. (Perhaps this was true. After we arrived at the Russian camp, some of the women seemed glad to see him.) He adds, however, that it would have been foolish for him to coerce his employees: if he had, they would not have worked as hard.

He tells us about the capture of Schwabach.

During the interval between the departure of German soldiers and Nazi officials and the entry of American troops, he and others tried to keep a semblance of order. At 6:00 A.M. a phone call came from the Americans, saying that if the roadblocks and other defensive barriers were removed the town would be spared.

Schmauzer and other civilians cleared the barriers and waited. The Americans did not arrive until 1:00 P.M. During the interval, there were reports of looting of homes and warehouses by Poles, but not by French or Russians.

I am surprised to hear that the looting was limited.

There are three different labor camps around the city.

The Russian camp houses about 1,200 people, with individuals and family groups living in run-down, flimsy wooden barracks arranged in a V formation. Each building is crowded with ten to twelve double-decker beds, many with straw-filled ticks, and covered by blankets or blanket substitutes made of pieces of burlap. No towels, pillows, or sheets are in evidence. Occasionally, ropes are strung between the beds, and from them laundry hangs, or torn, coarse rags or even cardboard for nocturnal privacy.

The shabbily dressed people flock about us, try to kiss us, follow us on our inspection, and chatter continuously. A clean kitchen contains four steel kettles, and enough food for about two days. The open-pit latrines are filthy. There are only twelve for the camp. In theory, sixty latrine seats would be desirable—5 percent of the camp population. There is one central washroom in which leaky pipes are noticeable. A Russian doctor takes care of the sick; I talk with him briefly and check some of his patients and supplies. No communicable diseases at the moment. There is no organization—the German *Lagerfuehrer* (camp master) has disappeared.

The second camp contains 400 French DPs and a few Italians. Almost half the French claim to be ex-prisoners of war. Their quarters are in buildings similar to those of the Russians —single-story, low-ceilinged wooden barracks, heated by pot-bellied stoves. The floors are littered by trash. Nearby is an identical building in which a dozen French women live.

These barracks are firetraps, I think, and particularly danger-ous during air raids. (Later I learn that an unknown number of DPs has been incinerated in buildings such as these in the large German cities subjected to Allied bombardments.)

Here the electricity works, and the *Lagerfuehrer*, a well-liked Czech, has remained. I meet a Sanitat, a POW equivalent of an aidman, and with his help I am able to make a cursory inspec-tion of the sick.

Poles, Italians, a few French and Russians, and small num-bers of people from other countries have inundated the third camp. Their beds are so close together that only a few inches separate them. The buildings are generally dilapidated with bro-ken windows, damaged doors, and leaky roofs. Clothes hang from nails driven into the walls. There is an insufficient number of latrines.

A medical student has been handling sick call. This camp, like all the others, needs basic medical supplies.

As we drive back to the center of town, I find the city attrac-tive, with a tiny river flowing through it. Picturesque, ancient houses look down at narrow streets. We pass a fifteenth-century Evangelical church; later I learn that it is filled with important art objects. The streets and nearby mountains remind me of Santa Fe, but the New Mexico mountains are more majestic.

Rain begins to fall, and Williams and I are assigned the job of finding quarters for the Team. We do not look too long, com-mandeering an immaculately clean two-story hotel and dining hall in the center of the city; we do not permit the German resi-dents to remain.

Williams hunts for rations and soon returns successfully. Now Aricer and Eastman concoct a late supper, after which Rosenbloom calls a meeting. He has provisional statistics for each camp, has made a judgment of existing DP leadership, and will begin the recruitment of camp and barracks leaders and in-terpreters. We decide that all three facilities can be maintained and improved. The next step will be the development of emergency work crews to start clearing the debris and trash that litter all the camps.

My report is accepted—the water supplies must be restored and the power lines to two camps repaired. As a temporary measure, it will be necessary to truck in chlorinated water for drinking, cooking, and washing. The *Guide to Assembly Center Administration for Refugees and Displaced Persons* (everyone has been studying his copy) says that each person should be provided with a minimum of five gallons of water per day, so Howcroft knows about how much to order.

New latrine buildings must be constructed. I deliver a short lecture on the subject. (Medical officers are drilled in waste disposal methods: we are familiar with pits, ditches, drains, and other intimate details; we must make certain that these structures are fly-proof, and remote from kitchens, dining halls, and water sources.) I also report the obvious—the dangerous overcrowding of sleeping rooms. Apparently, the German landlords have not read the *Guide*, which specifies that "thirty (30) square feet of floor space should be allowed for each single bed and forty-five (45) square feet for double-tier beds in dormitories . . . which should be adequately heated and ventilated . . . and kept clean." [1]

We talk about these recommendations and decide that we will have to find additional living space, beds, and bedding. The washrooms will have to be enlarged and the laundry facilities expanded.

From our population figures we estimate food needs, and Howcroft and Morivant add 10 percent on general principles.

Howcroft has been taking notes of all the supplies that are mentioned, and I am sure that his list is beginning to look like the index of a Montgomery Ward catalog, especially when dresses, skirts, corsets, and layettes are included. Obviously, none of us has thought of these unmilitary commodities in a long time.

It is midnight, but we are not finished. Morivant is worried about the men: they are restless and irritable. They have had very little to do because most of the work has been done by the officers. The mess personnel have not worked until this evening. The drivers have not done all the driving. The maintenance people have not had anything to maintain. He warns us that we can expect trouble with the men because they have been idle for too long a time.

I have noticed that some of the men are jumpy, but I feel that such reactions are to be expected during a period of adaptation to a new outfit, especially to one entirely different from anything they had been exposed to in the past.

Williams and Howcroft think that the sergeant worries too much. They are not concerned about the lack of work for the men; they predict that soon the men will have too much to do, and then they will complain about overworking. They attribute everything to the natural tendency of infantrymen to gripe.

The CO seems to agree with this opinion, but after adjourning the meeting, he arranges to talk with me privately. He is upset. Some of the remarks at the meeting make him think that there is something wrong between him and the men. What might it be? Religious bias? Perhaps some idiosyncracy of his? Or do some of the men resent him because he is an officer, a symbol of the caste system?

This is the first time a commanding officer has asked for my opinion about his leadership ability. What is there to say? I do not think there is a problem, but suggest to him that he seems too efficient and impersonal. He does have a reserved manner, but this is not a deadly sin, and, in many situations, it is an asset. I tell him about the remarks I overheard about the officers driving cars; he makes a note about this.

We chat a little longer; finally he relaxes. I tell him that I am unaware of any serious difficulties in the Team, and I doubt if anyone wants to apply for a transfer. He agrees.

Early the next morning we park in the main square, which is lined by a few small inns, a large church, and a fifteenth-century Gothic-type *Rathaus* (city hall). Hundreds of Germans are milling about, trying to read the newly posted declarations of occupation. My carbine-carrying teammates and I force our way through the crowd, march up the wide stairs, note the dark oil paintings of prominent citizens of the past, and walk into the office of the MG captain who is talking to the burgomaster and several other Germans. The captain tells the Germans who we are and what is to happen and then leaves.

The burgomaster, a tall, thin, graying man with a long, purple-veined nose, is obviously nervous, possibly as nervous as we are. But we have the security of our firearms. Two other men are supply controllers. One is a thick-necked man in his fifties; the other, plump and red-faced, is in his thirties. A well-dressed, pretty young woman is present, an interpreter.

The office is luxurious: rich drapes and a massive oak desk seem to symbolize authority. A faded painting hangs on one wall, and from it a gloomy Hessian soldier stares down at us. In a corner is a statue of a nude on which Howcroft deposits his helmet.

Rosenbloom, Howcroft, and I sit behind the desk, the Germans in front.

The important business is presented by Howcroft. The DPs are to receive a minimum of 2,000 calories a day. On a per hundred basis, this will amount to so much flour, meat, fats, coffee, biscuits, cheese, potatoes, and vegetables. Milk will be delivered to each camp every day for the infants, children, and pregnant and nursing mothers.

The burgomaster tries to make a point: in the past, the foreign workers were as well fed as German civilians. One of the controllers says that sometimes the foreigners received better food—when they worked hard. I find this hard to believe as I think about the lean and sallow DPs in the camps.

Rosenbloom cuts off the discussion. We have not come here for a debate, he says, and Howcroft continues to read monotonously from his long, detailed list of other necessities, such as soap, clothes, blankets, utensils, beds, buckets, and brooms, and the required medical supplies, headed by paregoric, sulfur ointment (for scabies), bandages, and a stethoscope.

After Howcroft presents the Germans with copies of the lists and they discuss them among themselves for a few minutes, the burgomaster says that most of the items are available, but sugar and coffee are hard to get, jellies and jams are scarce, and soap is impossible to obtain.

One of the controllers asks how they will be paid for these provisions; what currency will we use?

Surreptitiously, I pull out my *Guide* and quickly search through the table of contents for the heading "Supplies"—"Methods of Obtaining," paragraph 23a.

The instructor at school was correct. The pertinent paragraph states that "Supplies/stores required for Assembly Centers will be obtained as far as possible from existing local resources, the indigenous authority being instructed to purchase the supplies."

Now for the first time I notice paragraph 23b: "Imported supplies will however be issued by the Army services . . . to the account of the CA [civil affairs] detachment concerned. It will then be the responsibility of the Detachment to 're-issue' these supplies to the indigenous authority receiving firstly, a quantitative receipt for them; and secondly, cash payment for them. . . ."

So, the poor indigenous authority (the burgomaster) cannot get off the hook even if the supplies requested are unavailable from German sources.

I wonder if the CO knows this. But he has matters well in hand and does not refer to the Guide. He tells the burgomaster that we are the military representatives of the United States. Our job is to carry out the policies of the government of the United States. American policy concerning displaced persons is simple: all material and services for their care will be provided by the German people, who brought them here.

Rosenbloom is very brief. I am beginning to learn that he is concise in all situations.

Then Howcroft reinforces Rosenbloom's statements, butchering the language of the occupation policy, but getting through: only after they have accepted their responsibility can the rest of the world treat them with respect. Howcroft is 21—just old enough to vote—but his voice carries authority and his blue eyes are stony hard; none of us sees anything incongruous in his presentation to the middle-aged Germans.

Payment to private individuals for supplies and services would come from the burgomaster, from his community funds. Obviously, adds Howcroft, the currency would be reichsmarks. Then he tells the burgomaster that all items being requisitioned must be on hand in twenty-four hours. The Germans promise to cooperate. We do not foresee any major difficulties—we know that the Germans have read the new "Articles of Government," which start with the ancient words, "We come as conquerors."

As we start to leave, I realize that Rosenbloom has conducted the meeting formally, according to the instructions in our special orders for American-German relations: "Contacts with Germans will be made only on official business. Immediate compliance with all official orders and instructions . . . will be demanded of them and will be enforced."

The Germans know we intend to enforce our demands. Perhaps they know this because we are in uniform. The special orders also say that the "Germans hold all things military in deep respect. That respect must be maintained habitually or the Allied cause is hurt and the first steps are taken toward World War III. . . ."

We intend to maintain that respect. We do not want to be responsible for starting World War III.

I return to the camps to spend more time with the sick people, and I find two patients with jaw abscesses developing from infected teeth, so obviously one of the services I will have to arrange for is dental care. I find other patients with infections that could be controlled with sulfadiazine or sulfathiazole, the two recently developed antibacterial drugs that have helped to reduce the death rate in war injuries. I will have to look for an American medical unit in this area and hope it has a cooperative supply officer.

There are patients here with diagnostic problems—a pregnant woman with abdominal pain, a man with the ominous combination of upper abdominal distress and a hard lump beneath his jaw, another man with night blindness, and two middle-aged men with severe heart disease.

And infants.

A medical practice here would be exciting.

I remember that there is overcrowding, and I write myself a note to check everyone in the camps for contagious diseases.

Twenty-four hours later all the supplies requested are on hand except for medical items. When this is reported to the burgomaster, he is surprised and insists that the medical items have been obtained and delivered. He has a receipt!

The matter is turned over to the harassed MG captain. But I cannot wait for an official investigation or a search for stolen supplies: the medical needs are immediate. I visit one of the line outfits in town and learn from a friendly sergeant that there is a depot somewhere east of us that may have medical supplies.

Morivant arms himself with his dependable carbine, and we leave in one of our trucks, hunt for the depot and find it, and load our truck with bandages, ampoules of vitamin B-1, C, D, and ABCD, some interesting surgical instruments, hypodermic needles, and small syringes. But still no aspirin, medicinal ointments, or alcohol.

So, early in our career, we demonstrate our flexibility: we are supposed to requisition all supplies from the local city government (*Stadtkreis*). If unsuccessful, we can apply to the district administration (*Landkreis*). We are forbidden the use of American Army property. Captured German military supplies, unfortunately for us, are reserved for German POWs, not DPs. (In practice, German and American military garments are beginning to be worn by the DPs in increasing numbers, satisfying an urgent need.)

We find it is difficult to obtain emergency supplies from proper channels until MG is solidly established. So we learn to question soldiers in neighboring units about the location of supply depots. Later we discover that our own clients, the DPs, have kept their eyes open: they know there is a cache of coats 4 kilometers to the south, or of blankets 15 kilometers northwest. They guide us to the warehouses or supply dumps, on which we clamp an Off Limits sign and where we fill our vehicles and, of course, give receipts for the supplies obtained. Thus we have changed the reliable Army adage to "stay away from headquarters and always give a receipt."

7

THE SLAVES

We make rounds several times a day at each camp. When we have time we listen to stories told by the DPs, repetitive tales about the conditions under which they lived and worked, not only here at Schwabach, but elsewhere in Germany. They tell about their own experiences and those of other DPs. Most of the stories are about the last few years, particularly 1943—a grim year because the war was going badly for their masters. The need for increased industrial production became a reality for the DPs when their working hours increased, their payments decreased, and their leisure time was sharply restricted. Punishments became more severe and frequent, including the death penalty for minor offenses.

Simultaneously, as Germany's armies swallowed more and more of its citizens, foreign workers were brought into the Third Reich in increasing numbers in order to replace native civilian workers. This meant that labor camps such as those here became more overcrowded, toilets more inadequate, food poorer, and medical care limited. Official labor recruitment policies became aggressive: organized manhunts began.

An Italian tells about labor raids in his country in 1944: sections of cities cordoned off by German soldiers and people abducted, sent to Germany without a chance to notify their families. A Dutchman describes the kidnapping of thousands of people a day from Amsterdam. He says that the Germans had a predilection for searching churches and cinemas. A Pole tells the most frightening story, about the day his small village was surrounded by Nazi troops, the villagers instructed to vacate their homes immediately. Thirty minutes later, all the buildings in town were burned down. The sounds of machine gun fire could be heard in the nearby forest as soldiers searched for escapees. Our Pole, one of the more articulate of the DPs, tells about the icy fear that froze his voice, caused him to tremble uncontrollably. He could not move. Soon the villagers were prodded into trucks, then into boxcars. Fifty, sixty people in one car, he said, with small amounts of food and water. The floor was cold, the sick people groaned, a woman delivered a baby; periodically, the German guards opened the doors of the car and pitched out the dead.

Most of the DPs say they came to Germany in boxcars. A few say they arrived in crowded trucks and wagons. Once in Germany they were assigned to quarters of varying size and quality: dog kennels, barns, rooms in private homes, large group dormitories as in the work camps here, and concentration camps.

A Frenchman tells a different story, about the soft sell technique used by the Germans after the fall of France in 1940. Many of his countrymen volunteered for labor service in the Third Reich, lured by offers of jobs that not only paid better than in their own countries but also included attractive health benefits. Others came because their families were starving: for many there were no opportunities to work in their own land because the Germans had closed the factories that they considered unessential to the German economy. Later, however, the hard sell began—the penalty for avoiding labor service was death.

In the last year or two, conditions for all the workers were about the same. Long hours, no privileges, no contact with Germans other than as servants or slaves. The little money they received was spent in the black market, usually for cigarettes. The workers could not walk freely in the streets. In certain areas, church attendance was forbidden. Even their sex life was regulated; sexual intercourse was forbidden to certain Poles.

Undoubtedly, the greatest pressures were exerted in factories geared for military production, the least in small shops such as Herr Schmauzer's needle shop. Still, people disappeared. Perhaps they had escaped. Perhaps they had been "punished."

The Nazi overseers had sentenced their expendable human beasts of burden to hard labor—for life.

There are millions of foreign workers in Germany now; the process of liberation is going on daily; soon they will all be free.

When the end comes, will they turn on their masters? Are the Germans filled with fear and terror?

Considering their treatment, it is surprising to me that so few of the oppressed slaves did rampage, loot, and murder, especially those we have seen wandering through the countryside in search of food and shelter. Perhaps their ability to take action, even vengeance, has been blunted by years of submissiveness.

Occasional violence does occur, however. The CO makes note of it on his first daily report form, which has two lines for comments on the conduct and behavior of our wards: "Russians and a few Poles wandering on roads through town looting and destroying property."

The MG office is concerned, and asks us to take measures.

Rosenbloom, pondering the problem of keeping order, decides on a display of force. He orders all the members of the Team to dress formally, fully armed. We find the Russian camp completely disorganized. Nobody is working. Adults and children tag along behind us; young girls throw themselves at our men, kissing them. Rosenbloom, who speaks German fluently, questions all the adults in the party. The man who answers the most questions is appointed temporary leader. Rosenbloom asks him to arrange for urgently needed labor details to clean the camp, particularly the latrines, to work in the kitchen, and to establish a supply area. Barracks leaders must be appointed immediately. We need an accurate head count, says the CO. We are here, he says, to help your people to go home. We can't help them until we know how many are here, and if they are healthy. We have supplies and we will distribute them. Then we must find out what else the people need.

The Russian acknowledges our orders. But he has a request to make that none of us anticipated. His camp needs protection! Could we post guards at the camp? Last night they heard the noise of gunfire in the vicinity and are afraid that German soldiers are hiding in the hills and will return and set fire to their barracks.

We cannot furnish guards, but Rosenbloom finds this a good time to organize police and fire protection crews. He tells the Russians not to worry about the Germans in the hills: American soldiers will take care of them.

So there is an unexpected meeting of minds on the necessity for guards at the camp. An entry and exit control system is established. Still another reason for patrolling the camp becomes evident when friendly American soldiers infiltrate the camp from all directions as soon as an Off Limits sign is posted: the notice is as encouraging to them as an Adults Only sign at a movie theater is to youngsters. Our touring soldiers are generous, leaving behind a trail of candy and cigarettes, but they are less interested in sightseeing than in girl-watching, and this disrupts the domestic tranquility. Guards become very useful.

During our early days at Schwabach, our CO finds it impossible to obtain official American security guards for the camps, but DP sentries are appointed who are obviously pleased with their new duties, and they perform diligently—and enthusiastically.

I meet a few Poles and Italians living in the Russian camp: they have many complaints. They object to the two large Russian flags that fly above the barracks. They are upset about their quarters, which they say are worse than the Russians', although this does not seem possible. They dislike Russian cooking. They do not have enough to eat. Their clothes are poor.

I can see that someone from the diplomatic corps should be on our Team. This is definitely a problem for Rosenbloom, not for a medical officer. I am sure he can solve it with his infantry experience.

8

THE RUSSIANS

The Russian leader, a civilian, is either inefficient or lacks authority. We decide this on our next visit to the camp, when we discover that nobody has collected population figures and that no work is being done except by the sentries and the camp doctor. Rosenbloom decides to replace the civilian with a POW. He assembles the POWs, and they designate a young captain as their spokesman, whom Rosenbloom accepts as the new head. The Russian officer does not waste time. He makes a brief, loud statement, and almost miraculously kitchen, garbage disposal, and latrine cleaning details begin to function. Apparently the Russian people, like the Germans, respect or fear military authorities.

The camp physician is Dr. Musenko, a thin and weary middle-aged man. Assisted by his wife, he conducts a busy sick call. Every morning I work with him and tell him about the new sulfonamide drugs and about penicillin, the panacea. He receives this information with proper amazement, but is kind or tactful enough not to show the skepticism he must feel. Next to his dispensary is a primitive operating room containing a wooden table and a few instruments; it is clean and light—and warm, because he has cleverly insulated the walls with packing box material. His greatest need is for bandages; for a long time he has been using coarse paper as a substitute. He has no sedatives, only a small quantity of morphine, and almost no codeine.

I notice that he sits behind his desk and rarely rises; his wife does all the physical work. He coughs often and I realize that he has intense chest pain. Frequently the pain must become unbearable. I watch him grimace and then break open an ampoule and quickly swallow its contents. Afterward, he seems to feel better, but the effect wears off in two or three hours and he has to open another ampoule.

He also prescribes the same drug for his patients. I ask him what it is, but I do not entirely understand his reply—his German is better than mine. I think it is an opiate, but I am not familiar with its use in this form. I recall De Quincy's *Confessions of an English Opium Eater*, and I have read that powdered opium (laudanum) and opium tincture can be taken by mouth, but I thought this practice was obsolete.

I cannot find any evidence to support the rumor that the doctor is a chronic alcoholic.

I note that he is familiar with one of the early sulfonamides, because he has a tube of prontosil which he tells me is "good for bad throats." I present him with five tubes of sulfathiazole ointment which I have obtained from a philanthropic medical unit that passed through Schwabach last night. Dr. Musenko will be delighted after using them on skin infections.

We talk about other things as well, particularly about books, and he turns out to be an admirer of the writings of Edgar Allen Poe, John Ruskin, and Herbert Spencer. I hear a little about Kiev, a colorful, historic city with ancient churches and monasteries, and a famous eleventh-century gate that partially survived the forays and incursions of invaders. A city that suffered from repeated Jewish pogroms. After its capture by the Nazis, its citizens learned what it was like to be butchered.

Dr. Musenko and his wife survived the initial occupation and then the boxcar transportation into Germany. He has been here about three years.

He wants to return to Kiev, but I am not sure if he will. He is undoubtedly seriously ill, and I elicit from him the disturbing information that he has recently lost weight. I tell him that he should be evaluated in the German hospital in town, but, as expected, he denies that anything is the matter. I thought that only American physicians were reluctant patients, but the characteristic seems universal.

The next day I observe the doctor again. He is obviously failing. I present him with the problem: he must know that he is being unfair to his patients and wife by continuing to work. I have made arrangements with the local hospital for his admission. There his symptoms will be investigated—with payments for such services to come from the burgomaster, of course. He grudgingly agrees that it is best. His wife packs a few things for him to take, and he slips into a torn, black overcoat with a big astrakhan collar. I ask him if he was able to take much with him from Kiev. He says that he was permitted to take the coat and whatever clothes he could carry.

He kisses his wife good-bye; she rushes out of the room weeping.

I can anticipate what will happen next, and it does. At the hospital, he tells me that he has changed his mind, that he is not going to stay in the hospital, that his wife can take care of him in the camp, and, furthermore, German doctors are no good.

But I am ready for his objections. I cannot go back to the camp. Gas is scarce. I have orders to visit a different camp. Tomorrow I will visit him and he will probably be ready to leave, which we both know is untrue. He has used the same words before on his patients. I shake his hand and drive away after consulting with the chief German doctor at the hospital, who seems very competent.

Although I am to meet many Russians during the next few months, Dr. Musenko is the only one I am able to talk with in a meaningful way. Perhaps this is because we share a common interest—our concern for patients. Despite this, I never discover anything about his politics. With other Russians, I seem to be limited conversationally to requests, orders, explanations, complaints. Sometimes I throw out a question: Who are the important people in Russia? The only name I hear is Stalin. Perhaps there is no one else of importance.

I thought that vodka was their only liquor, but I discover that where there is no vodka, they will drink whatever is available.

Another illusion is shattered. I assumed that all Russian property was communally owned, but I note that each Russian DP has his own chattels and a well-developed protective and proprietary interest in them. Nobody is going to steal *his* possessions! He has forgotten that whatever he now owns once belonged to German military or civilian sources, or to the American Army. But this is irrelevant. He would also deny that he has a preoccupation with material things. Only capitalists are guilty of that.

No religious services are held at the Russian camp, but our physical examinations (and later delousing sessions) reveal that about half the old, and some of the young, wear religious medals.

9

POPULATION CHANGES

Each night Corporal Ferris, the company clerk, slaves over the Daily Displaced Persons Center Report. He huddles over his typewriter, entering onto the form—in triplicate—information about the organization, conduct, and health of the DPs, the camp sanitation, and the supply situation. There is also room for special remarks. Then the CO reads and signs the original and sends it to G-5 of 7th Army.

The capacity of the center is estimated at 2,200. Every day, population figures are brought to Rosenbloom's office by each national leader, who receives his statistics from his barracks leaders, who in turn procure their data from room commanders.

The table is a compilation of population data obtained from four separate reports covering the days from April 23 through 26, 1945.

POPULATION STATISTICS, SCHWABACH, 1945

	April 23		April 24		April 25		April 26	
	DPs	POWs	DPs	POWs	DPs	POWs	DPs	POWs
Russians	700	100	913	50	837	50	835	5
Poles	150		175		182		187	
French	440	258	310	385	240	381	165	417
Belgians	50		50		52		54	
Dutch	50		1		1		0	
Yugoslavs	6		5		7		15	
Czechs	6		6		6		5	
Italians	300		16	221	25	231	31	243
Greeks	5		5		5		5	
Others	1		1		161		306	
Total	2065		1907		2267		2270	

During this interval the figures fluctuate mysteriously.

There is a reduction in the number of French, never adequately explained, and a dramatic decline in the number of Dutch, who disappear entirely. We presume that they have abandoned their camp in order to start the homeward trek. Neither of these groups is responsible for the significant increase in the number of "others." They increase because new DPs are found and brought into the center and because some Poles, Russians, Estonians, and Latvians are beginning to shed the countries of their birth in order to become stateless people.

Some of the other variations are caused by people wandering in and out of the barracks and the camp during the roll call, abetted by a lack of proficiency in arithmetic and counting by our DP census takers. But they are not the only ones who cannot add. The failure of the "total" numbers on the bottom of the table to match the true sums of the individual, daily columns cannot be blamed on the DPs who supplied the figures: somebody in our office made these mistakes and nobody ever detected them—not even G-5.

It is remarkable that the number of Greeks remains the same every day. Perhaps they never leave their quarters. They seem to be happy playing dominoes hour after hour.

But there is nothing constant about the number of POWs. During the four days of operation covered in the table, the total population increases 10 percent. But, simultaneously, French POWs increase 75 percent, Italian POWs multiply like rabbits, and Russian POWs decrease almost 95 percent.

It is difficult to explain these gyrations. A reasonable explanation is based on the DPs' lack of proper identification papers. Because of this, they think they can claim any background that might be useful to them. We speculate whether the Italians and French are convinced that former POWs will be repatriated first and perhaps be given better food or quarters; hence their flocking into the ranks of military personnel. But reverse thinking exists in the minds of the Russians, in whose barracks we hear the rumor that the Soviet government might take a dim view of their former soldiers permitting themselves to work for the Germans—even though such labor was compulsory.

The daily report form has an entry for supply shortages, and the same items are listed during the first two days: medical supplies, beds, blankets, mattresses, DDT, spray guns, maintenance equipment, and plumbing material. On the third and fourth days medical supplies are "good," but kerosene is added to the other listed shortages, because DDT in kerosene is an important agent in the purification of latrines.

In the daily report of the third day of operation the following comments appear in the section labeled "Remarks (use back of sheet if necessary):

"Arrangements completed to delouse DPs. Recommend that the Military Barracks (formerly used by the German Signal Corps) be converted to a new DP center to solve problems of housing and control." (The CO had recommended previously that many administrative problems could be remedied by operating a single, large, adequate camp. Now he repeats his recommendation.)

The report ends with the statement, "a fourth location of approximately 150 DPs discovered in vicinity of Schwabach."

The newly discovered fourth center is in a canning factory, *Konservenfabrik*, and this intelligence spreads quickly through the camps. As soon as we hear the news we drive out but are too late. From a distance we can see what appears to be a column of ants trudging slowly toward us, each ant burdened with a load about twice his size. As we reach the column, we see that it is made up of hundreds of DPs from the three camps, each carrying canned goods and jars of fruit preserves in bags and improvised sacks.

They can use the extra food: we are not about to force them to return their treasures. But Howcroft is disturbed. He had understood that there were not supposed to be any jams or jellies in this area. Now he will have to reevaluate his information about other presumed unobtainable supplies.

There are about 150 DPs living in the factory, and they look better nourished than the ones closer to town. During my customary inspection, I discover a young Polish woman walking the floor; she has been in labor for ten hours. I examine her and then wait for a short time and wonder if I will deliver her baby; it has been about four years since my month of obstetrics as a medical student. But the whole process slows down, the pains are only every five minutes. There is plenty of time. I drive her to a civilian hospital, where she later delivers a normal baby.

I suppose that she could have delivered in the factory with little trouble—there were sheets and hot water there. But the hospital is more professional. My former professor of obstetrics used to say that primitive people could easily deliver in the fields, but I do not think any of the medical students believed him.

It seems strange after all these years of taking care of young male patients to have to start thinking about the conditions and disorders of women and children.

Although there are very few Poles in the mixed camp, we are experiencing difficulties with them. They say that they will co-operate and follow orders and recommendations, but they do not. They start a job but do not finish it. Their appointed leaders seem ineffective. They do not want to help themselves. They seem to be hostile toward us and there is friction within their own group.

One day a Polish-speaking MP drives into the camp and presents us with a short, shriveled, ill-tempered lady of about 40 whom he found wandering in town with no place to go. Nobody wants her. She has been thrown out of the Polish quarters. The Polish leader is annoyed when he sees her and says she claimed to be German when the Germans still ruled, but, now that the enemy has been defeated, she has become Polish. She is a woman without a country, he says dramatically. She has made her bed and they (the Poles) are not about to take her back.

We deliver her to the MG office for interrogation, despite her verbal resistance—she won't go where there are soldiers because once a soldier tried to rape her. Eventually MG clears her of charges of collaboration and she is grudgingly admitted into the Polish compound. Her prospects there do not seem promising.

Other DPs also appear to have grim futures, but not because of suspected collaboration. They are the ones who have given up all hope of ever seeing their families again. They say that their wives and children are dead or that their families are missing from their home towns.

How do they know, I wonder. They have not received any letters in recent years.

But apparently there was a communication system in which incoming slaves—particularly Poles, because they constituted the greatest labor reservoir for the Nazis—would bring the news. From them, husbands learned of their wives' fate, of their doomed little villages, homes, or shops, even of the destruction of their cows and sheep.

These are the beaten, spiritless people, with no capacity for productive work, no interest in community life, and no desire to return to their former homes.

I watch one of them: he sits for hours, holding a loaf of bread on his lap, his jaws moving monotonously up and down as he breaks off a small piece of the hard bread, then another. . . .

There are others, particularly the young, who pursue a post-liberation policy of retaliation for the mistreatments they received from the Germans. Still other DPs adopt an "I want to forget" attitude characterized by bursts of frenzied hyperactivity. Reckless driving on patched-together motorcycles and in uncertain cars, wild parties, and excessive drinking happen too often. (All kinds of alcoholic beverages were consumed indiscriminately. As a result, there were 2,000 deaths in the first month after liberation, thousands of cases of illness, and some of blindness following the ingestion of methyl alcohol. [1])

The VD incidence increases.

Our efforts at providing recreational facilities are unsuccessful, possibly because we are amateurs but partly because of the lack of proper material, such as movies and books and magazines in the languages of the DPs. One of our men finds some soccer balls, and these help. A dance is arranged. We look for radios. However, our efforts are unimaginative; we have not been in the business long enough to think about kindergartens, occupational therapy, and vocational training.

10

DUSTY DAYS

April 24. A public health officer, Colonel Hopkins, and a United Nations Relief and Rehabilitation Administration nurse, Miss Gregg, arrive for an unofficial visit. They are studying camp management and would like to inspect our facilities.

Our visitors compliment us on the appearance of the camps, but I think they are only being friendly. I must admit, however, that even the Polish quarters look better today.

In the evening, when we make rounds at the Russian camp, we are greeted effusively. The cooks and kitchen supervisors tell us how grateful they are to the Americans for coming out every day and being interested in them, and bringing provisions. The food supplies have been arriving regularly, and the compliments bring a trace of a smile to Howcroft's usual grim countenance, but Morivant is embarassed by the exuberance of our welcome.

The Colonel has a supply of DDT and asks if I would like to have our people disinfected. I am delighted, because I have been trying to obtain this highly regarded powder since our arrival.

Large rooms are selected for the dusting, each with doors for entry and exit. The national leaders are notified. Explanations are given. Appointments are scheduled for the next day. The enlisted men are instructed on their part in guiding the customers through the dusting rooms and the method of dusting, and that night they keep busy stamping little cards, 2,000 of them, saying "DDT" and the next day's date.

Two of the men gripe about being overworked. Life is back to normal.

Festivities begin the following morning. The French are first, and cooperate fully. Their leaders tell them that no one can cross the Rhine unless he has his little DDT card. No difficulty with the Italians, who seem to understand and accept long lines. The other Western European and Balkan guests move through without turmoil.

But when the hour arrives for the sprinkling of the Poles and Russians, no one is present.

Their leaders are found, the necessity for dusting reexplained—typhus, lice, bedbugs, flies, pestilence—and the leaders apologize, then leave to search for their constituents. Soon about a hundred people appear. The Russian chief is furious. Flanked by Eastman and Mace, both fully armed, he visits each barracks building and excitedly informs his people that if they do not have the little cards, they will not be given supper that night. This is a powerful weapon, more potent than the carbines, and soon the rest of the Russians march in reluctantly and receive the treatment.

Reactions to the dusting are mixed. Most of the men accept stoically and bravely. But many of the women, and some of the men, are uncertain; they are afraid that the dust will settle in their hair or spoil their clothing. Mothers resist bringing their infants for the procedure. A few of the older people think they are being poisoned. They unwillingly submit but immediately afterward rush to the washrooms to rinse off the magic white powder.

Only one person refuses to submit, a fearful middle-aged Polish woman who decides that she will die if she is dusted. Adjacent to the main dusting room is a small side room, and into this sanctuary she flees, clutching her rosary, her countrymen in pursuit. She climbs a dresser and leaps out of a high, narrow window crying, "The Gestapo are here," and sprains her ankle. Her defeat is total. After we tape her ankle, she is dusted. (This is the only casualty recorded during our extensive DDT experiences.)

Some of the supervising DPs, instrumental in making the arrangements for their countrymen, think that because they are important camp luminaries they do not need to be dusted. Their illusions are promptly pulverized.

Once the dusting has started, the NCOs and enlisted men find the work challenging. Sergeant Morivant becomes enthusiastic. Soon everyone, regardless of his specified job as driver or cook, becomes proficient at inserting the tip of the hand duster into specified crevices between the skin and clothing, and then aiming the duster properly. Men are easier to handle than women, but women are more fun to dust because they have skirt problems which induce considerable hilarity—the more the hilarity, the more thoroughly dusted are the recipients.

Usually only one dusting is sufficient to convince the DPs of the desirable qualities of DDT, and often they request a personal supply for their blankets and beds. (Later, at another camp in which we are using power dusters capable of handling 6,000 people a day, we find that 1,000 pounds of DDT disappear—some of the DPs have raided a warehouse, loaded the cans on carts, and distributed them to each of the barracks. Despite the theft of U.S. Army property, nobody is unhappy because by then we are fighting a grave typhus fever epidemic, and the distribution of the DDT is considered helpful in curbing the spread of the disease.)

I studied French and German in high school and college but never attained conversational fluency. In the camps, however, many words and phrases come back, and I am soon able to converse in both languages. I even acquire idiomatic phrases in Polish.

Eventually, I am able to weave French, German, and English together, using gestures. The result sounds something like a hesitant faucet. "Dub jay, Buddy. Wo ist der Schmerz? Sprechen, tout de suite." And the DP, also with his limited knowledge of these three languages, responds in kind, and somehow we understand each other.

Listening to these alien sounds, particularly German, and attempting to speak them myself all day, produces a corrupting effect on my English and this becomes noticeable when I the verb at the end of the sentence begin to put. This is followed by spelling inaccuracies. Great concentration is required to remember correct letter sequences, and I have to poll my colleagues about individual words: Is it "ordnance" or "ordenance" or "ordinance"? The votes are usually evenly divided.

Unquestionably the DPs learn English faster than we learn their tongues, particularly those like Edgar, who works in our office. First they learn the essentials—the obscenities—and later the less important words.

Edgar, a tall Lithuanian, had worked in that country's merchant marine before the war. Afterward, he was "recruited" as a laborer and sent to Berlin for a short time, and then to Heidelberg for three years. He speaks Russian, Polish, German, and Lithuanian competently, and his English improves in tremendous spurts.

Each morning he brings us a daily report:

> Yesterday night, eight Estonians into small camp come. One is no good-sonamabitch; I tink he is Gestapo man. Trouble maker. Bad for displeased persons camp. One room must be deloused. One sack of potatoes steals away in night. Water closets goddam no good canals. Big dancing tonight. Need greens for painting.

It is always a pleasure to return to our quarters for supper and listen to English again, even though it is punctuated by local idiom. However, this respite from the concatenation of alien languages lasts only until April 24. A horde of French soldiers joins us, and now our meals are bilingual.

"Pass the bread, the bread. *Le pain*, you stupid frog!" And their leader, Lieutenant Chaudon, would be convulsed with laughter, and reply with choice Gallic expletives straight from the Casbah. We become great friends, and he invites me to visit him someday in Casablanca.

Chaudon brings trucks and drivers; one of the drivers is married to their cook. I note that she carries in her belt a vicious-looking knife, emblazoned with swastikas. All the French have prodigious, enthusiastic appetites and the evening meals become festive, prolonged excuses for reminiscing and guzzling. One of the Frenchmen supplies noisy background music from a foot organ, which is in the dining room. On the organ is a book of Lutheran hymns, but the music that comes out is worthy of Maurice Chevalier.

We Americans are too subdued.

The French drivers are put to work immediately, picking up and delivering supplies. They are very diligent. I notice that when they are not on the road, they spend an inordinate amount of time checking, washing, oiling, and greasing their vehicles—four-ton, lend-lease Dodge trucks. I am told that they do this because each of them has signed away his life now and hereafter for his truck; if his negligence causes any damage, he is required to pay the expenses himself, or be thrown into the Bastille.

Accordingly, each driver looks after his conveyance with the same attention he would give his current mistress. He strokes and perfumes it; he watches it jealously; he sleeps with it, for there is a large comfortable bed and mattress in its rear.

But when he is behind the wheel, his legal commitments are forgotten and the grim specter of Devil's Island fades away. Passion replaces concern. He drives as fast as he can, whether going forward or backward. He manipulates his strident horn and squealing brakes with the enthusiasm of a concert pianist at work on his keyboard and pedals. Once embarked on his irrevocable course, *le bon Dieu* help anyone in front of or behind him, whether it be an American soldier bemused by an attractive young woman, or General de Gaulle momentarily lost in a daydream.

About the time the French arrive, Williams, our adjutant, leaves. He has been ill, and finally I have to send him back for hospital care. After a few days of headache, chills, and fever, he develops a yellow hue in his eyeballs and, although there are several diagnostic possibilities, I think that most likely he is afflicted with acute catarrhal jaundice.[1] Army doctors have been alerted to the presence of this disease in the last few months, with cases appearing in many different divisions. Williams is unhappy about going to the hospital. He fears that he may not return to the Team—and he does not. Rosenbloom, Howcroft, and I take over his duties.

11

NEW ORDERS

DPs are being discovered all over. Reports arrive of ten Poles in a barn, forty Russians in the hills, some Italians in town and on the roads, seven Frenchmen in a field—and our men go out to bring them in, or the Military Police collect them.

One day the CO tells me that 200 Ukrainians are living in a farm about 5 kilometers from Schwabach. After the German troops fled the area, they organized themselves into a small farming community. They were given, or somehow acquired, cows, pigs, and chickens. They make their own bread and are now living independently.

My medical-sanitary inspection reveals no major problems, but I advise attention to their latrines and promise them garbage pails. Their leader is a tall, handsome young man. I inform him that when we have space we will move his people into one of our camps, and I arrange with him to return that evening with our crew for a delousing session at 7:00 P.M.

The young man accepts the appointment but says his people will not be happy about moving into a new camp. They like it where they are, and, furthermore, our camps have Russians, and they do not like Russians. Now I become aware of people living in Russia, and part of Poland, who do not consider themselves Russian or Polish. The Ukrainians seem to have their own traditions. They fought everyone for hundreds of years and regard themselves as a distinct national entity.

This is informative, but not our problem. If the Russians, Poles, and Czechs could not resolve the problem of the Ukrainians in 800 years, it is unlikely that we can in the next few days. Our concern is with health and sanitation.

At 7:00 P.M. I return with my crew, and there are only ten people in the camp. The others have gone into town for a night of carousing. A middle-aged woman greets me. Neither she nor the others know they are to be dusted. We have wasted our time. Out of humor, we drive back to Schwabach.

At our regular staff meeting that night I inform Rosenbloom of the bungled arrangements. He is not upset. He tells me that the man I talked to earlier is not the leader. The woman I talked to is! Most likely she had not received any message from the man.

No great harm done. The dusting will be rescheduled.

After supper, a young British officer arrives as our guest for the night. He has been in a German prison camp for a long time, and has just escaped. Aricer brings him some reheated supper and apologizes.

"Lieutenant, this is all I have left, this poor plate of salmon croquettes. That's the God's honest truth."

"I'll bet it has not been waiting for me as long as I have been waiting for it," says our guest, who seems amused by Aricer's Deep South accent. The sergeant is equally entertained by the young man's clipped British speech.

We have hosted other escaped prisoners in the last few days, all of whom have told exciting stories. Now, everyone on the Team sits down to listen to another tale.

The lieutenant was captured at Dunkirk five years ago, and since interned in a POW compound in Silesia. When elements of the Russian Army neared his camp last week, the German guards decided to leave, hoping to reach the Bavarian Alps; they took along a handful of the POWs as hostages, but some of them escaped, including our guest.

His story might have been written in Hollywood. While in the prison camp, some of his friends had constructed a crystal radio, which they kept in two parts—in a canteen and mess gear. The components for the radio were obtained from German guards in return for cigarettes and delicacies from their International Red Cross packages. (Incidentally, says the lieutenant, we could not have survived all these years without these wonderful packages.) With the radio, the POWs were aware of the changing nature of the war; even so, they had not been able to avoid being forced out of the camp. Why did the German guards want to escape? asks Private Eastman, who sometimes seems unaware of the nature of evil. The lieutenant answers his question: the Germans were trying to avoid being captured by the Russians; they feared their retaliation for the way the Nazis had mistreated Russian POWs. (Of the 5.7 million Red Army soldiers who reached POW camps, only one million survived.[1])

Tomorrow we will take our British lodger to MG to start his final trip home. At the moment he is weary, dirty, and ragged, but excited; he cannot stop talking.

Late that evening I have a request for a house call. I drive out to the mixed camp to examine an elderly French lady whom I had previously treated for a badly infected finger. Now she has developed a cough, pain in her chest, and fever. I do not have a regular stethoscope, but several months earlier I "liberated" a small wooden stethoscope, about five inches long, with a single earpiece. It has the same shape as the stethoscope invented by the great Laennec (René Théophile Hyacinthe) early in the nineteenth century, and I am surprised to discover that I can really hear the diverse sounds of the lungs and heart through it.

But tonight I hear too many extraneous noises when I try to listen to the patient's chest: passing vehicles, the kaleidoscopic sounds of people in the six-family bedroom she shares, people saying, in French, "Doctor, do something!"

As an intern I learned that it is sometimes best to give sedatives to relatives of the patient so that they can sleep and not disturb the patient, but all I have is a German inhalant containing a combination of chloroform, ether, and ammonia. The only thing I can do is load the old lady into my car and deliver her to the local hospital for treatment of her pneumonia. The German doctor there resents being awakened in the middle of the night. He behaves just as I would.

Great activity at our quarters when I arrive at 1:00 A.M. Orders have arrived for us to leave immediately. Our vehicles are being packed. Our acquisitive supply sergeant has somehow stockpiled enough gasoline to fill the trucks and the spare cans. We learn that we must take all the gasoline we can obtain with us; otherwise we may be marooned. (There are gasoline stations in the cities and towns of Germany, some with the familiar red Esso and Standard signs, but at this time they do not have any fuel for sale.)

We have been in Schwabach for five days, long enough to

learn several fundamental truths: how to judge DPs for executive ability, how to obtain supplies and get along with German burgomasters and American MG officials, and how to use psychology for the greater benefit of health and sanitation. We have not learned how to motivate some of the DPs so that they will have a sense of communal responsibility.

We are surprised—and pleased—to hear that the DPs are sorry that we are leaving. They have become increasingly cooperative during the last few days. They respect us, not only because we work overtime at our jobs, but because we are genuinely concerned about their well-being, an attitude they have not encountered for many years. The malevolent world in which they have survived, terrified and lonely, is beginning to vanish. We, the Americans, care. Perhaps there is hope.

I am unhappy about leaving so suddenly. What has happened to Herr Schmauzer? I have not seen him since the first day. Will the missing medical supplies be found? What will happen to Dr. Musenko? Will he be able to practice again? Will the Ukrainians be dusted? Will my little old French lady with pneumonia recover and rejoin her neighbors?

MG is given a complete report of all the loose ends and will tie them up, but I have no one to write to here in Schwabach, and I never do find out.

At dawn the next morning, a clear sharp day looms. The convoy is assembled; each of the American and French vehicles is in its proper position.

Our destination is deep in southern Germany.

12

CAMARADERIE

On the first leg of the trip, I am invited to be a passenger in one of the cars brought by the French. Innocently, I accept. After being wedged between an assortment of guns, oddly shaped sacks, framed pictures, a stovepipe, and an apprehensive cocker spaniel, a great truth dawns on me: survival in a Frenchman's automobile depends on the plasticity and malleability of the passenger.

Our new comrades love to accumulate property. This explains why many of the French ride on top of their trucks—there is usually no room inside the vehicles for passengers. In addition to beds and mattresses, their conveyances bulge with things like chairs, tables, a bathtub, bicycles, boxes of food, dogs, cats, bowls with goldfish, crates of chickens, toys, miscellaneous bric-a-brac, and useless antiques.

An exciting ride for me, but at the first stop, I politely thank Chaudon for letting me ride with him, ooze out of the car, and transfer to one of our own sedans. The cocker spaniel seems to have become fond of me during the trip, and tries to enter our vehicle, but I would not think of depriving our friends of their pet. A good dog, but lacking sphincter control.

The remainder of the journey is less exciting. Even the normally exuberant French soldiers lose their gaiety as our convoy creeps along roads of uncertain substance, their condition unimproved by a heavy rain that starts about noon and continues through the rest of the day. Sometimes we have to back up and hunt for connecting roads; this increases our depression. We drive through a gloomy forest; ominous, dark clouds cling to the hilltops.

"*Comme artillerie*," says Chaudon of the thunder and white flashes of lightning.

Not far from the forest is the small town of Pappenheim, where we look for lodgings, hoping to find a building large enough for everyone. But there is nothing suitable. Finally we move into two houses after giving their occupants the customary two-hour eviction notices.

The house to which I am assigned is comfortable. In the living room are restful chairs and a good radio. A bookcase with a glass door is filled with interesting works, including a few volumes on psychoanalysis and a German edition of *Gone with the Wind*. Tonight, I will browse through them. This prospect cheers me; so do the sounds from the kitchen where dinner is now being prepared by our French and American cooks.

The CO decides that this is a good opportunity to welcome our French comrades. We had little time for fellowship in Schwabach. We decide to celebrate in order to cement (plaster would have been a more appropriate verb) Franco-American relations.

Everyone crowds into the dining room. Last to arrive are Rosenbloom, who walks in laboriously, and Chaudon, who strides in briskly. (Like many other heavy and muscular infantrymen, Rosenbloom seems to find every step an effort.)

After an unfestive dinner, the CO stands up and welcomes everyone. He seems embarrassed: speechmaking is not his forte. Furthermore, he knows that he will not be able to match Chaudon's ready wit. But he tries. Speaking in English, he mentions the long history of cooperation between the two great Allies, the help they have given each other in perilous times, the Statue of Liberty, and the good relations among the men. The great applause is for the brevity of his remarks, and the opportunity to sample more champagne. Then Chaudon speaks in French, and says about the same thing; his reception is equally enthusiastic.

Afterward, each Frenchman arises in turn and sings or chants unselfconsciously and unaccompanied. If one of them forgets a line of a song, the whole group huddles and then advises him of the correct words, and he continues. Between songs there is rhythmic applause—two successive bursts of three rapid hand claps, followed by three slow claps. If a song is not forthcoming as rapidly as desired, everyone sings *Silence, pour la chanson* to the refrain from the end of *La Marseillaise*.

We hear ballads of love and hate. Love of France, women,

wine. Hatred of the Germans. The *Song of the Maquis* has to be repeated; it tells about the young men who fled from the cities to avoid being deported to German labor camps. Living off the countryside, these men became part of the French underground movement. The ballad brings back memories: we hear heartrending, tearful tales of courage, treachery, torture, and executions. Apparently our new comrades have been in the Resistance, or members of their family have. (I am beginning to learn that all Frenchmen claim membership in the Resistance, just as all Germans claim nonmembership in the Nazi Party.)

Then it is our turn. Rosenbloom obliges with a school song whose purpose is to spur the members of its football team to greater glory. I manage to get through *Home on the Range*. It is Howcroft's turn, but by this time we have made significant inroads into the wine and champagne. Tempers begin to flare. A brawl erupts between two French drivers. Chaudon ejects them both.

He explains that the bloodshed was caused by the driver wearing glasses. He is no good, that one, always a troublemaker. He hit Joseph (the good driver) because there was no more cognac.

"But why did you also throw Joseph out?" I ask naïvely.

"That Joseph, he is no good," he replies. "Should not let anyone hit him at an international celebration."

By this time, the party has lost its *élan, joie de vivre*, and *esprit de corps*, so we bid each other *adieu* and stagger to our beds.

Howcroft and our men have lost their opportunity to sing in public. They do not seem to mind.

In the morning, our French friends tell us that the party was *magnifique*. But the food was *impossible!* Not only last night, but ever since they arrived. Their *estomacs* are being poisoned by our packaged rations. They have dyspepsia. They may not be able to work because of heartburn.

We are not overjoyed about the food either, but as patriotic soldiers we only gripe about it.

Not so the French. They are prepared for action. They would like to take charge of the cuisine; if this is permitted they will transform the C and K rations and other tasteless monstrosities that we draw from Army commissaries into irresistible Gallic delicacies. Aricer and Eastman will not be out of a job; they will work with the French chefs and learn all their secrets. Some of our men are hunters; they can roam the German hills and bring in deer and rabbit. But the important ingredients—eggs, cheese, cream, beef, and veal—can only be located by knowledgeable Frenchmen.

This is the proposition. We listen, think about the problem of divided authority, balance our administrative misgivings against our gastronomic expectations, and succumb.

Immediately, the dagger-carrying Amazon, Madame Colette, takes over the kitchen and dispatches her countrymen on secret errands. She is experienced; she once managed an inn in a small town near Marseilles. I hear that the Germans destroyed her inn, and since then she has been destroying Germans.

With her dagger, I wonder? Was she skilled at cutting Nazi throats in the quiet French night?

But there is no question about her ability with a knife in the bright, noisy kitchen. For lunch she plans rare *biftecks*, for supper *coq au vin*. For our next breakfast we will gorge ourselves on *omelettes aux pommes de terre*.

Suddenly the kitchen has become a social center, with Madame Manger the main attraction. This is what our men call her, and she is pleased with her new name.

We were supposed to continue on our way today, but this morning a message arrived from G-5 HQ telling us to remain where we are until further notice. Our temporary assignment is to search the countryside for facilities for housing thousands of DPs.

So we separate and drive in various directions, but we are always sure to return for lunch and supper.

My travels take me through thickly wooded country and green fields. I stop at a castle, where I meet the Count of Pappenheim, a mild, thin English-speaking gentleman, surrounded by oil paintings of Pappenheims dating back to the Middle Ages. The Count cannot help me in my quest.

In another area I find a colony of beautiful uniformed Hungarian cavalrymen taking care of handsome, disciplined white horses. They also do not know of adequate facilities in their area, and, for my efforts, I am bitten on the leg by one of their ugly, undisciplined dogs. The Hungarian chief assures me that the dog has been healthy, and is a peaceful, law-abiding citizen of his colony, so I give myself first aid and do not consider the Pasteur treatment.

For two days we survey the district for suitable, large-scale living quarters, but find none.

Our brief on-the-job baptism of training is over. On the afternoon of April 29 we receive orders to move into Dachau the next day. We pack that night and early the next morning our convoy leaves.

We cross the Danube into Bavaria. I am surprised by the Danube, because its beautiful water is green, and I will record this observation in my letter tonight to my wife, although I expect her to respond by accusing me of blue-green color blindness.

I will also tell her about how much more interesting our convoy is now than before the French joined us. All of their vehicles are painted with the Fighting French symbol, the double-barred Cross of Lorraine. In addition, small tricolor flags wave from their right front fenders. When the French sight DPs on the road, they listen for the ecstatic cry, "*Vive de Gaulle.*" Now they know that the DPs are French nationals, and they sprinkle them with cigarettes and parts of K rations. But their *fraternité* does not extend to other DPs.

Dachau: The First Week　3

13

LIBERATION

April 30. It is still early in the morning as we approach the 1,000-year-old city of Dachau. In the distance we see pillars of black smoke fading away in the cold, cloudy sky, and we hear the pounding of artillery and the screaming of planes.

Dachau, with a population of about 15,000, seems to have the same attributes as other cities its size. There are flower beds and trees, small shops, bicycles on the ground, churches with steeples, a mirrorlike river. Many old-fashioned wooden houses are built on terraces, and from their windows we can see faces peering at us from behind curtains. Above the houses gloomily sits a weather-beaten castle. There is no intimation in this innocent-looking city of the activities a few minutes away.

The narrow streets are filled with tanks, jeeps, and other military vehicles, and DPs and unhappy German civilians, now refugees. Small clusters of forlorn, disheveled German soldiers trudge wearily toward rear area POW enclosures. Some are under guard, others are unguarded, their resistance gone.

Hailstones begin to fall as we drive toward our destination: the concentration camp outside the city. We are slowed down by roadblocks where American soldiers check our identification and orders.

We brake to a stop at a railroad unloading point.

An unbelievable sight. Flatcars and open boxcars contain hundreds of emaciated bodies piled on top of each other, bodies of men, women, and children, lying in grotesque positions. Their cadaverous arms and legs seem disproportionately long compared to their sunken abdomens, narrowed bony chests, visible ribs, protruding shoulder blades, and withered necks—all signs of starvation.

Some of the bodies are covered by pajamalike cotton uniforms with vertical blue and white stripes, the official clothing of concentration camp prisoners. Some are covered with coats. Many are naked. Because of the intense cold, the bodies and cars are now lightly coated with white frost, Nature's shroud.

Refuse and excrement are spread over the cars and grounds. More of the dead lie near piles of clothing, shoes, and trash. Apparently some had crawled or fallen out of the cars when the doors were opened, and died on the grounds.

One of our men counts the boxcars and says that there are thirty-nine. Later I hear that there were fifty, that the train had arrived at the camp during the evening of April 27, by which time all of the passengers were supposed to be dead so that the bodies could be disposed of in the camp crematorium. But this could not be done because there was no more coal to stoke the furnaces.

Mutilated bodies of German soldiers are also on the ground, and occasionally we see an inmate scream at the body of his former tormentor and kick it.

Retribution!

An incredible sight, a stench that is beyond experience. Horror-stricken, outraged, we react with disbelief. "Oh God!" says Rosenbloom. Ferris is silent, and so is Howcroft, his vocabulary inadequate to describe this circle of evil. I hear Hollis, our car-counting driver, say that even primitive, savage people give a decent burial to their own dead and the dead of their enemies. I shut my eyes. This cannot be the twentieth century, I think. I try to remember the redeeming attributes of man. None comes to mind.

"Lieutenant," says Private Eastman, our young driver who has never voiced his feelings before. "Maybe we should occupy this country for fifty years."

We drive past an ornate lamppost mounted on a cement base, bearing a large sign reading *SS KonzentrationsLager* (concentration camp). Above it are six brightly painted figures, each with a grim, unsmiling face. Of the three on the right, two wear peasant clothing; one plays an accordion and the other holds an umbrella. The third is a soldier holding a cello. This part of the sign indicates the road to the prison compound. The trio on the left, consisting of a bugler leading two other helmeted, marching German soldiers carrying full packs, indicates the road to the peripheral administrative area.

Then down SS Strasse with its large residential homes, surrounded by a vast complex of office buildings, warehouses, shops, and rows of barracks. This area is landscaped, but now the grounds are strewed with bodies of prisoners, guards, and large Alsatian bloodhounds.

We reach the prison area, which is surrounded by a water-filled moat about fifteen feet wide, and a ten-foot-high barbed wire fence mounted on solid pillars, each pillar capped by electric lights. Strategically located around the fence are watchtowers with pointed roofs and small windows, and from them white flags made from bed sheets wave in the strong wind. I can see many of the inmates inside the fence, wistfully looking at us.

The guarded prison compound occupies about a fourth as much space as does the administrative section. Above the entrance to the camp sits an imperial German eagle, its wings spread, its talons clutching a swastika. I note the large iron grille gate, in the midst of which are the wrought iron words: *Arbeit Macht Frei*—"Work Makes One Free." [1]

Rosenbloom enters the gatehouse, now taken over by American troops. After twenty minutes, he emerges. "A lot to do," he says. He sends Sergeant Morivant to the outer area to search for housing for the Team, and Sergeant Aricer to establish a kitchen. He gives us entry passes, which we show to the sentry, who opens the gate and then closes it behind us.

How many terrorized, fear-drenched men have entered here? I wonder.

To the left of the entrance are the prisoners' barracks, which occupy most of the enclosed area. To the right are operational buildings: the kitchen, storage rooms, laundry, and locked cells and interrogation center—the bunker. A large, barren field is interposed between these buildings and the barracks; here prisoner formations took place.

We get our bearings. Rosenbloom and Howcroft, accompanied by Ferris and Eastman, begin their inspections. Mace and Hollis have been assigned to me. My job is to survey the medical condition of the inmates, the medical facilities (and manpower), environmental conditions, such as waste disposal, water supply, living conditions, insect control, food handling, and anything else pertaining to health and sanitation.

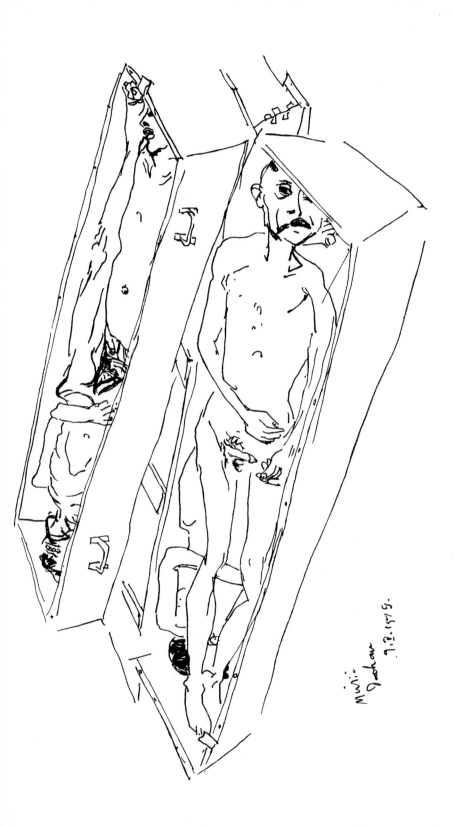

14

THE INSPECTION

Not as many inmates are standing at the fence as I had thought, probably because it is too cold. A few walk slowly over to us, and I see from their gait and then from their pinched features that they have been starved. They crowd around us, finger our insignia. One of them, listening to the distant cannon fire, asks if they are safe. Yes, I reply. The Nazis are gone; they will never come back; we have driven them away; soon the war will be over. They try to smile.

Yesterday, the day of liberation, must have been a great day for these men, I think. I wish I had been here. How they must have rejoiced!

The inmates volunteer to be our guides, to show us the sights. We head toward the barracks and reach them before our guides because they cannot walk as fast as we do. We detour around more bodies in their blue-white striped uniforms; there are bodies in front of and between these buildings.

There are thirty-two one-story, low-ceilinged wooden barracks, or blocks, arranged in two rows separated by a wide dirt street. Most of them have eight rooms filled with triple-tiered wooden beds, some of which have rags or filthy straw ticks thrown over them. Now, lying head to foot, as many as three men are crowded onto each narrow bed. Each building holds from 1,000 to 1,900 men; if each person had his own space in which to sleep there would be room for only 650 men in each block.

These are not really beds, but shelves measuring thirty-two inches wide and seven feet long. There are no places for the inmates to sit, so most of them lie on these slabs. As they look at us, their bald, shaven, or partly shaven heads jut out, and we can see part of their shoulders and chests. The rest of their bodies are hidden by the bedsteads. Some try to smile, but emaciated, sallow faces do not convey emotions.

The feelings are there, however. Some of the inmates come over and touch us; others, too weak to stand, wave their hands feebly; others weep.

Here are healthy prisoners, others who are sick, and some who are dying—too weak to get up for the biologic necessities: to eat, urinate, or defecate. When they are in an upper berth, the excreta drip down over the men below. They are dying of starvation, or are afflicted with a disease or combination of diseases made more serious by the starvation. There are no opportunities here for diagnosis and treatment, obviously. Why are they here? I ask some of the healthier men. Because there is no room in the hospital for them. In some of the berths are the recent dead. The well, the sick, the dying, and the dead lie next to each other in these poorly ventilated, unheated, dark, stinking buildings.

The washrooms have too few troughs, the water mains are inoperative, and the number of foul, deep-pit latrines are inadequate. There are no clothes closets but this is no deprivation because the only clothes the internees possess are the ones they wear; all other items were checked into the camp on admission and stored. Some of the barracks have lockers.

What do these people need? Everything. They have only their prison uniforms, inadequate, torn shoes, some have coats and caps. I should start making notes, and I pull out of my pocket a small German diary, a *Taschenkalender* for the year 1940, that I found somewhere. As I look for a blank page I find a list of important German dates, and I read that tomorrow, May 1, is a legal holiday for the German people. I wonder if it will be celebrated here? Richard Wagner was born on May 22, 1813. Hitler became the leader of the Nazi Party on May 29, 1921.

I find an empty page and start my list; these people will need underclothes, overclothes, shoes, socks, towels, bedding, beds, soap, toilet paper, more latrines, new quarters.

How have they survived? The human body has a greater capacity for endurance than I thought. Of course, my experience has been with the weak and the sick, people under attack by their natural and synthetic enemies: bacteria, cancer, faulty chromosomes, the aging process, battering automobiles, penetrating bullets, extremes of temperature, excesses of food, liquor, and drugs, arteriosclerosis, viruses, allergens, psychoses, malnutrition, accidents—deputies of death by the million, their pernicious intent to injure or destroy the marvelously intricate protoplasmic labyrinth we call the human body. My training and background have taught me that people are vulnerable and fragile, but they must be tougher than I have suspected in order to have survived this camp, these conditions.

But the survivors don't look tough. Some are skeletal in appearance, like the corpses outside—the walking dead. Others, in better condition, are still pale, lean, and unhealthy looking. I ask them questions and receive different responses. Some cannot understand my German, some talk about their gnawing hunger, some stare vacantly with a deathlike indifference, some clutch my hand.

How long have these men been in the camp? Are the best nourished prisoners those who have been here the shortest time? I find out that this is not necessarily true. Some without the strength to hold their heads up are recent arrivals from other concentration camps. I write more words in my notebook. But how am I to describe the dark shadows of disease, starvation, and imminent death?

I am escorted to the prison hospital, consisting of eleven converted barracks, some quarantined by the prisoners themselves, others open. I can see little difference between them and the ordinary barracks except for the presence of medical equipment. The sick lie in the same kind of triple-tiered beds, but they are more comfortable than the "healthy" inmates because there are only three patients for every two beds. Again, the sick, the dying, and the dead share space with each other, not only on the slabs but on the floors and in the latrines. Everywhere is the stench of decomposition and excrement. Some of the patients are too weak to reach the latrines, or, if they do, too feeble to crawl back to their beds.

Here are thousands of patients ranging in age from 12 to 65, all malnourished and emaciated, their diseases in all stages of development: early, late, and terminal. There are patients with typhus fever, dysentery, erysipelas, pneumonia, scabies, and a host of other infections. A great many inmates have infections of their skin, or of the tissues beneath their skin: abscesses, furuncles, sinuses, and ulcers. These are probably caused by many factors, among them the lack of cleanliness, the thinness and fragility of their skin, and the pressure exerted on the skin by the unpadded wooden slabs on which they were forced to sleep.

Diarrhea is ubiquitous.

Tuberculosis, the great killer, must be widespread.

There are many surgical patients, some with fractured limbs in makeshift slings, others with gunshot injuries. There are many instances of infected wounds and bones. There are cases of gangrene.

The injuries were accidentally or deliberately incurred.

There is supposed to be a castrated Jewish boy here.

It has been impossible to separate those with communicable diseases from those with ordinary disorders.

The sick are being helped by prisoner-doctors and volunteer inmates, and I am so stunned by the number of patients that I fail to appreciate the care given to these people by the doctors and orderlies. They have aided many patients; they have performed life-saving operations, though how they did this is beyond me—it seems impossible to keep anything free from infection. From these doctors I try to obtain some estimate of the number of patients and the varieties of disorders, but I find them apathetic, discouraged, confused.

A Spanish doctor, here since the Spanish Civil War, is helpful. A Yugoslav physician says that he is a former professor of public health. A Russian public health physician and a French doctor who served in World War I supply me with background information. From them I learn how to recognize typhus fever, a disease that I have never seen. These doctors are exhausted and need help themselves. Their supplies are primitive. Nursing care is essentially lacking. I start to add to my list of needed supplies and services. Every item makes me think of another. I absorb the impression of hopelessness that permeates these barracks.

What am I going to write in my notebook? Everyone is touched. One of my men weeps. Even my callous, death-hardened county-hospital exterior begins to crack. We would like to give these people something to indicate our concern. We were so emotionally moved when our inspection began that we have already given away whatever we had in our pockets that was edible or smokable. Our loose rations, candy, and cigarettes went to the first group of ambulatory inmates; now we have nothing left. We can do nothing for these half-dead people except find out what is going on, let them know we care, and then look for help.

I find it difficult to sort out my thoughts. A primitive instinct warns: Be careful. This place is loaded with dangerous epidemic diseases. Remember—handwashing, face masks. Instruct the members of the Team. Begin disinfection. Another mental relay says: Get the figures, the number of patients, the morbid statistics, and get out. Another thought: How these men have suffered! I cannot believe this is possible in this enlightened age. The gaunt faces and trembling, supplicating, dirt-impregnated hands. Is there any future for them?

I think incoherently, shocked by the insignificance of the human being in this mad Nazi world. But then I remember that the Nazis did not consider the prisoners to be members of the human race. I am appalled by the extent of the physical and mental suffering and anguish in these blocks. I cannot understand why our inexperienced Team was selected for this job. I feel sorry for our men, for myself. What is happening in this camp is beyond anything I have ever read about, imagined, or anticipated, and suggests to me that I was sheltered in my training by the scientific medical school I attended, by the sophisticated, departmentalized, specialized hospital where I interned, and by the modern, expense-is-no-object Army Medical Corps. The tools and brains of the medical profession have always been nearby, available for consultation and guidance, and with these one could face Death down for a while. But here there is not only the smell of Death, but his actual presence, and there are no weapons with which to fight.

I do not have the missionary spirit—I cannot think of how to combat epidemics and famine with my brain alone. Nor do I seem to be able to discard the principles drilled into me, that one does the right thing as a doctor by taking care of an individual patient, by lavishing diagnostic and therapeutic attention on him. I cannot conceive of mass management, and I have to restrain myself from sitting down with one of these wraiths, obtaining a history, a complete physical examination, a battery of diagnostic tests. That is the way that all sick patients should be handled, but it is impossible now. I cannot even examine a patient here.

What are we going to do about these starving patients? How will we care for them without sterile bandages, gloves, bedpans, urinals, thermometers, and all the other basic material? How do we manage without an organization? No interns, no nursing staff, no ambulances, no bathtubs, no laboratories, no charts, no orderlies, no administrator, and no doctors—the ones I see here are too weak to handle patients.

I feel helpless and empty. I cannot think of anything like this in modern medical history, but undoubtedly this is happening in other concentration camps in Germany and probably nothing really evil, like this camp, is new. Undoubtedly desecrations of this nature have occurred before, perhaps during the days of the Black Plague or the depradations of Genghis Khan or Attila the Hun.

I remember shreds of *Paradise Lost:*

> With shuddering horror pale, and eyes aghast
> View'd first their lamentable lot, and found
> No rest . . . shades of death . . .
> Where all life dies, death lives . . .
> Abominable, inutterable, and worse . . .

Out in the cold air I breathe more easily. The stench of feces, vomit, and decomposition is less suffocating. I want to flee to the Team quarters outside the camp, to the security of people I know, and my disturbed men would also be glad to leave this nightmare, but there is more to do. Self and group discipline are reasserted. We continue to the central kitchen.

In the kitchen are the strangest-looking chefs in the world —pale, emaciated bald men without chef's hats, wearing blue-striped camp trousers, stirring enormous kettles filled with a potato-vegetable-meat soup. Food has been brought here from the SS warehouses. Thirty-five kettles, with a capacity of 1,000 liters each (I finally have a figure I can write in my notebook), are being used for cooking, and these are now heated with wood fires. Ordinarily they were electrically operated, but the electricity is *kaputt.* There is no incoming water, and something will have to be done about this today. At the moment water is being delivered in small carts.

I make notes of the supplies on hand. It will take time for a complete inventory, but I see many desirable items here, including Ovomaltine. I learn that the present kitchen workers are not the same ones as several days ago. Changes have already been made. I think the labor detail will have to be enlarged and storage facilities expanded.

After the soup has been prepared, it is transferred to metal containers that are transported on carts to the barracks. Howcroft or the CO will have to see that there is no favoritism in their distribution, to be sure that responsible people call for and serve the food.

I am glad I had this thought. It tells me that my planning lobe is back in operation.

Our escorts take us to the disinfection building. Here, while prisoners were bathed in antiseptic solution every two to four weeks, their clothes were put into an apparatus in which they were exposed to two to four meter radiowaves and a temperature of 182 degrees Centigrade. So I am told. This is an experimental method, and I cannot ascertain its effectiveness. My recommendation will be to use soap, water, antiseptic solutions, and DDT.

Nearby is a concrete building in which 300 prisoners could shower at a time. I am told that each prisoner was permitted one shower every two weeks. (The building has been closed for the last three weeks.)

The grand tour must include the crematorium and the gas chamber, and our escorts lead us to the large concrete and brick building with the high smokestack. The smell here is stronger even than in the quarantined barracks. Outside is a small hill of bodies. In storerooms within, the corpses are piled high. Deaths have exceeded storage space.

The technique used by the Nazis is explained.

Prisoners scheduled for liquidation were marched to a point near the gas chamber and processed in the same way as those who were to serve prison terms. Then those to be executed were ordered into the building, told to undress, handed soap and towels, and directed into the *Brause Bad* (shower bath). That is what the black letters say on the sign that hangs over the door, and the prisoners believed it. The door through which they passed is made of smoothly fitting steel; when it closed, the victims were sealed in. They stood beneath innocent-looking shower heads, evenly spaced on the ceiling; from them the invisible lethal gas (carbon monoxide and hydrogen cyanide) flowed for ten to twenty minutes. I notice a thick glass window in the rear of the chamber: I am told that through this window a supervisor witnessed the executions so that he could decontaminate when they were over.

After the gas had dissipated, special inmates wearing protective clothing entered the chamber after opening another airtight door, then, using grappling hooks, dragged the bodies into storerooms. Other workers cleaned and hosed the chamber. Our guide calls attention to the floor, gently sloped for proper drainage.

From the storerooms, the bodies were moved into the crematorium, whose four furnaces were capable of consuming 150 corpses a day. The metal doors to the furnace are narrow, about two feet wide. They did not need to be larger. Coffins were not used.

In the rear of the crematorium is another sign, depicting a man riding a monstrous pig. "Wash your hands," says the caption. "It is your duty to remain clean."

The inspection has taken a long time. Emotionally exhausted, Mace, Hollis, and I return to the entrance, show our permits, and pass through the gate. I feel like Ulysses leaving the house of Hades.

Outside, we sit and talk with members of the guard unit. What was it like yesterday? asks Mace. Was it rough getting in?

Not bad, says a sergeant who has seen action in Africa, Sicily, and Italy. We were mad; we got those bastards. . . .[1]

The sergeant participated in part of the action, which began about the time I was searching for quarters for DPs sixty miles away. Was that only yesterday? It seems a hundred light years away.

15

Our new quarters are in the home of a former SS officer on SS Strasse, where, after a quiet supper of C rations and coffee —nobody complains tonight—Rosenbloom, Howcroft, and I get down to business. They have had a busy day too. In addition to their inspections, they have been talking with 7th Army, Military Government, and civilian affairs officers, as well as certain knowledgeable inmates who are members of an organization, the International Prisoners' Committee (IPC). If this group is effective, says Rosenbloom, then we have the nucleus for an internal administrative structure. Very interesting men, he says; he promises to tell us about them later.

We learn from him that there had been many "honorary" prisoners in the camp: Léon Blum, the former French premier, and his wife; Kurt von Schuschnigg, the former Austrian chancellor, and his wife and child; Stalin's son, Jacob, supposedly captured in 1941; many others. They are not in the camp now. G-5 is very anxious to know what happened to them. Some of the inmates say they are probably dead—that they were evacuated from the camp several days before liberation. A death march, the same day that 6,000 ordinary prisoners were removed, for the same purpose.

If we hear anything about these notables, we are to let Rosenbloom know at once.

For the moment, he continues, we are to concentrate on the census figures supplied by the IPC; he has three mimeographed sets of these papers. I hope they are more accurate than the ones we studied in Schwabach.

My copy is on cheap, flimsy white paper; the edges are beginning to fray. The first page lists the number of prisoners in each block, and in the prison hospital, a total of 32,600, of whom 376 are women. (We have heard that most of the women are political prisoners; some are alleged to be prostitutes.)

The bottom of the page carries the red stamp of the camp secretary, and his indecipherable signature. The same stamp is on the bottom of page two of the census report, which provides us with nationality information.

Poles predominate in the camp—about 9,200. There are 4,200 Russians, 4,000 French, 2,900 Yugoslavs, 2,200 Italians, 1,600 Czechs, 1,200 Germans, 900 Belgians, and about 600 each of Dutch and Hungarians.

I am surprised to learn that there are also about 200 Spaniards in the camp. There are the same number of Greeks and Austrians, and about 100 each of Croats, Luxembourgers, Norwegians, and Albanians. A handful of others from the Balkans are also here, people who identify themselves as Serbs and Slovaks.

Every country in Europe is represented except Monaco. There are small numbers of people from Denmark, Great Britain, Estonia, Bulgaria, Portugal, Latvia, Lithuania, Romania, Malta, Armenia, Switzerland, and Finland. There are a few who say they are from Alsace-Lorraine, and others who label themselves as Annex-Germans or Sudetens.

Other countries represented are Turkey, Iraq, and Iran. There are supposed to be two Chinese in nearby satellite camps. Rosenbloom explains: he has found out that many or most concentration camps had subsidiary units filled with prisoners used as slave laborers in regional factories. Dachau, for example, had satellite units as far away as Augsberg—30 miles distant. One of the inmates had told Rosenbloom that there were 70,000 prisoners in the Dachau camp system at the time of liberation.

According to the census report, there are six Americans in the camp.

I do not meet them. I hear that most of them were men who had lived in Germany for many years. One, however, was a POW, a Major Rene J. Guiraud from Cicero, Illinois. Captured about eight months earlier, he was brought to Dachau where he lost fifty pounds. He was quoted as saying that he worked in the hospital, helping treat prisoners who had been clawed by the savage dogs of the SS troopers—some had been brought to the hospital in a state of unconsciousness. For excitement, said the major, a guard would set his dog on a prisoner, "just for a little sport." [1]

The figures show only 2,700 Jews in the camps. They are not listed as members of a separate group, but included in the national figures.

We are surprised by the small number. Several explanations are given. One is that, by this time, most of the European Jews had been killed. (In Dachau, Jews constituted 8.5 percent of the inmate population. This was comparable to data from other concentration camps, assembled by Proudfoot: at the time of liberation, there were roughly 600,000 in the camps; 10 percent were Jews. Many of these survivors were to die, as at the Bergen-Belsen camp, where 13,000 expired in the six weeks that followed its seizure from the Nazis. Proudfoot's figures showed that six million people were killed in the camps; three-quarters were Jews.[2])

Another explanation for the small number of Jews in the camp was that those who avoided extermination camps were deemed useful to the German war effort, hence sent to labor camps. Most of the Jews in the Dachau camp system are said to be at the satellite camp at Allach, a nearby town.

The census sheets end with the information that 286 inmates have been assigned to jobs within the camp, and 54 Allied enemies are now locked up securely in the bunker, the fortresslike prison behind the kitchen.

At our meeting we do not waste time on an analysis of the national statistics. Our concern is with total numbers that we can use to estimate supplies. Probably the figures we have been given are as accurate as can be expected in the circumstances.

Top priority is given to the procurement of food. Howcroft assembles lists that are breathtaking in their magnitude. We are fortunate to have been in Schwabach where we learned to order for a few thousand—which shocked us at the time because we had not previously thought of food in quantities greater than can be carried in grocery bags. But, despite that experience, we are still astounded by the amount of food and other supplies that we will need.

According to the IPC, there are 4,205 patients in the camp

hospital and another 3,866 bedridden. I am glad to get these figures, for they give me the information that I need for my report, which is next on the agenda. I estimate 900 inmates with typhus fever, 800 with open tuberculosis. There are thousands with starvation and severe debility, but it is difficult to assess these as to prevalence and whether they are primary disorders or secondary to other diseases. There are also many other infectious diseases and traumatic conditions, and, according to some of the prisoner-physicians, there is a mysterious, new acute disease characterized by uncontrollable gangrene developing in areas of trivial infection. I recall vaguely that such complications can follow illnesses such as typhus fever. Perhaps malnutrition contributes.

In addition to all these disorders, I think there may be patients here with typhoid fever. They are difficult to detect in this jungle of clinical material, and to separate from the thousands of people with dysentery-like symptoms.

A prediction of the number of probable deaths can be made from the number reported this week. Today, probably 135 people will die. A 7th Army OSS Detachment is also at work here. They think there are about 200 deaths a day.

It is obvious that we need hospital beds, nurses, doctors, trained specialists such as epidemiologists and sanitarians; a dietician would be helpful. We need medical supplies. A strict quarantine will have to be established. The men of the 45th Division recognized this problem when they arrived and are now guarding the camp. Inmates voluntarily patrol the hospital area. Despite these efforts, many of the internees have escaped, and cases of typhus fever can be expected in the countryside.

Trained people who can seek out those afflicted with communicable diseases are urgently needed. Ideally, everyone here, with or without symptoms, should be evaluated medically. Those suspected or proved to have typhus fever, tuberculosis, and the other diseases I fear—epidemic meningitis, typhoid fever, dysentery, and diphtheria—should all be isolated.

I report this at the meeting, and it is agreed that a top priority goes to the medical needs of the inmates. Still another priority is given to the restoration of electrical and water pathways and to the emptying of latrines and the construction of new ones. Priority must go to identification and burial of the bodies that are scattered all over the camp grounds. To the formation of special labor details to clean the camp physically of the tons of debris everywhere in evidence. To the procurement of decent living quarters.

Everything seems important enough to deserve a high priority. Everyone contributes items for Howcroft, in case he forgets something—now we think of buckets, dishes, forks and knives and spoons, towels, containers. His list is endless.

The CO says there are significant security problems within the camp, where SS guards, criminals, collaborators are present. Some of these are dressed in prison garb. We must be vigilant. Nobody is sure of anyone at this moment.

Tonight I must make out a written health and sanitation report, incorporating my findings and listing shortages. In the health report I will emphasize the importance of obtaining sulfa drugs, vitamins, calcium compounds, digitalis, and dressings. We must have hospital facilities for 10,000 patients. In the sanitation report I will emphasize obtaining water, disposing of human waste, rubbish, and bodies. We need living quarters for 20,000 people, DDT by the ton, spraying equipment.

Nothing had been said at the DP school about this kind of situation. There is nothing in our *Guide* to help us, except for the admonition to be flexible in order to "meet the widely varying situations and particular problems which will be encountered."

I am flexible enough to know help is needed, and it will have to come from the American Army. I am certain that enough material and professional help cannot be procured from the countryside as fast as we need it here. Munich MG cannot possibly be organized yet.

We must report our needs immediately to the high-ranking 7th Army officers who are in the camp and area now, and to the higher echelons of G-5.

Right now is the best time to start hunting for trained men to repair the water and power lines.

It is late at night, but the reports, consultations, and appeals for aid cannot wait.

16

THE FAMISH'D PEOPLE

Only a few hours of sleep. After breakfast, Rosenbloom briefs us. He has already been in contact with G-5 this morning. The information we transmitted through channels last night went all the way to the Supreme Commander, General Eisenhower, who promises total assistance.

In the meantime, we are to leave the camp in the same condition as when it was liberated, so that representatives of agencies concerned with war crimes can investigate and record what has happened here. The public must be informed about the camp; bulletins have been sent to the communications media. Members of Congress have been notified, and our allies.

We can expect a flood of visitors.

The news arrives after we have attempted to start housecleaning; some of the bodies have been moved to a storage area.

No further effort is to be made, says Rosenbloom. I am reminded of the standard orders given by a policeman at the site of a crime: "Don't touch anything until we get fingerprints, measurements, and photographs."

I am annoyed by our inability to do anything about the physical situation here. But, after thinking about it, I realize the General and his staff are right—mankind can best be served by knowing about the atrocities committed here. My appreciation of the position taken by Supreme Headquarters does not prevent me from chafing at the restraints imposed on reconstructive efforts.

It is cold and bleak. Snow is falling. There is no central heating. Trying to keep warm, ambulatory inmates huddle over small fires on which they heat pots and bowls filled with scraps of food. Some of them, running out of wood scraps, begin to burn their bed boards. Fuel—one of the items nobody has thought about.

Piles of debris on the large treeless field near the barracks (there are poplars elsewhere) and throughout the camp grounds need collection and incineration. Some of the inmates wander through the camp, rummage through these piles, hunting for treasures—bits of wood for their fires, windblown papers, clothes? Others ransack storage and administrative buildings. A few visit barracks other than their own. Some stand at the fence and look at the hills, the distant marshes, the nearby bodies. Because of the cold, most of the internees remain in their own quarters.

The coldness is an asset, I think. It prevents further decomposition of the dead.

Suddenly there is a parade. It is May Day, a legal holiday for the German people, an important day for those of many other countries. Inmates capable of walking carry flags of their countries; there are many Red banners, but those of Poland predominate, not because they are the largest national group but because they operated the sewing machines in the camp.

No one carries a Norwegian flag. The answer to my question is simple: Norway is still in the hands of the Nazis. Some of the inmates carry signs reading, "For a New Democratic Germany," and "For a Free Democratic Spain."

An American colonel and some inmates are surrounded by flags. The colonel—I hear he is with the 45th Division—salutes each passing flag, then speaks briefly. A few more speeches and the ceremony is over.

Patients in the hospital watch the celebration from windows and doors. Others, on crowded slabs, are unaware of the festivities.

I spend part of the day in the hospital trying to find out more about the prevalence of diseases, and part in a study of the mechanics of waste disposal. My interest in latrines keeps growing. They will have to be cleaned manually. In the past there were manure-cart details. They will have to be reactivated.

The remainder of my time is given to an exploration of the water system, which, I discover, begins at the Amper River and ends at two pump houses in the camp, one of them out of commission. After emergency repairs of the water lines it becomes possible to chlorinate the water, and with the help of an Army engineer, Major Trigg, a concentration of one-half part chlorine to three million parts of water is achieved, ordinarily a satisfactory level. Here, with bodies floating in the river and with dysentery-like disorders everywhere, it is unlikely that even the treated water is safe for drinking.

Fortunately we have been able to locate essential maintenance workers to operate the pump houses and others to repair the power lines. Now we have incoming water and electricity.

Today Rosenbloom and Howcroft have been in conference with the burgomaster and MG officers in Dachau, who now know that the situation here is critical. They have begun to amass the lifesaving items on Howcroft's lists.

After consulting with some of the inmate physicians and Howcroft, I have set up three different diets: one for the healthy, one for the weak (soft), and one for the ill (fluid). Theoretically, everyone receives 2,000 calories a day; in practice, this amount cannot be measured. Many of the camp inhabitants supplement what they are given with provisions liberated earlier.

May Day is not yet over. The final, cheering event of the day is the arrival of our French drivers with large supplies of food. The Army has broken its own policy that we must procure all supplies from German sources! The trucks are filled with massive quantities of wonderful-looking corned beef—24 tons; 13 tons of rye soup; 15 tons of beets with potatoes; 22 tons of biscuits; large amounts of sugar, marmalade, sausage, evaporated milk, coffee (ersatz), soap, and other supplies. All from G-5, I hear.

May 2. Forty-eight hours have passed. The death report arrives from the secretary of the International Prisoners' Committee. In the last twenty-four hours, 129 people have died. We are encouraged by the reduction in the number of deaths. (In another two days there will be fewer than 100.) But it is depressing to watch while people die of starvation and sickness, even if many of them could not have been saved with the most sophisticated techniques.

The Army continues to move swiftly. This morning the XVI Corps Surgeon, Colonel George Hathaway, arrives with his staff. I accompany them on their exhaustive inspection of the camp; I try to answer their questions. The colonel tells me that on the basis of the information we provided, he has ordered several American hospital units to the camp, as well as the famous ETOUSA Typhus Commission. They should be here soon.

Rosenbloom, Howcroft, and I spend an hour with the colonel discussing the treatment of starvation. Optimally, patients with this disease should be under careful medical management; good nursing care is essential. It is important to be gentle and deliberate in all phases of treatment, to remember to institute a program of mild exercises to promote physical recovery, and later to stress psychological rehabilitation. The mortality rate can be high (as we know), and some who recover may be left with permanent aftereffects.

Obviously we are more interested in the emergency care of starvation, compulsively so. This has already begun with the introduction of soft and fluid diets reinforced with vitamins and important nutrients. To overcome the protein deficit characteristic of this condition, we will make great use of eggs, condensed and dry milk, cheese, beans, and meat.

Even in this phase, warns the colonel, gentle handling is important. Food must be given cautiously. The principle also applies to the use of intravenous fluids and transfusions—if they are given too vigorously, some patients will die in heart failure.

Everyone who has seen a western movie knows the horrible fate of the cowboy who staggers across a desert with his canteen empty, collapses into a water hole, and drinks excessively. The starved person is in a similar predicament. Lord Byron knew this:

> Famish'd people must be slowly nurst,
> And fed by spoonfuls, else they always burst.

We have been admonishing the inmates not to overeat. But they have not been to the western movies or read Lord Byron or the medical texts, and they do not heed our admonitions. "The belly hath no ears when hunger comes upon it." Izaak Walton was referring to the aggressive behavior of the pike, the "fresh-water wolf"; in extreme hunger it had fought an otter for a carp. The description applies here, except that the inmates are not fighting each other for food. (One such incident was reported on the day of liberation.) But they talk about it and think about it all the time. They eat and eat and eat, not only what we give them, but whatever they can promote. Every time I see them they are nibbling and chewing and crunching and gnawing and drinking and swallowing. Or watching some-one else eat.

How many have died because of overeating? Probably not too many, judging from the gradual decline in the death rate.

Starvation diminishes physical differences, and thus the ema-ciated inmates look alike: faces without expression, eyes lifeless and sunken, cheekbones prominent, lips cracked, hair (when present) unkempt, skin ashen. Their legs are often swollen; this interferes with knee bending. Starved people find walking diffi-cult or impossible. They shuffle along, seem to droop; their breathing is labored. Their limbs are so thin that they look like acute angles when flexed. These patients are more sensitive to cold than well-nourished people. Their reflexes are sluggish, they lack mental and physical stamina, they seem to be mentally dull, exhausted, and depressed.

Diarrhea is common in starvation, and I think that many of the people whom I have suspected of having a bacterial form of dysentery may only be exhibiting a complication of their miser-able nutrition. Proof of this will have to await the opening of the hospitals and the availability of laboratory tests.

As the need for food overpowers a starved person, his desire for sexual satisfaction declines; eventually impotence develops. Homosexuality, common in penal institutions, is thought to be uncommon here. Two stories circulate about the prevalence of masturbation: one that it is rare, the other that it is common-place, not for the purpose of releasing sexual energy, but to re-assure the individual that he is still potent.

The inmates talk not only about the food they hope to re-ceive, but about the abominable provisions doled out in the past. During the six months preceding liberation, the food declined in quantity from about 900 or 1,000 calories a day during the preceding winter to as little as 500 or 600 calories a day in April 1945. Breakfast consisted of one-half liter of ersatz coffee or tea. At noon, the prisoners were given one liter of thin soup made from dry vegetables and potato parings. For supper they were permitted one-eighth of a loaf of a sour, coarse black bread (182 grams, about 6½ ounces) and a small amount of poor quality sausage (20 grams, about ¾ ounce). Sometimes soup was substituted for the sausage. Twice weekly this meager fare was augmented by a little less than one ounce of margarine. Additional amounts of bread and sausage, of about the same quantity, were given to working prisoners.

The stories are not identical, however. Some say that each day one loaf of bread was issued for eight people, supplemented with a ladle of gruel made from oats. Or one-quarter or one-seventh of a loaf of bread was given each person each day for dinner, and a bowl of soup twice a week.

In earlier days, 500 grams of bread per person had been distributed, with sausage and margarine several times a week, and marmalade, small slices of cheese, or ersatz honey on Sunday.

Receiving a few extra crumbs of bread, or some of the solid material in the soup—sometimes at the discretion of the inmate dispensing it—meant the difference between life and death. The general rule was to eat everything available, and quickly. If an extra slice of bread could be obtained, fine. The source was unimportant. If it belonged to another prisoner, this was unfortunate, but not a cause for concern.

What sort of prisoners were most likely to survive? Many inmates believed that the unluckiest persons in the camp were those who were tall and strong, for they needed more food to survive than the smaller and less muscular ones.

There were no reports of cannibalism in the camp. However, a Polish inmate said that he saw two mutilated corpses in a boxcar in which the other bodies all showed signs of starvation. He thought it had occurred in 1942.

The stories told by the inmates are so gruesome that, after listening for a short while, I have to don my invisible armor, a shield of objectivity and detachment. Otherwise I would not be able to function. Several of the internees say that they must relate these stories, that the only reason they forced themselves to live was so that they could tell the world about what happened here. About hunger—and death.

The inmates whispered about the extermination camps where large gas chambers had been used, permitting the Nazis to process thousands of victims a day using assembly-line methods. But

Dachau was not a death factory. Here, despite their inefficiency, older, more conventional methods continued to be useful: shooting, hanging, clubbing, and bayoneting.

Special techniques were developed. One was exposure to the elements—rain and heat, but particularly to the winter cold during the deliberately prolonged roll calls and snow removal, and during boxcar transports. The electrically charged fences, the savage dogs of the guards, the intravenous injections of gasoline and other lethal agents, and the medical experiments all took their toll. Many prisoners were assigned to hard labor in regional factories; deaths among these internees were described, resulting from floggings and beatings administered to assure a high level of productivity. Prisoners who were unable to keep pace were either executed on the spot or scheduled for extermination.

The living conditions were deadly. There was no privacy during work or sleep. The sleep period was generally reduced to five or six hours. Exhaustion was universal, and an important cause of death. The poor medical care, limited number of latrines, overcrowding, inadequate clothing, general filth, and starvation or semistarvation diet all reduced the prisoners' resistance to disease, and caused the mortality rate to increase.

Dr. Ali Kuci, an inmate with whom Rosenbloom has been in contact, tells us that in the last few years of the camp's existence the death penalty was invoked more often for a man's national or religious affiliation than for infractions of camp regulations. He told of a group of ten or twelve prisoners removed from their quarters and asked what kind of death they preferred. They could choose between being hanged or shot. After thirty minutes of grace, the prisoners were forced to strip and then were executed by the method they selected.

This tale did not correspond with other stories: it seemed unusual for the SS to give their victims a choice of anything. The more common account is of a group of men being sent to a vacant site on a cold winter night, forced to strip, then hosed with water. In the morning a labor detail would be ordered to collect the bodies. Or a convicted group would be escorted to the crematorium and executed there, for greater convenience. Another method, greatly feared by the inmates, was deportation to other camps for extermination. Apparently the two centers to which many prisoners of Dachau were sent were the Hartheim Castle, near Linz, and the Mauthausen concentration camp.

Activities in the crematorium and gas chamber were kept secret. At one time, the prisoners assigned to work there, usually Jews, disappeared after six weeks and were replaced by others. In recent months, the men who worked in the crematorium survived. Rosenbloom has plans for them as soon as we are permitted to begin housecleaning.

There are conflicting stories as to the use of the gas chamber. An Albanian tells me that it was used only four times since 1942, but a Pole says that it was never used during that time. Another Pole reports that 100 or 150 people were put to death each day in the chamber. A Yugoslav says that thousands were gassed in the last three years. A Frenchman believes that the chamber has never been used.

Dr. Franz Blaha, a Czech physician inmate, a member of the IPC, and a valuable source of information about medical conditions in the camp, believes that the gas chamber was used many times. Later he testified at the Nuremberg trials. Between June 1942 and April 1945, Dr. Blaha supervised 12,000 autopsies. Out of eight or nine bodies that he examined in 1944, "there were three still alive and the remainder appeared to be dead. Their eyes were red and their faces swollen. . . . Afterwards they were removed to the crematorium where I had to examine their teeth for gold. . . ." According to Dr. Blaha, lethal intravenous injections were administered to hospital patients. Sometimes mentally ill patients were brought to the gas chambers, where they were either injected or shot to death; they were not gassed. He testified to seeing people shoved into the ovens of the crematorium while still alive.[1]

Many of the stories described the shedding of clothes before execution. This was purposeful. The clothing was collected and later issued to newly arriving prisoners.

Regardless of the extent of the use of the gas chamber, its presence in the camp contributed to the pervasive fear of death; so too did the constant column of black smoke rising from the chimney of the crematorium.

Who would be next? they asked themselves. One of the inmates says that he used to look at the smoke pouring from the chimney and think: That is the way to escape from this camp.

Dr. Kuci tells us about the toothpaste incident, an example of the crime of "sabotage," for which the death sentence was mandatory. A group of prisoners were unloading crates of toothpaste into a warehouse. Two of them pocketed a tube apiece. This was noted by a civilian employee, but she thought it too insignificant to report.

Two weeks later she mentioned it as a joke to a friend, an SS guard, but he did not think it funny, and reported the theft. Records revealed the identity of the laborers; their barracks were searched and the two tubes were found. The "saboteurs" were hanged—ceremoniously, with all the prisoners at attention.

17

CAMP FEVER

April had been a difficult month for the men, nurses, doctors, and CO, Colonel Lawrence C. Ball, of the 116th Evacuation Hospital. They had moved four times that month; none of their locations was desirable. It required a vast amount of labor and paperwork to discharge patients, close, pack, move, and reopen at its usual size, 450 beds. Four changes of location were exhausting. The hospital had traveled 315 miles in the move across Germany and had received a total of 2,070 patients during its twenty-four days of operation. Its trucks and ambulances had been strafed many times by the enemy, despite the red crosses on their sides and roofs. The long hours on the gutted roads, the large number of casualties, the need for sharing its trucks with other outfits, and the lengthy supply and evacuation routes all contributed to a nerve-wracking month. Perhaps the only high spot was when three German soldiers surrendered to some of the corpsmen, but even this had created a problem of disposition.

These hardships were minor compared to the difficulties that were to appear soon: medical and administrative difficulties that the experienced men and officers of this outfit could not even imagine.

On May 1 the hospital was in Ottingen, Germany, in support of the 42d and 45th Infantry and 20th Armored Divisions. Emergency orders arrived to move into Dachau. At midnight, the corpsmen began to pack, and today, May 2, the long lines of trucks and ambulances filled with weary nurses, doctors, and other hospital personnel reach the camp gate, where they are greeted with demands for each of them to show proof of previous typhus fever immunizations.

After surveying the sites that might be suitable for a large hospital, the CO selects the least of the evils, eighteen one-story frame buildings in the administrative area, former SS barracks now filled with debris and trash. If partitions are removed, the barracks can be converted into large wards with latrines and washrooms.

The urgency of the situation evident, the dedicated though not uncomplaining corpsmen begin the renovation and purification of these buildings. Aided by a detail of inmates capable of work, they remove tons of muck and scrub the rooms, beds, and furniture with a 2 percent cresol solution.

The staff moves into quarters in an SS administration building. Fortunately, a large mess hall is available for them, with good cooking facilities, a cooler, and steam from the central power plant for dishwashing.

A race against time: the hospital is scheduled to open for patients tomorrow. How will it function? The orders specify that only patients with typhus fever will be admitted; the staff doctors have never treated such patients before; they spend hours trying to work out a method of selecting and transporting patients. Physicians, including inmate doctors, will determine the presence of typhus fever clinically—by history and physical examination. Litter bearers will then place the patient on a litter and carry him to an ambulance, and from there to the receiving section consisting of large ward tents. Here his filthy clothes will be removed and burned by corpsmen and nurses using strict isolation techniques—caps, gowns, masks, and gloves. Then orderlies will scrub the patient with soap, water, and cresol solution, shave his scalp, and help him into clean pajamas, property of the United States Army. After DDT dusting, the patient will be carried by new litter bearers and ambulance to the converted wards, stopping first in the X-ray department for a chest film obtained with mobile units: it is anticipated that many of the patients with typhus fever also have tuberculosis.

Eleven wards of 1,200 beds are to be in operation as soon as possible. The plans also call for 600 more beds without latrines in about three more weeks, and the recruitment of 50 more enlisted men from other American units, and 50 trained inmates from the camp.

The 127th Evacuation Hospital (semimobile), under Colonel Aubry L. Bradford, was also busy in April, putting up and striking down its tents, treating 210 starved and maltreated Allied POWs, many well-nourished German POWs, and a large number of battle casualties, totaling 4,684 admissions and 11 deaths. The unit was at its normal strength, approximately 40 nurses, 40 officers, and 220 enlisted men. Supplies had been a problem all month; its trucks were forced to haul food hundreds of miles. Everyone hoped that life would be easier in May, so they were disappointed yesterday to receive orders to move into Dachau immediately. They planned the move in three stages. The first contingent arrives today; the other two are expected tomorrow and on May 5.

Here, they face the same problems as the men of the 116th Evacuation Hospital. Like them, they work overtime with the customary Army overtime pay. Soon the rubble disappears from other SS barracks. The hospital, normally 400 beds, plans to expand to 1,200. Beginning tomorrow, these beds will be filled with patients with ordinary disease, and women with typhus fever. The CO has put a request through channels for a quartermaster laundry company, a sanitary company, an engineering unit, and a bath and sterilization company; he also plans to recruit interpreters and inmates to work as ward men.

I hear from Colonel Hathaway that the 10th and 66th Field Hospitals are on their way and a mobile unit of the 1st Medical Laboratory, as well as special personnel from the 59th Evacuation Hospital.

May 3 is to be a long day.

The hospitals open. Someone attaches a sign with the words "127th Evac. Hosp." to the main signpost below the three German figurines with the cello, accordion, and umbrella and the words *SS KonzentrationsLager*.

We are overjoyed by the arrival of many of the members of the United States Army Typhus Commission, headed by Colonel John C. Snyder. They will occupy administrative and consultative positions in the management of the epidemic and will also participate in patient care.

We have heard of their success in Naples in 1943 when DDT, then a new insecticide, was tested for the first time in a major epidemic. Five weeks after dusting all the people in that city, the disease was contained.

A historic event. The first full-scale epidemic of typhus fever to be arrested by the efforts of man.

Now DDT is to be tried again, in an infinitely more serious and dangerous epidemic than the one at Naples.

One of the interned physicians says that the typhus fever was present in the camp during the winter of 1943–44. Another believes that the outbreak began in the fall of 1944, brought in by Hungarian prisoners. The presence of the disease was reported by the SS doctors, but the Germans took no action. Other physician-inmates say the same, that the Nazis deliberately encouraged the spread of communicable diseases as another method of population control.

Toward the end of 1944, control measures were put into effect after the epidemic flared out of control and into the SS camp, but they were ineffective; thousands of deaths occurred. I am told that twenty-one of the interned doctors succumbed to the disease—typhus fever is as unkind to members of the medical profession as it is to the laity, unless preventive measures are taken. I do not think that any of us on the Team will contract the disease: we have been inoculated, and we dust ourselves with DDT every few hours. Fortunately G-5 sent several hundred pounds of the dust for our use.

In the past, epidemic typhus fever has been called jail distemper, camp fever, Old World typhus, and ship fever because it has appeared during evil times, times of war, famine, and overcrowding. Its catastrophic destructive power was demonstrated in eastern Europe and Russia after the end of World War I when tens of millions were stricken and three million died.

For the disease to spread this explosively, human misery must be extreme and personal cleanliness impossible.

Leon Malczewski, a Polish member of the IPC whom we have met several times, has been interned for five years. He explained how impossible it was to change one's shirt.

"I try to keep clean. I trade some of my bread for a second undershirt so after a day's work, when I go to bed at night, I can take dirty one off and put on clean one and let dirty one air out. But what do I do with second one during the day? If I keep it in the barracks, it might get stolen." (This happened twice.) "If I hide it in mattress, it might be found by the guards when they inspect and they take it away." (This happened.) "Finally, I put it into pocket of my coat and keep it with me all day."

It was characteristic of the concentration camp that a prisoner could not keep clean, dry, or warm. This was part of the physical maltreatment to which he was constantly exposed, stress factors beyond his control intended to make him feel helpless.

The inadequacy of the medical care also contributed to this feeling.

Several inmates tell us that, until the end of 1942, physicians were not permitted to take care of patients in the prison hospital. Instead, untrained prisoners, usually German criminals, were assigned this task. According to one of the Poles, the prisoner in charge of the hospital several years before performed major operations; he was completely ignorant of medical techniques. Later he was permitted to become a member of the SS. Another inmate reported that a different chief "surgeon" had been a carpenter by trade.

In one of the barracks, patients with diarrhea were tied to beds and placed under cold showers for the night. In two of the barracks, the dying, the sick, and those who had soiled their beds were moved into the lavatory. If they did not die quickly enough, they were killed by their block chief.

Medical care improved in 1943, when trained physicians were permitted into the prison hospital, but only because the Nazis realized that the prisoners could contribute to the war effort by their labor, and therefore something should be done to keep them alive.

At the same time, working hours increased. In the summer, the prisoners awoke at 4:00 A.M. Their frenzied day began with supervised bed-making and a scanty breakfast. Roll call was at 5:15 A.M., followed by assignment to a labor squad and the march to work. Working hours were from 6:00 A.M. to noon, and from 1:00 to 6:30 P.M. The noon hour was for dinner and additional marching. In the evening, the prisoners were permitted their skimpy supper. At 7:00 P.M. they reported for another roll call, often lasting for a long time—up to an hour. Then the final collapse into the oblivion of sleep after lights-out at 9:00 P.M.

During the summer, the prisoners of Dachau worked an eleven-and-a-half-hour day. In the winter, they awoke at 5:00 A.M., and worked only until dusk.

Despite the long hours, the arduous labor, the inadequate rest periods, the flimsy and ragged bedding, the rough, abrasive beds, and the overcrowded bunks necessitating side-sleeping, the prisoners slept without difficulty. Complaints of insomnia were rare.

But there was no oblivion during the day. The stories emphasized sudden, savage acts by the SS guards. I look at the drawn, pallid face of a wizened Frenchman. The air reeks with the death smell as he tries to tell about one of his countrymen shot to death for walking too slowly when returning from work.

"Sadistic beasts," says the Frenchman. I agree, and so do my teammates.

I have heard several accounts of the vicious, criminal behavior of some of the block chiefs and Capos, the prisoner-foremen responsible for the amount of work accomplished by members of their labor crews. They were said to be even more brutal than the SS men. These tales predominate because the prisoners had more contacts with their own leaders than with the SS troopers.

Such behavior of the prisoner-leaders was deliberately fostered by the SS command because it made it easier for them to control the inner compound with a minimum of German personnel. If the camp leaders could carry out their orders pertaining to labor assignments, and punishment and execution of internees, fewer SS men would be needed to supervise the camp.

This principle worked well at Dachau, says Rosenbloom. From contacts with the inmates, Rosenbloom and Howcroft have become familiar with the structure of the camp, which, for administrative purposes, was divided by the Nazis into five sections. The same system was also in use in other concentration camps.

Section I consisted of the offices of the camp commandant and his staff, the guard unit, and the mail censors.

Section II was the political department, headed by a Gestapo or police officer. Here the prisoners' dossiers were kept up to date. Members of this section, or Gestapo agents from Munich, interrogated the prisoners, and, when appropriate, arranged for their release, transfer, evacuation, or cremation. The bustling officials of this department kept in constant touch with Berlin, checking and counterchecking all orders, death sentences, and activities of the other sections, including Section I.

In Section IV, administrative, fiscal, housing, engineering, and supply matters were handled.

Section V concerned the hospitals and the malaria station.

Section III, responsible for the operation of the prison compound, was staffed solely by prisoners. The key person in this section was the Nazi-appointed camp senior or elder (*Lageraelteste*), who, aided by a secretary and a cadre of inmates to handle the records, executed the orders sent to him from Section I. Under his jurisdiction were barracks (block) and room (cell) leaders (seniors) and secretaries, and his police chief to whom the prisoner-police were responsible. At one time, the police force numbered 600 men.

We heard many stories about the cruelty of these hated men in green uniforms.

The heart of Section III was the Labor Allocation Office (*Arbeitseinsatz*), headed by a chief (*Arbeitseinsatzfuehrer*) and his staff.

The composition of the death transports out of the camp was often determined in the Labor Allocation Office. The chain of command began with the camp senior after he received orders from the SS commandant. The instructions were simple: have so many men ready at a specific time to be shipped to another concentration camp or undesignated location. The order might say that they should be Jews, or Poles, or Italians. After consultation with block or cell leaders, certain prisoners were selected for their last trip.

A similar process was used for the major activities of Section III. The selection of members of work gangs and their leaders, the Capos, was affected by the consultations with the camp senior and block leaders.

At one time, more than 160 work details (*Arbeitskommandos*) were commissioned. They were dispatched to the camp grounds, workshops, warehouses, and maintenance and custodial areas. Some reported to a large experimental farm on the camp grounds, the *Plantage*. Others were sent to regional factories and shops producing small arms, SS uniforms, paper, and porcelain. (About 8,000 prisoners in the Dachau complex were employed in the Air Force and aviation industry in many different cities. The Praezifix, a factory in Dachau manufacturing airplane parts and screws, employed 356 prisoners.[1])

Copies of an affidavit, signed by many inmates, reach our offices:

> We, the antifascist prisoners of [this firm] . . . accuse the former prisoner . . . at Dachau . . . of committing the worst crimes a prisoner has ever committed. By caning and torturing prisoners he increased production in favor of fascist rulers. He denounced many prisoners to the SS-team-leader, and these comrades were then sent away on death transports. . . .[2]

We receive many accusations of this sort. Rosenbloom turns them over to other units of the 7th Army.

Each will be investigated thoroughly, we are told.

One of the 7th Army investigating teams is an OSS unit assigned to probe charges of cruelty and inhuman behavior on the part of certain Capos, block leaders, and other inmates. Their report describes the process of conversion of inmates into spies.[3]

Although Dachau was a center for "protective custody" for political prisoners, at one time real criminals whose offenses ranged from misdemeanors to major crimes were incarcerated in the camp. Their number was always small in proportion to the number of political prisoners.

It was usually these real criminals who were persuaded by the Nazis in Section II, the political section, to act as lackeys and informers in return for special privileges.

No great effort was required by the criminal to become indistinguishable from the majority of the inmates—he disguised himself by exchanging his green identification patch for a red one.

All prisoners wore triangles stitched onto their uniforms, color coded for their offenses so that ordinarily a political prisoner or POW (red triangle) could be distinguished from a common criminal (green), a religious "fanatic" such as a Jehovah's Witness (violet), a recaptured prisoner (blue), a homosexual (pink), or an antisocial person (black). Jews wore a yellow triangle combined with a colored triangle so as to form a Star of David. Nationalities were indicated by appropriate letters, such as P for Polish or F for French, these letters placed within the triangles. Recidivists, or those who had been to a concentration camp before, wore a crossbar above their triangles.[4]

When a criminal was able to become a Capo, or block or cell leader, or policeman, he achieved control of the lives of the political prisoners within his domain; many of the atrocity stories relate to acts of people with this background. But other camp leaders who had been interned for political reasons also were said to be guilty of cruel and savage practices, probably in order to hold their positions.

Many prisoners learned that they could improve their chances of surviving by becoming part of the organization: if they succeeded, they obtained security of sorts—a negotiating ability and some personal power that could be used to obtain more food, better clothing, easier work, tobacco, and, sometimes, better housing.[5]

According to the OSS investigating team, the limited power of the men in the upper class was sufficient incentive for other individuals and cliques to vie for their positions, and the battle for control began. In 1937, a group of Austrian and German Socialists ruled the inner compound. After their leader, Brenner, was released, a German Socialist-Communist combine took over until 1944, when one of its key people, Schaetzle, was suspected of treachery and sent out of the camp. The other leader of this group, Rieke, died shortly afterward. Other Germans then took charge but were swept from power by the members of the future IPC: Arthur Haulot, a Belgian journalist, Dr. Ali Kuci, an Albanian public official, Lieutenant Commander Patrick O'Leary, a British-Canadian officer, Leon Malczewski, the Pole with the shirt problem, Edmond Michelet, a French Resistance fighter, Captain Willem Boellaard of Holland, and several others of different nationalities.

Being the oldest inhabitants of the camp, the German prisoners had ruled for a long time, and people of other countries became increasingly hostile toward them. Unchecked power breeds tyranny; tyranny spawns fear and hatred. These feelings intensified over the years and transferred from the prisoner leaders to the German prisoners as a whole. An exception was made for Oskar Mueller, the choice of the IPC for the position of camp senior. Mueller, a fairly recent arrival at the camp, was almost universally respected because he did not abuse his power.

In office he was nonpolitical, but so too had been all the other Section III leaders during the reign of the Nazis.[6]

Organized groups did not exist during this time. The pressures of the concentration camp environment had obliterated the backgrounds and distinctions between individuals—political, religious, social, national, or intellectual bonds between prisoners became almost insignificant. The only objective was personal survival.

Despite this, several prisoners organized a small group, later to be called the International Prisoners' Committee, in September 1944, when news of the Allied advances reached the camp. For a short time, the group consisted of only four men— O'Leary, Kuci, Haulot, and Malczewski—who met in great secrecy in the prison hospital.

For several months they contacted other potential members representing many nationalities. Their hope was to keep the prisoners alive during the days before the Americans came. They recognized that this would be a critical period in the life of the camp. They enrolled carefully selected cell and block leaders in order to control the genuine criminals during the time of transition. They made plans to prevent any acts of the prisoners that might provoke SS reprisal. They succeeded, in part, in taking over Section III. Their "press bureau" became active when they decided to disseminate news about the progress of the war to all inmates. They began to compile records of criminal activities by the SS and others. When the Americans reached Augsburg, certain prisoners from the camp who toiled on nearby farms were instructed to inform the Americans about conditions within the camp.

The Committee offered its services to the Americans on the day of liberation.

18

THE IPC, THE VISITORS, AND THE "PIGS"

The International Prisoners' Committee (IPC) has been meeting regularly since April 30; copies of the minutes of their meetings, either in the original German or in their English translations, have been sent to me. After reading them, I begin to realize that control of the thousands of inhabitants here would be impossible without the tireless and continuing efforts of the members of this organization.

The first meeting was held shortly after liberation, Lieutenant Commander Patrick O'Leary presiding. (The minutes often refer to him as Sir Patrick.) An American lieutenant colonel, attending this historic session, conferred on O'Leary "all powers concerning the management of the camp." Two vice-presidents were elected: General Nikolai Michailow, a Russian, and Arthur Haulot. Oskar Mueller was confirmed as camp senior. Dr. Franz Blaha was made head of the important sanitation committee. Disciplinary problems were to be handled by Oscar Juranic, a Yugoslav.

The Committee restricted itself to matters concerning the prison compound. "Outside" protection and the feeding and safety of the camp residents were to be the responsibility of the Americans, and a motion was made to turn over the SS men imprisoned in the bunker to the American military authorities. Some of the inmates still had guns and rifles, obtained not only from American soldiers but also from dead Germans and from ransacked SS quarters and warehouses. All firearms were to be forbidden in the camp; they would have to be turned in immediately. Inmates were not to take the law into their hands, say the minutes: "Any kind of personal dealings like vengeance or similar deeds will be immediately severely punished."

The minutes also say that two ex-prisoners who collaborated with the SS "have been arrested, and, on order of the American commander, shot according to the law." [1]

The minutes end with the announcement that they will be published in the most important languages. The meeting was opened at 20.30 and closed at 22.30. The only hint of emotion appears in the title: "Minutes of the 1st Meeting of the International Prisoners' Committee in the freed Camp Dachau."

At the second meeting, held the same day, subcommittees were formed to take care of matters such as clothing, culture and information, mail service, laundry, food, and labor assignments—"division of work." Then the IPC began to expand by electing national leaders into its ranks: Rasmus Brooch, a Norwegian, and Comrade Yocarinis, a Greek. It was agreed that the Lithuanians would be represented by the USSR delegate, an unpopular decision in certain quarters.

Dr. Blaha was made chief of the hospital subcommittee.

An announcement: "Tomorrow, the 1st day of May, will be a holiday due to the liberation of the camp by the American Army as well as in connection with the probable end of the war which is approaching. The American CO [a Lieutenant Colonel Fellens, whom I never met] will be invited to this feast." The Section for Information and Culture was designated to handle the festivities.

A 7th Army officer, Captain Martin A. Agather, attended the third meeting (May 1). Registration is about to begin, he said, demonstrating a questionnaire printed in German and English. The replies are to be printed, then signed. Difficulties are expected because most of the inmates cannot understand either language: at the moment many do not have the strength to sign their names. Further, many of the inmates will be suspicious of any request for vital data. They will be reluctant to give information on account of their treatment by the dossier-minded Nazis. National leaders will have to help their people with these forms and appoint interpreters and transcribers.

Nothing is simple. The captain exhibits great patience as he explains the entries on the form, item by item. Name, place and date of arrest, date of arrival in Dachau, particulars of any ill treatment received, past criminal offenses (again dates of arrest, court appearance, and release; legal details), past military service—World War I or II? A critical entry asks the inmate where he wants to go. Who does he know there? What are their names and addresses?

A question-and-answer session then followed in which many of the queries were directed toward determining an individual's nationality. The official position seemed straightforward: a person would be a citizen of the country in which he lived on January 1, 1939, before borders were eliminated or changed by the Nazi wars of aggression. So, the Poles would no longer be Germans or Russians, but Poles again. Yugoslavs from Trieste and Gorz, at one time Austrian citizens, would become Italians. Yugoslavs from Istria, who had been under Italian rule, would be Yugoslavs again. (Before Istria had become an Italian province in 1918, it had been under Austrian and French rule.) Austria was an exception to the present policy; its annexation by the Third Reich had occurred before the critical date, so its people would be Austrians, not Germans. Similarly, the Sudeteners would no longer be Germans, but Czechoslovakians.

There were individual problems. People from Greece, Albania, and other Balkan countries who had been arrested in Italy had been registered as Italians. What would happen to them? They would revert to their original nationalities. Then there were Hungarians who had become Romanian citizens before January 1, 1939, and wished to remain in Hungary. But they would have to become Romanians again.

The minutes disclosed other difficulties:

> MICHAILOW: Is military service to be understood only in the Russian army or in the German one?
> AGATHER: Only in your Army, the Russian one. . . .
> MICHAILOW: How should one fill out the item on nationality, for example, for the citizens of a particular state of the USSR—a Ukrainian, etc., or simply Russian?
> AGATHER: They should mention that they belong to the USSR, although they may have a nationality other than the Russian one.
> MICHAILOW: The next to the last question: does one indicate just the country one wants to go to, or also the place?
> AGATHER: When some parts of a country are so destroyed

that it is impossible to live there, the place cannot be mentioned exactly, but everyone has to show where he wants to go. Later we will discuss if this is possible.

MICHAILOW: Should only the country be mentioned, or something more?

AGATHER: The town and village as well.

MICHAILOW: What regulation applies to those who left Russia during the Revolution and would like to go back to Russia now?

AGATHER: After they have changed their citizenship, they are no longer Russians. In such a case, Russia will have to agree to take them back. We can only send papers to the Committee, which will decide. [In reply to a question from Michelet, France.] People evicted from their country for a political crime are no longer citizens of their country, and should be treated as not belonging to any country, but should mention the country to which they once belonged.

BOELLAARD: Our country [Holland] has said that Dutch people fighting for the freedom of Spain now belong to no state. We will try to right this wrong, but what country should these people name on their form?

AGATHER: We want to know this. Put the previous country. They should be sent home.

HAULOT: There are Poles and Yugoslavs, etc., who were living in Belgium and would like to go back there. What can they do?

AGATHER: They may go where they like. [Later, this is made conditional—if the Belgian committee agrees. Another question asks where Norwegians are to go, so long as Norway is not free.] To a port. From there home, as soon as possible.

MELODIA (Italy): Should Italians, first taken as POWs, then put into a concentration camp, give the date of the first or second arrest?

AGATHER: The date of the first arrest. [In reply to Parra, Spain.] The first date applies to Spaniards arrested in Spain. Or France.

MUELLER (Germany): Many Germans have been punished for political reasons. Should this be mentioned?

AGATHER: This is exactly what we want to know.

JURANIC (Yugoslavia): What regulations apply to Italian citizens who have served in the Yugoslavian Army and were incarcerated as POWs?

AGATHER: They are considered Italians, but should mention circumstances. . . .

MICHAILOW: Should the women in the camp fill out these printed forms?

AGATHER: Yes, and in the same way. . . .

The meeting continues a little longer. Captain Agather states that the one function of the Americans is to look after the internees; he is at their disposal twenty-four hours a day.

Discussion of citizenship problems recurs at the next few IPC meetings, particularly the status of people who do not wish to remain in or return to the country of their birth. Approval for migration must be given by the country in which they wish to live. Rosenbloom, who has become liaison officer to the IPC, says at a meeting that stateless people should be represented in the organization, and this is approved. The names of two inmates are submitted to become representatives; both are stateless people who hold Nansen "passports." [2]

What will happen to a person who is not permitted to enter a country of his choice? Will he be forcibly moved elsewhere? The American position is clearly stated by Captain Agather: a person will not be forced to go to a country against his wishes; he will be allowed to go wherever he wants to, provided the government of the designated country does not object.

But what can be done about a person considered a criminal in his own country but not in another? Edmond Michelet, as active on the IPC as he was on the original underground committee, clarifies the situation: a person who is considered a criminal in Russia and wants to live in France should be approved as to his acceptability by the French. Many people want to go to France: those from the Saarland, and the Spaniards whose families live in France. One of the Dutchmen on the IPC mentions that there are young student priests in the camp, mostly Poles, who cannot continue their education in their native land. He would like them to come to Holland to continue their education. Captain Agather thinks this may depend on whether they can show they have means of support. A rumor circulates at the meeting that the Romanian government has announced that it will accept all those who say they are Romanian. Everyone agrees that such an attitude would be exemplary.

The ultimate decision to admit anyone into a new country will be made by the government of that country.[3] This expresses the majority opinion at the meeting, which has been another long one. The presiding officer, visibly tired, reminds everyone that the purpose of the Americans is to evacuate the camp as quickly as possible.

An excellent hint. Someone moves to adjourn. The inmates return to their tasks, the Americans to their offices.

The first few days of May bring increasing demands from many sources. Members of the Team, particularly Lieutenant Rosenbloom, are under great pressure to attend to the needs of certain individuals or national groups ahead of others. Many demand better and more food than we can give them, better medical care, and improved housing. The internees want to go home immediately—I don't blame them. They ask for interviews, each has his case to present. Some think they have important contributions to make to the war effort.

The IPC helps, as its minutes show:

> Especially it is not allowed to hear all people who believe to be more important than the other ones or who believe that the tales which they intend to produce before the American commander are of special interest. There cannot be any talk of such things. Of course, this does not apply to such cases [as] the French parachute fighter who jumped over Munich some weeks ago and was delivered to the camp some days ago.

This information clarified a story I had heard earlier, that brave parachutists were seen floating into the camp several days before the Americans came. One of them was said to be an exotic American woman underground fighter!

Visiting dignitaries begin to arrive from the Allied countries. They make their first stop at my office because they have to be dusted with DDT. Senators, congressmen, generals, editors, national leaders, all submit to the handgun, and afterward to inoculation. I even have my picture taken while spraying a congressman.

I am frustrated by this intrusion on my time, and by having to explain and reexplain the medical and health situation.

Reporters and photographers roam the camp freely; they carry small cameras and movie cameras. Their questions are probing, to us and to the inmates. Some of the visiting luminaries interrogate the internees exhaustively, as if they were witnesses in a court. Rosenbloom has to squire some of these special visitors through the camp. He, too, has his picture taken, with the American ambassador to France, Jefferson Caffery, a tall, distinguished-looking man. As he is being escorted through the camp, an inmate suddenly dies in front of him.

Many of the internees willingly conduct the tourists to all the usual sites, and to others that they know intimately—the dog pens, the medical experimental station site near one of the blocks, the restricted area for the interned clergymen, the rifle range where Russian POWs were executed, and the gravel pits where prisoners were forced to kneel and were then shot, their blood draining through a convenient grate into a ditch.

All the visitors are shocked, their sensibilities stunned, just as ours were.

The quarantine is also being shattered.

Rosenbloom and Howcroft are working overtime with the IPC and their designated people on the reorganization of labor teams and the procurement and distribution of supplies, particularly clothes. Food supplies are improving. New latrines are being constructed. The water continues to be contaminated, and I consult with public utility specialists on this problem. I meet with supply officers from the evacuation hospitals who cannot comprehend that our material comes from German sources.

Then there is a meeting with Harry D. Pires, the American Red Cross representative. I am cheered because he promises more of their wonderful supplies. He becomes indispensable in his own quiet, unassuming, dedicated way.

Many of the consultations are held in my office in one of the SS administrative buildings, in a room next to the office of Colonel Barrett, a Military Government officer temporarily in charge of the camp. I have taken over a comfortable room in a former SS library with a huge map of Europe on one wall and a calendar on another. In one corner is a cracked, empty safe.

There are also desks and chairs, a coat tree, and a bookcase filled with Nazi brochures and books containing hideous propaganda and teaching material—lantern slides of the *Untermenschen*, the subhumans such as the Jews, Slavs, Orientals, and others, subhuman because they were inferior to the members of the Master Race. With each slide was correlated written material.

These teaching guides have been studied intently: there are many marginal annotations and exclamations. In one of the pamphlets entitled *Das Judentum* (Judaism), picture number 5 shows in its upper left corner an army of tall, blond, muscular, seemingly invulnerable Nordic men, four abreast, dressed in shorts, wearing boxing gloves, striding resolutely forward. The companion illustration in the lower right-hand corner shows bearded black-hatted gaunt men, many using canes— orthodox Jews from Poland. The caption says: *Young German Sportsmen—Disgusting Eastern Jews*. The sixth picture shows *Der Jude, Ein Bastard*. Three centrally placed heads— fat, bearded, bald. Four marginally situated show their unsavory cousins: Negro, Hamite, Asiatic, and Oriental.

In these brochures, the Jews are described and caricatured as short, furtive, odious, nonhuman creatures with sinister devil's faces, thick lips, fleshy eyelids, hooked noses, and horn-rimmed glasses. Their evil deeds stemmed from their materialistic, Marxist traits and their ability as international bankers. They were responsible for all the disasters of the past and the present: the slaughter of 75,000 Egyptians at the time of the Pharoahs, the Black Death during the Middle Ages, the surrender of the German fleet at Scapa Flow, the detestable Weimar Republic, the burning of the airship *Hindenburg*.

"Pigs," they had been called by the SS guards; they had no other names.

Other racial, national, and ethnic groups were also stereotyped. Uncle Sam was depicted as carrying two guns and waving a flag of imperialism, or characterized as a mongrel money grubber or a greedy shopkeeper. The American soldier was portrayed as an ignorant, loutish savage, with dollar bills hanging from his pockets.

In contrast was the Germanic superman, an overtly heroic, bold, determined, powerful giant, the personification of all desirable physical, cultural, and intellectual attributes. He was a member of the elite, the Chosen, the ruling class of the future. In comparison, other people of the world were suitable only for menial chores.

Or for extermination.

This must have been the thinking of the men who sat in this room a few weeks ago, and for others like them throughout Germany, men obsessed with their own racial superiority. The books on the shelves told them that they were pioneers in the brave, new Germanic world, that they were scientists searching for new strains. To accomplish this, they had to be ruthless in stamping out inferior variants, those detrimental to the German people, the subhumans who could be eradicated like vermin.

I put the Nazi books and brochures back into the bookcases. It is impossible to understand how intelligent people could believe their contents, let alone teach their contents to others.

I make my first visit to the labor camp at Allach, ten miles away, where there is one enclosure for 3,000 Jews and another for 6,000 non-Jewish inmates. They have the same pinched faces, labored gaits, and stooped backs as the ambulatory inmates at Dachau. They live in overcrowded, flimsy barracks. They wear the same blue-white striped uniforms. One man, perhaps 40 years old but looking considerably older, walks slowly up to where Hollis, my driver, and I are standing, and asks suspiciously, "Are you Jews or Germans?"

Here a Frenchman tells us that all the Nazis are beasts and all the SS men murderers, a not unexpected opinion, although some of the inmates of Dachau are surprisingly objective about them, feeling that they behaved as expected of people trained under their system. This particular inmate tells us that the German anti-Nazis are wonderful people. But from others I hear the old refrain, *the only good German is a dead German*, which I have heard so often in the past, the last time when our infantry battalion was being mangled by SS troops. It is difficult to think otherwise in these camps.

When I can be objective, perhaps in the quiet darkness of night or in a sudden rare, time-stopping moment of reflection, I know it is wrong to utter these parrotlike sounds, imitating the monotonous chorus of the Nazis themselves—there are no good Jews, Poles, priests, churches, Frenchmen, black men, yellow men. Their list was endless, their minds rigid, their fears overpowering, and they welded all their anxieties, biases, distortions, and desires into a racial "science" that they considered to be the absolute truth. The "vermin," "lice," and "spiders" were "soulless" and "slavelike"; they were to be destroyed—emotionally, intellectually, or physically.

The psychic deterioration of many of the inmates is most evident when they knock timidly on the doors of our offices, edge fearfully inside, come to attention, and then remain rigid even after we tell them to relax. Their hands shake. They find it difficult to express their thoughts.

They have not yet overcome their fear of authority.

We tell them to put their hats on again. We even magnify our relaxed attitudes by putting our feet on our desks, offering them cigarettes or wretched German cigars, or by attempting light, bantering multilingual jokes. We swear at them—and they know that our words are pleasantries.

But usually they are unable to unbend. It will take time for them to become human beings again.

Their behavior was essential to their survival. The SS had decreed that in front of guards and German visitors, a prisoner was to stand at attention, doff his cap, state his prisoner number, and ask permission to have his request granted. If this were not properly done, or quickly enough, he was marched to the shower room and forced to kneel with his arms thrown back and lashed to a post. The punishment lasted for one hour. Prisoners returning from their daily work were searched; if cigarette butts or tobacco shreds were found, the same humiliating penalty was invoked.

The Nazis had planned to make the prisoners lose their identities. When they had forgotten their past and had become incapable of making decisions, they had fulfilled the goal set for them by their German overseers: they were slaves, entirely dependent on their guards.

The methods used were not new in human history; they consisted of a series of events designed to instill fear into the individuals who were to be transformed into slaves. The first occurred when a person was kidnapped from his home, or arrested and subjected to brutal treatment. The second came during the trip to a new land. Savage treatment was customary.

Again, the prisoner had no recourse; he saw others like him die. The final shock occurred in the concentration camp, when he realized he had no control over anything. He was exposed to starvation, torture, constant labor, sudden death, unceasing supervision, unceasing harassment; cruel and degrading experiences lasted from morning to night; visitors were not allowed; lawyers were banned.

Survival depended on absolute obedience, but was not guaranteed by it.

According to Bettelheim,[4] prisoners unsuccessfully attempting suicide were whipped and then placed in prolonged solitary confinement—they were punished for making a decision! On the other hand, a guard might so torment a prisoner that he would throw himself into the electrically charged fence. But this was on the guard's initiative, not the prisoner's. The inmates were also assigned to pointless tasks: they were made to dig ditches by hand when tools were available; meticulous, repetitive bed-making often occurred; a prisoner was hitched to a wagon and forced to gallop; another carried rocks from one site to another; inmates were required to request permission to go to the latrine in the daytime—these were usually denied.

One of our incarcerated priests sends us a description of the ordeal of snow cleaning; he was forced to carry snow from place to place on an inverted table. When he asked his guard the reason for this punishment, he received no answer.

In the evenings we sip wine in our quarters, talk about the internees, and wonder how we would fare if we were subjected to forces similar to those that existed in the camp. Would we behave differently? Would we cooperate?

One of the men says that he would remain loyal to the end. Give his last crumb of bread to a starving comrade. Die bravely under the hot afternoon sun, with distant, muted bugles sounding "Taps." Another says he could not withstand the pressure.

Nobody really knows.[5]

19

THE BURIAL DETAIL

Many of the big guns of the Medical Corps are loaded, and on May 3, seventy-two hours after our arrival in the camp, the barrage begins that will bring victory against the body lice, the misanthropic, parasitic insects responsible for the transmission of typhus fever from person to person. The Army has contributed enough DDT so that dusting of all the inmates at Dachau and Allach can start. By a superhuman effort the task is completed in five days. In addition to the inmates, the official quarantine calls for the dusting of all other individuals—Army personnel, guards, visitors, Allied officials—when they leave the inner camp for the outer area. Furthermore, these persons are required to show their immunization records and be given typhus vaccine, unless they have received the vaccine during the previous thirty days. We would like to inoculate the inmates at this time, but such action will have to wait. Despite the mighty resources of the Army, there is insufficient vaccine on hand.

The order for the quarantine is issued by the commanding general of 7th Army. But it is awkward to manage the camp from a distance, and the Army establishes a permanent camp administration here, temporarily headed by Colonel Barrett. His General Order, No. 1 announces the appointment of Colonel Bradford, CO of the 127th Evacuation Hospital and highest-ranking medical officer in the camp, to the position of Camp Surgeon of the Dachau and Allach concentration camps.

Decisions about health and sanitation can now be made on the spot.

The Team's relation to the new organization is hazy. There is another high-ranking officer here, Colonel Myron P. Rudolph, Surgeon of 7th Army; I have talked with him several times. I think I am to work under Colonel Hathaway, who is at Corps level, even though he is not in the G-5 section. But the Team remains responsible to the G-5 representative here, Colonel Kenneth Worthing of Fond-du-Lac, Wisconsin.

Even though the chain of command has some weak links and authority is divided, the medical job is being done, and quickly. Many other military units are here for different purposes; they, too, are semi-independent. So far, I have not heard any grumbling about the looseness of the organization.

I am glad that the new medical units are headed by full colonels. It is important to cut through red tape, and chicken colonels carry sharper scissors than do first lieutenants.

After Colonel Bradford moves into his new office, a loud explosion resounds in his building, and the occupants exit rapidly. Sabotage? Later I hear that an American soldier accidentally nudged a German "potato-masher" grenade in the cellar of this building.

In another room used by an investigating unit, an inmate being questioned is suddenly revealed as a Gestapo agent and tries to escape. He is shot four times.

"Is there a doctor in the house?" The old cry echoes, and a soldier dashes into my office and tells me that the German is dying. Can I come over and try to save him—for questioning?

When I reach him, I find that one bullet has passed into the right side of his chest. I give him first aid and ship him to one of the American hospitals for surgical management: the surgeons there could use a clean, fresh gunshot wound for a change. This man should recover, I think, and I reassure the interrogators.

Almost daily SS men and collaborators are flushed out of buildings and hiding places in or near the camp. Yesterday one was discovered and impaled on the front gate. Some are believed to be in the inner compound, dressed as prisoners, but they should be easy to detect: their healthy appearance will give them away.

This morning, on my way to see the burgomaster, my driver and I stop a short distance from the camp in order to see what interests a crowd of American soldiers. They have formed a circle around and are watching three blue-striped inmates beat and kick two screaming green-clad prison guards—collaborators. We observe for a few minutes, then continue to our destination. About four hours later we return; the act of vengeance is continuing. The swollen, bruised victims are still alive, but no longer screaming because they need their breath to gasp feebly. The inmates still curse and kick. The American soldiers—in the crowd is a high-ranking infantry officer—still watch silently.

Little drops of rain fall from the sky, but they are not filled with mercy.

Ex-prisoners are not the only ones who pursue the enemy. Corporal Ferris tells me that one afternoon, at lunch, one of our French ex-Maquisards poked his head into the door of our quarters and shouted "SS!" All the Frenchmen in the dining room interrupted their meal (an unusual state of affairs), and joined in the chase. The hunt was victorious: the victim was kicked to death.

It is easy to sympathize with our French comrades. I have listened to incredible tales about the plundering of their country and the severe hardships and deprivations endured by the civilian population. Most striking were the stories of the lack of fuel and food, the closing of factories, the unemployment, and the brutality of the German occupiers. "Sous la botte des Nazis," said our French friends.

Now the boot is gone. It is time for revenge.

The French drivers are armed, as are all Allied personnel except those in the Medical Corps. But my teammates do not think that my Red Cross markings are sufficient protection in this treacherous environment. They have presented me with a .25 caliber Mauser automatic with a handsome mahogany hilt. I hope it works. I have not had time to try it. (Months later I do, and discover that the firing pin is *kaputt*.)

On May 4, three Polish liaison officers arrive, each wearing two stars on his collar. We think they are major generals until one of them explains that they are only insignificant first "lef-tenants" in the volunteer Polish Army. After Rosenbloom studies their credentials from the Polish government-in-exile in London, they become official members of the Team. The senior officer, Lieutenant Junghertz, is a short, tough, very correct man in his thirties who has spent his life on military pursuits; most recently he has participated in infantry and paratroop action, the latter at Arnheim.

After touring the camp and talking with many of their compatriots, the three officers return silently, appalled by what they have seen.

When I meet with Lieutenant Junghertz, he again apologizes for his inexperience in the area of civilian affairs, but, even so, he is not worried about the new assignment because he has decided how to handle his people: he will determine which of them require medical care, then tell me who they are, after which he will permit me to examine them and admit them to the hospitals.

What can I accomplish by getting angry? The day has been depressing from the moment I awoke and discovered that one of my faithful fountain pens had disappeared. So I take a deep breath and count to ten. I know that Junghertz has more problems than most people. Gently, I try to define lines of authority, and explain about priorities in the selection of patients for admission to the hospitals. He seems upset.

Afterward, I discover that Rosenbloom has talked with him at length, and found out that Junghertz is discouraged by the privations of his people and the lack of hope for the future. He also seems frustrated by his own inability to communicate. In the evenings he strides back and forth in his room, hands clasped behind his back, repeating that he is a line officer. His English is formal. He abhors slang. Unfortunately, our English is 100 percent slang.

One of the VIPs arriving at the camp today is not a sightseer. His Royal Highness Prince Jean of Luxembourg, a short thin man with a trim moustache, dressed in a simple dark uniform, walks into my office to find out if he can see his brother, Prince Charles, who came to Dachau to help escort his liberated countrymen back to their homes. I did not know that Prince Charles was in the camp, nor that another member of the royal family, Prince Felix—the father of Princes Jean and Charles—had accompanied the American troops into the camp on April 29. Prince Jean is a friendly, unpretentious person with whom I enjoy chatting for a few minutes. I refer him to Rosenbloom, who tries to keep track of the many visitors who are filling the camp.

Later I learn that when Prince Felix arrived at Dachau he had hoped for a reunion with his brother, Prince Xavier de Bourbon de Parme, for a long time a prisoner of the Nazis. But Prince

Xavier had been in the group of special prisoners taken out of the camp several days before its capture. No word has yet been received about what happened to them.

It seems impossible to understand why Luxembourg, a tiny neutral country with an area of only 999 square miles, should have been invaded and occupied by the legions of the Third Reich. One of the Luxembourgers says that it was for strategic reasons, that Hitler needed Luxembourg, as well as Holland and Belgium, in order to mount his attack on northern France and England. So, like his predecessor, the Kaiser, he violated their neutrality.

Another inmate says that Hitler was also after booty, which is why the steel mills, the major source of employment in Luxembourg, were seized by the occupiers. It was a time of hunger, grief, and terror. A gauleiter was appointed to govern the new German province, the members of the government fled to England and Canada, and the picturesque streets of the cities of Luxembourg were filled with prowling Gestapo agents, collecting data for the dossier assemblers in Berlin. The French language was banned after hundreds of years of use. The streets were renamed: the Avenue de la Liberté became Adolf Hitlerstrasse. Men of military age were impressed into the German Army and sent to the Russian front. About 30,000 Luxembourgers, 10 percent of the population, were forcibly deported to Germany. (Of the 407 Luxembourgers imprisoned at Dachau, 60 died.[1])

Today, May 5, will be a memorable day: a Jewish service is to be conducted by an Army chaplain. This should be an unforgettable experience. If time permits, many of us will be attending, including one of the new Polish officers who says he would like to help the Jews because "they saved his family once."

Although the Jewish service is historic, one of the 45th Division soldiers says that the first public religious ceremony held at the camp was on the day of liberation when some of the imprisoned priests said Mass for American infantrymen and inmates.

I am no longer a scout for Colonel Hathaway. Today is his last day here. He has completed his mission of determining which Medical Corps units should be sent here, and of integrating their relations with each other. An energetic, tireless individual, he strides out of here after shaking my hand and wishing me luck. I am sorry to see him leave. From now on, some of my orders will be arriving from the camp surgeon's office.

The quarantine has been difficult to maintain. Despite all efforts, there are some restless inmates fleeing from the camp; this has been happening since the day of liberation. Word is sent to the IPC to emphasize the necessity for keeping the inmates in the camp. The members of the IPC have been helpful and clever in their approach to this major problem. Now their spokesman says that General Eisenhower has spoken: anyone leaving the camp must first be disinfected for typhus fever. This gambit should be effective because the General is loved and respected. But the spokesman does not take any chances. For the benefit of those who may not care what the General thinks, he warns that any internee found in town without a proper pass or valid reason will be shot without delay.

Nobody is ever found without a valid reason.

Now the principal need is for adequate living space for ten or fifteen thousand people. Everyone should be provided with his own bed. How can this be done?

The IPC believes that additional space for six or eight thousand men can be found in the outer compound. The camp chief is concerned about control; he knows that his room elders cannot keep order because of the overcrowding. A letter from him under the heading of "Order and Discipline" stresses the need for alleviation of the overcrowding and the importance of restructuring the camp along national lines:

> . . . . because of the great number of asocial elements living in the camp, friction, thefts and disorders are inevitable. The fact that the different nationalities are not separated is also a constant source of friction because only a few of the camp's people have the attitude that the first principle of [coexistence] is the maintenance of order and comradeship. . . .

I think it will take too long to convert the suggested facilities into useful barracks. Instead, I recommend a tent city. The space is available, the amount of canvas required is quickly calculated, the distance between tents is computed and my report is submitted—and pigeonholed.

Later the general principle of the IPC recommendation is accepted and implemented.

Two additional bulletins arrive from the IPC. One states that 3,000 beds have become available. Mattresses, blankets, and sheets can be obtained but need disinfection. All these items are on the premises.

The second bulletin states that their sanitation and health committees have cleared sixty doctors and one hundred male nurses for services in the hospitals.

The camp surgeon puts them to work immediately.

On May 6, near our quarters, a sedan carrying three Frenchmen, one an abbe, sideswipes a jeep and ploughs into three DPs who cook and clean for us. We rush out to do what we can, and one of the women dies in the arms of Mace, our stoical, combat-experienced driver. He faints twice and is so shaken that I send him off to bed for the rest of the day.

His reaction surprises me because, while we have all been disturbed and shocked by the atrocities in the camp, no one has lost consciousness. Nor can it be the blood at the accident that triggered Mace's response; he has been exposed to similar gory scenes before.

Perhaps tragedy only becomes a significant experience when we know the individual involved.

HEADQUARTERS
FOOD; HEALTH
INTERNAL ORGANIZATION

All orders or memoranda sent out of our office bear this typed heading, and now the number of these communications increases because the visitors are going home and the important work of cleaning the camp can begin.

The camp laundry, to the left of the camp kitchen, operates eight hours a day and keeps sixty-three men busy. It can function at night if necessary. The disinfection squad consists of sixty men who are to collect and burn the clothes lying around the camp grounds and buildings, including those in the crematorium. A detail will be appointed by the labor committee for the unpleasant but essential chore of collecting and burying the excreta, which are still present in the barracks and on the grounds and date back to the time of insufficient latrines. Two squads of thirty men each collect the camp debris and burn the rubbish; still another detail scours the administrative area for trash. Unfortunately, smoke is carried into one of the hospitals, disturbing the patients with lung diseases. A new incineration site will have to be found.

Rosenbloom issues the appropriate orders, which wind through the usual channels: to the IPC, to the camp senior, to the Labor Office headed by Captain Boellaard, and then to the Capo of the labor squad, who notifies his men. The chain of command is the same as in the days before liberation.

It is time to dispose of the bodies.

Some are carried to the gravel pits. Then the furnaces of the crematorium are stoked and reignited. By increasing the work day for the operators from four to ten hours, 710 corpses are cremated in the next four days.

Too slow! A top-level decision is made to bury the dead.

Identification is usually impossible because what is seen now is difficult to relate to appearance before imprisonment, even if anyone could make such a comparison. There are no fingerprint records. Color of hair? Many corpses have shaven heads. Color of eyes? Faded. Staring. The triangles and other symbols on the clothes of the dead—if they are clothed—are of little help.

At the American commander's request, the burgomaster sends townspeople to the camp to handle the corpses. On entry, the Germans are vaccinated and dusted, instructed to scrub their wooden horse-drawn wagons after use, bathe thoroughly, burn, boil, or bury their clothes, don clean garments, be dusted again, and return in one week and every day thereafter for ten days to be examined by a medical officer.

They fill their carts and walk alongside them through the silent streets and roads to the burial site on a hilltop where the bodies are transferred to a bulldozed excavation. Here inmates dressed in blue-striped uniforms, their emotions hidden by surgical face masks, serve as pallbearers. Three chaplains administer the graveside service. Someone throws a handful of flowers over the bodies. The German soil is replaced.

When identification is possible, proper markers are erected on the German soil—Mr. Pires, the American Red Cross representative, has been partly responsible for this action. Here, it is said, a monument is to be built by the Germans at the instigation of American military authorities.

Eventually 2,400 bodies are buried.

An agonizing, unbelievable procession in the middle of the twentieth century. There are some men whose hearts are not touched by other people's suffering. But they are not on our Team. We stand outside each day to support the marchers. To let them know that we care.

Corporal Ferris, who is more articulate than anyone else on the Team, expresses all our feelings in his poem *Dachau, Germany:*

> Through quiet Dachau's cobbled streets
> The bull-drawn carts plod on their way,
> Past shops, cafes, and cool retreats,
> Past churches where the townfolk pray.
> On through the town they haul their freight
> Of starved and naked dead—
> Up to the hill where mass graves wait—
> At last the end of fear and dread.

Now memories of previous burial details are recalled by some of the inmates. During the winter typhus fever epidemic, and during the previous winter, the crematorium had not been able to keep pace with the number of corpses, so huge pits had been excavated by the prisoners. The method of burial was a simple, no-nonsense administrative matter. Only relevant information was requested: How many corpses? How many men for the pick-up detail? How many carts? No query as to names, identification, numbers, or other vital statistics.

The prisoners who were members of these special crews must have seen the large white sign painted on one of the buildings: "This is the Road to Freedom. Its Milestones are: Obedience, Cleanliness, Sobriety, Industry." They could see the words on the gate: "Work Makes One Free." Did they think about these slogans as they carted away the bodies, as they weighed the chances for their own survival?

I am told that these slogans were posted to suggest that a submissive and industrious prisoner might yet be released and allowed to return home.

Did the prisoners believe they would be saved?

Sometimes. They oscillated between despair and hope, like men in a death cell, like patients dying of cancer, thinking of a miracle. In moments of clarity they knew the slogans were lies, that by toiling they contributed to the Nazi cause and therefore to their own doom—by working they were committing suicide. At other times they believed the words, the signs. The only hope. If their masters wanted them to work, they were evidently important, they might be permitted to live. But most of the time they did not think. They did not see the painted words. They lived and worked mechanically, instinctively.

Prisoners had been used for years in the crematorium in this and other concentration camps in Germany. Here, the chief of this service is Ludvik, a heavy, powerfully muscled Czech who has labored in the crematorium for a long time. After liberation, he was appointed chief of the undertakers. Now his special hardworking crew prepares the bodies for burial. At the peak of their activities I receive a letter from him:

> To: Lt. Smith, Room 4, HQ:
>
> This Team, consisting of ten people, is doing heavy and awkward work. Therefore we always have had a privileged position as to food, alcohol, tobacco, clothing and footwear, even during the SS rule.
>
> We feel that after our liberation, at least the same standard of living should be maintained. But our position is worse than then as to food, drinks and tobacco.
>
> Therefore, I take the liberty, on behalf of the whole team, to beg you to provide us with
>
> 1.) jam or sweet of any kind.
>
> 2.) alcohol drinks, especially brandy and wine not in order to be drunk, but to be even able to stand it out
>
> 3.) sufficient quantity of tobacco (20 cigarettes a day per person).
>
> Please do not misunderstand this petition, but it is a hard job to wrap daily from 60 to 100 corpses in linen blankets, to disinfect them and to do the whole work that cannot be

done by everybody, but only by people which are thoroughly healthy and vigorous and which are well fed. . . .

Thanking you in anticipation, we remain
yours truly

We surely did not want them to have poorer working conditions during our tenure than under our predecessors', so we did what we could.

20

THE LAST DAYS OF DACHAU

Many of the stories we hear are about the frightening weeks before liberation, a most perilous time for the prisoners who believed that their lives were in greater jeopardy than ever before. They had endured years of cruel confinement. Now they knew they were doomed; they were certain that the victorious American troops would not reach the camp in time to prevent their slaughter by the SS. With dreadful clarity they foresaw the moment when the prisoner-police would whip them into line and the SS troopers would prod them through the gate, march them to a gloomy Bavarian forest, and remorselessly riddle them with machine gun bullets.

For them, every hour that passed was a sweet victory over death. Not yet, they would think. They did not foresee that most Nazi attempts to evacuate the camp would fail because daylight travel was almost impossible; convoys and trains were constantly tortured by American fighter planes. Nor could they know that a torrent of contradictory orders and counter-orders were pouring in from Berlin, compounding the confusion.

They reacted intensely to every omen and rumor; waves of fear, anger, depression, frustration, confusion, hopelessness, hopefulness, and joy washed over them, then receded. They were cheered by American planes strafing the outskirts of the camp, by news that part of the camp at Allach had been bombed, and by the distant sound of artillery. They began to peer through the fences, looking for the Americans, dejected because they had not yet arrived. Now, every act, word, or mannerism of the guards and prison policemen was weighed and measured, as if each might signify the presence of victory or defeat.

As the sluggish minutes crawled by, the prisoners sensed the increased probability of freedom; for them, elation replaced concern, even momentarily transcending their indescribable hunger pains. They experienced a sudden, powerful life-wish. I did not understand, they explained: they had always wanted to stay alive, but knowing that their chances of dying were great, they had adapted by becoming indifferent to continued existence or death. Now with the possibility of liberation a few days or weeks away, it became important to live.

Dr. Ali Kuci, a man of great energy and ability, is a repository of information about these difficult days. With Arthur Haulot, he has written an account, *The Last Days of Dachau*, printed by the Central Press Bureau; he presents me with a mimeographed copy. I find it absorbing. I tell him this, and offer to correct the faulty spelling and grammar, but Kuci will not permit anyone to edit his written material: he has too high an opinion of his own literary abilities.

Kuci's story begins with a copy of an order received at the camp from the Reichsfuehrer SS Heinrich Himmler: "Handing it [the camp] over is out of the question. The camp is immediately to be evacuated. No prisoner should fall into the hands of the enemy alive. . . ." The message was in response to a query sent to Berlin by the camp commandant.[1]

There was no doubt in Kuci's mind about the intention of the Nazis. The first threat to the lives of all the prisoners occurred early in April. At ten minutes before midnight of April 9, everyone was awakened and ordered to line up outside the barracks. SS men and members of the prisoner police force searched the buildings so thoroughly that even mattresses were slashed. After ninety minutes, the prisoners were permitted to go back to sleep. The inspection was over.

"We were all pale and nervous out there," said Kuci, who had not expected to last the night.

The day before, the commandant and his staff had worried about the possibility of concealed knives and firearms in the prison compound; they feared an insurrection. Knowing that the prisoners were getting out of hand, they made plans to massacre them. At the designated time, the barracks were surrounded by SS troopers, their machine guns ready.

But the SS camp surgeon protested strongly. He believed that there should be no more killings. The commandant decided to search for weapons; if they were found, he could justify the executions.

Nothing was found.

As the weeks passed, the disorder and commotion increased. On April 23, Kuci and other members of the underground committee began to initiate action designed to create confusion within the camp; they had been planning these steps for several months. They wisely chose to remain anonymous for the moment.

In the morning, a list was compiled by the SS of all invalids capable of travel. Then, SS men packed military and personal equipment and burned documents.

A menacing development at 1:00 P.M.: all Jews were ordered to the assembly area—all 2,400 according to one account, all transportable ones according to another. Most were feeble, many could not stand. Some prisoners tried to disrupt this formation, but were whipped by the green-clad prisoner-police as they approached the column. At the assembly point there were boxcars, but no engines. Here the Jews were to wait.

At midnight, 400 Jewish women in poor condition arrived from the concentration camp at Landsberg. They had walked all the way, receiving the usual treatment.

Early in the morning—April 24—the Jews waiting outside were forced into the boxcars. All except sixty, who had died during the night. The engine had not yet arrived. (The Jews were to remain in this spot for three more days.)

The leaders of the underground movement ordered certain prisoners not to report to work. There were signs of loss of control by the SS—camp policemen were not in evidence, but by noon they appeared. An SS order was received that all valuables brought the previous August by prisoners from another concentration camp (Natzweiler) were to be loaded onto trucks. This was ominous, suggesting that prisoners would be on the move soon. But the order could not be implemented; vigilant American planes discouraged all highway traffic.

Alerts all night. No one slept. It was rumored that the Jews were kept in the outer area in the hope that they would be bombed by the American planes. Two sources advised that the SS intended to move everyone out of the camp this afternoon and evening. Some inmates became distraught when they heard this, because night transports were particularly frightening; furthermore, it was believed that no one returned from convoys leaving on Wednesdays.

Now the native-born German prisoners were summoned to assembly point. At the rifle range near the crematorium gunfire was heard. Here a group of French Resistance workers were executed, as well as a French leader, General Delestraint, and eleven officers.

Alerts continued. The American fighter planes constantly swept over the camp, and the prisoners waved to them. They bombed and strafed around the camp and the railroad station at Dachau, then searched for targets near Munich. Everyone was overjoyed, says Kuci: "Something like exultation is in the camp. . . . The alerts bring enormous joy to the people of Dachau. If [the air raids] would cease for some hours, we know what would happen: the camp would be evacuated. This question occupies all. . . ."

Later, frantically, the SS began to load machines and supplies onto trucks; they were observed putting civilian clothes into their packs; they took for themselves passports belonging to the prisoners. Again, the prisoner-police disappeared. Some of the inmates took advantage of this respite to steal the valuables of the newly arrived prisoners, whose possessions had been stored in a tent. After a while, the activities in the tent became riotous, and all the property disappeared. SS men appeared again and removed medications and instruments from the prison hospital. Even the sterilizers were loaded onto large trucks.

During the confusion, the underground committee placed its people strategically, in the labor office and prisoner-police force, and in barracks.

Food supplies dwindled still further. Some of the prisoners were repulsed by the smell of the food; the soup resembled "dirty water." I was surprised to read this; from other stories I had gathered that starved people were undiscriminating; that for them, disgust did not exist.

The number of deaths increased. The "Moorexpress" service, special wagons used to convoy bodies to the crematorium, was unusually active.

Despite the death rate and food shortage, a feeling of hope swept through the camp. Kuci reported that most of the prisoners were "in a good humor."

More disorder on April 26. Prisoners ransacked the trains, canteen, kitchen, and warehouses for food and civilian clothes.

Nine A.M. The dreaded SS order was announced: total evacuation of the camp! Prisoners were to assemble at the roll-call place at noon, carrying their possessions.

The underground committee moved quickly to sabotage the SS plans. All records in the camp labor office were burned, and now prisoner identification data no longer existed—the SS had destroyed their own records earlier. Furthermore, the committee ordered that the letters on the prisoners' identifying triangles be changed.

By 2:00 P.M. the SS were able to assemble only about 1,000 prisoners. The day was beautiful—the sun was shining, there were no clouds. The SS increased their efforts, and the dominant mood of the prisoners turned to fear. By 8:00 P.M., more prisoners had gathered—Russians, Jews, Austrians, Gypsies, and Italians. There were now 6,700. Small amounts of food were distributed to them as they passed the kitchen: bread, cheese, and margarine. To hasten the process, the SS whipped the prisoners who were parceling out the food.

Just as the assembled inmates were ready to leave the camp, the front gate opened and 120 barefoot women with swollen legs stumbled into the prison area. They were all that remained of 480 women who had walked all the way from the Auschwitz concentration camp; the others had died along the way or had been shot by their guards because they could not keep up with the main group.

The incoming women were a temporary distraction. The SS would not let anything stop the convoy from leaving, and at 10:00 P.M. it left the camp.

It was the morning of April 27. "Another twenty-four hours had passed! And we were still living!" says Kuci, expressing the thoughts of the jubilant inmates. By this time, thousands of them had donned civilian clothes. On the backs of their coats were identifying cloth crosses, which could be easily removed. Picking a moment during which SS guards were packing their possessions and prisoner-police were not on duty, many prisoners ripped the crosses from their coats and escaped from the camp. The policemen soon reappeared, using their whips to force a formation of Poles, Czechs, and other Italians and Russians. Another convoy? The police efforts, however, appeared half-hearted. By this time, the members of the underground committee felt more secure. They were determined that no one else would leave the camp.

At noon, another transport from Buchenwald appeared. A column of walking skeletons entered the main gate, 1,600 gaunt, barefoot, half-naked men, survivors of the 2,400 who had started. (Later figures were different: 2,000 to 2,500 arrived at Dachau; 6,000 had left Buchenwald.) Six hundred were taken to the hospital immediately. Two hundred never reached the hospital. They died that afternoon on the camp grounds, beneath the clear sky and the burning sun.

According to one account, each prisoner had been given one loaf of bread, the only food for the two weeks it had taken them to reach Dachau. Probably many of the bodies scattered over the camp grounds and stacked in the crematorium were from this last convoy to arrive.

Some of the prisoners believed that they were saved by the Buchenwald survivors, who, by distracting the prisoner-police, gave them ten precious hours.

Despite the distractions and the determination of the members of the secret committee that no other prisoners would leave the camp, a group of men, women, and children was hurried through the camp and out the gate by a heavily armed SS escort. These were the "special" prisoners whose identity no one knew.

The next day, April 28, the battle front was only ten or twelve kilometers away. The nearer it came, the fewer the number of Nazi soldiers in the camp. About one hundred remained; most of the officers were gone.

Members of the prisoners' committee moved into the open, distributing a bulletin saying they were taking command. All prisoners were to remain in their quarters, to refrain from contact with the guards. (Some guards had been helpful in the last few months. They, too, were aware of the progress of the Allies.)

At 6:00 P.M., three of the committee leaders, Arthur Haulot, Captain Willem Boellaard, and Father Phily, a French priest, were summoned to the office of the camp commandant. Four others, Patrick O'Leary, Leon Malczewski, Ali Kuci, and Edmond Michelet, waited nervously in the hospital.

About two hours later the three reappeared, smiling.

The commandant had conceded, they said. He had introduced them to an official of the International Red Cross, who had just arrived with five truckloads of supplies.

"We had a long conversation with him concerning its distribution," said Captain Boellaard.

The Last Days of Dachau ends here, although there was one more day to wait: armed SS guards still patrolled the camp.

Sunday afternoon, April 29, bright and sunny. The SS men had removed their insignia and decorations. Suddenly a prisoner ran toward the gate. Others followed.

Americans!

The word raced through the camp, repeated in Polish, Russian, French, German, Italian, and all the other languages, the most beautiful word in the world on the most beautiful day that ever dawned—the Last Day of Dachau.

An end to the waiting.

What was the fate of the convoy that left on April 27? The column of prisoners forced to march out of the camp numbered 6,700; those who could not keep up were shot. In a quiet forest glade 20 kilometers from Munich, dark clouds gathered and bitter rain fell. The guards turned their machine guns on the prisoners. Then they searched for survivors and killed them.

But they were careless; a few survived. "Only sixty could escape the transport," wrote one of the survivors, who sent us each a copy of his affidavit. "The rest had been murdered. . . ." [2]

21

DR. ALI KUCI

Dr. Ali Kuci is a short, thin, dark man with a long face, whose doctorate in philosophy from the University of Florence was preceded by special training in political science at London University. He claims to have been the former minister of propaganda in Albania, or so I am told, and I can believe this because he has a nimble brain and a fertile imagination. At one time he impulsively recorded for posterity his opinion of Mussolini's birth and shortcomings, and after that was confined at Dachau. The years of imprisonment do not seem to have limited his mental and linguistic dexterity. He retains a capacity for warmth and humor that is welcome in this dreadful place.

A man of many talents, Kuci admits to being a master of contract bridge. In his country, where bridge is very popular, he was known as the Culbertson of Albania. Later I discover that his bidding is so deceptive that neither his partner nor his opponents have the slightest intimation of his holdings. When he is declarer, he changes from a cunning fox to a charging tiger, exposes his hand after the second or third playing trick and claims the remainder—the Kuci Coup. When he is challenged and forced to continue the play of the hand, he usually makes two tricks fewer than he originally claimed.

Sometimes he is saved by a telephone call, which he answers in a soft, singsong voice: "Kuci speaking," followed by a machine-gun delivery in German, Albanian, Italian, or Turkish.

He has an unusual talent for discovering hidden automobiles and concealed gasoline containers.

One morning he rushes into my office and shakes hands with everyone twice.

"My friend," he says, "last night I come to visit you. It is late at night, one in morning. But there are no lights. I have a problem. Should I wake you? No! My friend must sleep at night; he works hard. So, I go way. I stumble over gas can. Is funny coincidence because my car runs out of gas in front of your house. So, I borrow some gas. Is all right? Some day you come to Tirana and run out of gas in front of my house. I show you good time."

I warn Kuci that the penalty for looting is summary execution in front of a firing squad. If gasoline is stolen, I add, the penalty is worse: the culprit is not given a handkerchief to mask his eyes.

He is not impressed. Perhaps because of his royal lineage. One of the inmates says that Kuci claims to be a direct descendant of Alexander the Great.

The IPC has decided that recreation and entertainment will help reduce the friction in the camp. Kuci's reputation as a treasure hunter par excellence naturally leads to his appointment as Chairman of the Committee on Entertainment. Kuci immediately discovers 3,000 propaganda-free books and has them delivered to the camp, the beginning of a library. He also searches for music—three orchestras have been organized. No one can find an adequate practice room for the musicians, so Kuci is given the task. His cameralike mind quickly scans each building and focuses on the shower room. Large enough so that each orchestra could practice there one hour a day, he says. His recommendation is sent through channels and is accepted by the shower room Capo.

Kuci's next assignment is to arrange for a theater in which concerts and stage shows can be given, and movies shown. No one can think of a suitable building, but we know that somehow Kuci will not only find one, but equip it lavishly.

He persuades the people who operate the radio station in Dachau to broadcast special programs to the camp inhabitants daily. Then he institutes a search for movie projectors and a public address system, finds an American radio transmitter that needs repairs, and, after estimating that it will take a week to have it fixed elsewhere, establishes a radio repair service in the camp.

There are very few radios in the camp. To alleviate this

shortage, Kuci dispatches four men to a nearby town. Unfortunately, American MPs arrest them on their return, and impound the "wireless sets." Kuci springs the men, but not the sets. Unperturbed, he says that others are to be found, and he knows where. A mild discussion follows at an IPC meeting:

Sir Patrick O'Leary asks where these sets are and if they are not by chance in a private home.

Kuci replies that they are in a shop and that his man is well informed about the whole matter.

O'Leary means that one cannot do with these apparatus what one likes because they certainly belong to somebody.

Kuci remarks that they were already there before the arrival of the Americans. All details knows his man.

O'Leary requests that Kuci's "man" be brought to the meeting, and a messenger is dispatched to find him. The radio expert soon appears and seems familiar with the number and location of sets in the camp and in nearby towns such as Schleissheim and Erding; he will soon be familiar with the resources in Munich.

O'Leary is not satisfied and demands an immediate investigation. He wants a report sent to the IPC to include the number of radio sets available, their distribution in the camp, and the number needed. (The members of the IPC would like to provide each block with two radios; Kuci also hopes to supply one to each national committee, and an adequate number for the hospitals. At the moment, some blocks are without radios, other blocks have more than they need.)

The radio expert points out that a report has been started but he doubts if it will be useful because everyone on the IPC knows that when an investigation is begun, anxiety develops. Some of the inmates will hear about it, and those who have radios will be afraid that they will be confiscated. It will only be natural for them to hide their sets and deny possession. Thus, the final report is unlikely to be helpful to the Committee.

Unmoved, O'Leary requests that the report be brought in the next day.

Kuci's insight, enthusiasm, industry, and fluency in many languages lead to his appointment as head of the Bureau of Press and Culture. Each day he issues nonpolitical communiqués carrying announcements of current activities, news of departures, and important information to the inmates from the IPC and American command.

On May 8, he editorializes:

> Twelve years have passed since this camp of Dachau was founded. Twelve years have passed since the Hitlerian beast [seized] the reins of Germany. Only twelve years. Years of suffering and of enormous tortures. A very limited instance in the vast space of innumerable centuries, but a very sorrowful and tiresome period in the history of humanity. . . . The ambitious creature of Hitler wanted to suffocate the world, and the German soil became the grave of Europe. A grave was also this Dachau of ours. And we live today. . . .
>
> Tomorrow we shall return to our hearths. We shall find our beloved countries free and independent. It is there we [should resume] our social activities. Not here. Here we are in Dachau in the place of tortures and massacres. And in this place we should be inspired by the shivering love of the past, no more. No further. We should allow time to our liberators to help us and to cure our wounds of the past. We should allow our representatives to fulfill their duties. No chaos, no anarchy. Those who betrayed our cause of yesterday will reply before the court of justice of the camp. But the lives of thirty-three thousand skeletons should not be sacrificed. Who will try to disturb this order will be punished by all. He will not be tolerated. . . . Here we want only two duties and one principle: *Friendship, Brotherhood* and *no politics.* . . .

Dachau: The Turning Point   4

22

FRICTION

The measures taken to curb the typhus fever epidemic—the quarantine and mass dusting program—are showing results. Now, sufficient vaccine has become available, as well as an organization to administer it, so that the third step in combating the epidemic can be taken: the vaccination of all the inmates. This began yesterday, May 7, at Allach, where 7,000 injections were given.

The Typhus Commission also advises an important fourth step in the fight against the disease: the "decompression" of the inner camp to relieve the overcrowding that contributes to the survival of body lice. Everyone has been in favor of such action since the very first day, but progress is slow. Perhaps the Commission's report will speed things up. Sometimes a picturesque word like "decompression" is more effective than a prosaic word like "overcrowding."

The admission of patients into the American hospitals has helped, but only a little, despite the transfer of 400 sick people daily.

When the epidemic struck the camp during the previous winter, the prisoner-physicians treated their patients with convalescent serum, which they believed to be an effective agent if given early. But, according to one of the doctors, even the earliest treatment is ineffective in patients over the age of forty-five.

This is not the attitude of the military doctors at the 116th Evacuation Hospital, where all patients, regardless of age, are being treated with current methods.

Additionally, the doctors of the Typhus Commission plan to take care of selected patients—half a ward—using special management. It will be another week before they get started, however.

Medically, these developments should be of great interest.

Another long-awaited development is the end of hostilities in Europe. Three days ago a rumor circulated that the war was over. Our enthusiastic French drivers became so exhilarated that they began firing their guns into the air like cowboys galloping into town after months on a cattle drive. Today, our eighth day in the camp, the surrender of the Germans is official; this is the historic V-E Day, May 8, 1945, one minute after midnight. A major celebration seems inappropriate with so many sick inmates languishing on their beds. In addition, a change in weather intensifies the usual gloom. Abruptly it is no longer cold, wet, and windy, but very warm; as a result, the stench of death seems more pervasive than before.

Despite the depressing environment, the reality of the surrender cheers the staff and the inmates, and we smile, shake hands, embrace, and offer toasts to each other. We listen to the radio, to speeches by Winston Churchill and the King, to descriptions of wild celebrations in England, to interviews with American soldiers and what they thought of the end of the war, and the impact of this historic day reaches me.

Our wounded men won't be coming through the collecting company; the American hospitals will slowly discharge their patients; we won't need to worry about strange sounds or shadows at night. We won't have to be constantly vigilant for snipers or booby traps. We won't have to check beneath the hood before starting our cars. The fighting is finished here, if not in the Pacific.

But our worries are not over. We find that we still need to be careful. There are still enemies in Germany—unreconstructed Nazis who sometimes stretch wires across the road or drive their trucks too close to our jeeps. There are mysterious car accidents, unexplained shootings, and looting and vandalism. We are particularly wary of the young men who have never been exposed to anything but Nazi propaganda.

Camp HQ announces that Lieutenant Colonel Martin Joyce, an artillery officer, is the new camp commander—a tough position for anyone. From the IPC comes news of the "regretful" resignation of Lieutenant Commander O'Leary; he is to return immediately to England.[1] General Michailow takes over as president; Arthur Haulot is the sole remaining vice-president.

Additional reasons are constantly being invented to persuade inmates not to slip away from the camp. A new one is that the war is over and this means that an increasing number of soldiers will now be guarding the camp—American MPs, who will make certain that no one leaves without permission. They will treat escapees with "utmost severity."

Furthermore, one of the four copies of the official questionnaire must accompany a person when he returns home. A person escaping now won't have his copy, and this will create many difficulties for him.

Some of these sly suggestions from the IPC must be effective, because many escapees are returning to the camp for normal processing.

They are not penalized for having fled from the camp. This is fortunate because there are more than enough disciplinary problems within the compound to require the full attention of those responsible for law and order: the members of the IPC. At its first meeting, they were authorized by the Americans to create a police force; this was confirmed at a later session. A police Capo had been appointed, and he and his men were permitted to arrest anyone who committed a crime, and to strike the suspected culprit if there was no alternative or if he resisted arrest. Individuals guilty of minor transgressions were to be locked up for a day or two; those guilty of major crimes were to be turned over to the Americans. At another IPC meeting, Oscar Juranic, the Yugoslav who had been head of the subcommittee on disciplinary questions, was reassigned as chief of the criminal investigation section. He was asked to confer daily with the Committee members.

Unexpectedly, his reports show that some of the inmates who have been taken into custody are innocent of the charges made against them. An example is a block chief, arrested after being accused of not giving bread to one of the men in his block. The allegation was shown to be groundless, as were others. Furthermore, it seems likely that some of the prisoners now languishing in the bunker on charges of being SS men or Gestapo agents are there only because they were hated by certain inmates whose false accusations were prompted by envy, spite, or jealousy.

The members of the IPC agree that such malicious acts should be condemned, that strong action should be taken to discourage them. But what sort of action? The discussants hope that the national committees that have developed since liberation, composed of inmates selected or elected to act for their people when dealing with the Americans, the IPC, or their own national commissions, can cooperate with the IPC in reducing the friction. Perhaps the national leaders might be in the best position to determine the nature and truth of the accusations made against their compatriots. A countersuggestion is made, that the reputation of the individual making a complaint should be investigated by one of the members of his national committee.

It seems obvious that these recommendations, if adopted, might lead to miscarriages of justice: a guilty person might be exonerated if his reputation was good, or if his politics coincided with that of his national committee (pamphlets espousing political causes are beginning to be distributed). Those whose reputations were bad, or whose positions on national issues differed from those held by their leaders, might be unjustly convicted.

However, under the circumstances, the proposals are not without merit because they are intended to act as a deterrent to deliberate falsification.

There is no real solution to these problems. Unfortunately, the inmates who unjustly condemn others do not realize that they have adopted a technique espoused by the Third Reich. Children in Germany were encouraged to inform against their parents, students against their teachers, suitors against their rivals, debtors against their creditors; many personal whims or grievances were satisfied in this manner. At one time about 20 percent of the admissions to concentration camps resulted from denunciations. Charges against these prisoners were euphemistically listed as "insulting the Fuehrer," making "subversive remarks," "insulting leading personalities," "defamation of the swastika," or "behavior prejudicial to the State." [2]

Prisoners in the bunker are being beaten. This news distresses the members of the IPC, who move decisively to end the practice.

The German soldiers captured during the battle for the camp are still imprisoned in the bunker. An attempt was made to use them on labor squads, but, because of inadequate supervision, the effort failed; some of them were beaten by the inmates. As a result, the inmates continue to be assigned to the work details. But working morale is poor. One day, everyone on the kitchen detail—sixty people—refuse to work. What can be done about this? The members of the IPC are annoyed:

MUELLER: It has been reported that two workers laid down on their jobs. One of them decided to take a sunbath on the roof, and the other left his job to "organize." If it is impossible to get a national committee to maintain order, then we will have to assign guards to work details.

BLAHA: The guards at the front gate are worthless; packages are handed through the fence or thrown over it.

MUELLER: The police department is filled with friends of the inmates. The policemen make too many allowances for their friends. The individual national committees should try to exercise voluntary discipline.

BLAHA: The Czech national group has suggested that the work details should be organized by the national committees, that poor workers should be fired. Thus, national pride could be stimulated. Poor workers, or those who behave badly, could be punished by being designated by their national leaders as the last ones for repatriation. Or, if they do not work diligently, they could be arrested and placed in the bunker. . . .

MALCZEWSKI: The American authorities say that looting and refusal to work must stop. For example, a detail was directed to clean a building, but the work was not done —all of the people on the detail were busy stealing! The Americans say that they will be here for six months, that they are making efforts to make life tolerable. They have introduced mounted police on horseback and other measures to enforce working discipline and morale. National groups will have to cooperate. . . .

MICHAILOW: . . . Supervisors of work details must be made responsible for the completion of the assignment. We need a list of the workers. Those who don't show up will be locked up. . . .

MUELLER: A member of a national committee should accompany each detail as supervisor.

BOELLAARD: Today I inspected the work being done on the

refurnishing of an SS building. The workers did not report until 3:00 P.M. because their food had not arrived until then. If things are not on time, order cannot be maintained. . . . Suspension of bread time is ineffective because everyone has enough to eat. Where there are rules, there must be punishment.

MALCZEWSKI: That is what the bunker is for, and Oscar Juranic. Furthermore, we still have a list to be published —of the people who will be repatriated last. But for this measure to be effective, we need publicity. . . .

MUELLER: To improve the morale of workers, I would suggest that only those who really work should receive their full allotment of tobacco. Those who perform very heavy or extraordinary work should receive additional rations. (Voted and passed.)

POPOVIC (Yugoslavia): Many members of national committees work very hard; they too should be rewarded.

MUELLER: Only those who work for the camp as a whole should be considered.

BLAHA: The services of many capable doctors have been lost because they work solely within their national committees. It would have been better if they had contributed their professional skills to the entire camp; the committee work could have been done by others.

To my surprise, some of the inmate physicians have refused to work. The problem is brought to the attention of the IPC.

BLAHA: There are great difficulties with block physicians. For the most part they won't cooperate. They send healthy persons off in ambulances, while sick ones are left behind to die. Right now, orderlies have been assigned to take the place of hospital doctors.

HAULOT: When Blaha calls a block doctor and the latter does not respond, he should be arrested on the basis of work sabotage.

BLAHA: It is difficult to send people with a diploma to the bunker. . . . Two block doctors have deserted!

HAULOT: It is requested that the two should be arrested. . . .

BOELLAARD: Several days ago, block doctors were told that they were responsible to the IPC for their work.

YOCARINIS (Greece): In one of the blocks, patients have complained that they have not been examined for five days. Where is the doctor's conscience?

MUELLER: We will be responsible for the punishment: fourteen days in the bunker. . . .

MICHELET: I saw a French doctor engaged in political activities instead of his work. He will be arrested as soon as he arrives, I assure you.

HAULOT: A letter of appreciation should be sent to all of the hospital personnel—doctors, orderlies—expressing gratitude for their self-sacrificing work. . . .

One day later, the distribution of the inmate physicians is again discussed. Michailow, presiding, states that there must be doctors in each block.

BLAHA (interrupts): At least two doctors have been assigned to each block.

MICHAILOW: There are none in Block 20.

BLAHA (interrupts): Two doctors and an emergency team are available.

MICHAILOW: Perhaps on paper. But their work is neither evident nor effective. . . . Despite Blaha's statement, there are no doctors in Block 20. The doctor from Block 28 has to help there. The two assigned doctors richly deserve to be locked up.

BLAHA: I won't go along with this. According to the order given to me, I have caused the arrest of two doctors from Block 21. As a result, forty French doctors went on strike to show their solidarity. Furthermore, all day long we receive delegations from the inmates who want to intervene in behalf of the two doctors. All morning I have done nothing but confer with the French delegates. I asked Colonel Bradford what to do, and he says, "Throw them out!"

MICHELET: Yesterday we were improperly informed. The derelictions were not by the two assigned block doctors, but by two doctors who were sick and they can't be held responsible.

KUCI: Was it true that these two deserted ill people? Did they not comply with Blaha's assignment?

BLAHA: I was opposed to their arrest. Both called on me last night and explained that they left their post because it was beyond their ability to examine patients because they were sick and old. They should be released from the bunker. . . .

MALCZEWSKI: The important goal is the emptying of the camp; when this is achieved, the other problems will solve themselves. Haulot, Lieutenant Rosenbloom and I agree.

ROSENBLOOM: The CO, Colonel Joyce, and the American authorities are working with all their might to accomplish the evacuation of the camp. Specific sites have been selected to receive patients. In a short time all the patients will have been removed. So far as the French doctors are concerned, I am astounded that doctors would refuse to work under these conditions—in a situation so sad and tragic that refusing to work is scandalous. Perhaps through the French major, and the American and French authorities, the world could be informed about this situation. . . .

MALCZEWSKI: We have talked for one hour and have made no progress. We are wasting time. . . . Next Sunday, the French national holiday of Holy St. Joan of Arc will be celebrated. . . .

BOELLAARD: Everyone here is invited to participate. . . .

It is evident that whatever unity existed at the time of liberation is beginning to dissipate. For a few days all the inmates loved each other. There were many expressions of sympathy for the Jews; it was obvious that they had suffered more, in every way, than the other internees. But now we hear that some of the Jews are being unfairly treated by other inmates: they are receiving less food; their housing is poorer. Similar complaints are trickling in from people beginning to identify with others speaking their own language, or coming from their own country. These inmates jealously study the food, clothing, and housing allotments of their neighbors—even their medications—to be sure that someone does not receive more than they do.

When shirts were distributed, the Greeks received none —according to one of their leaders. When they went to a warehouse to ask for their share, they were chased away. A Frenchman says that the clothes were unfairly distributed: his people received none. The only inmates not to receive passes to leave the camp were the Poles, according to one of their spokesmen.

Even rumors lead to complaints. A Yugoslav leader has heard that his people will remain in the camp longer than anyone else. An Italian committee member believes that the people of "preferred" national groups will be moved to the new, advantageous outer compound quarters, while those belonging to "inferior" groups will remain inside the compound where they will continue to be miserably overcrowded and surrounded by disease and death.

There are outcries about the IPC, probably because its policy has been to cooperate with the Americans in keeping the quarantine, helping with the registration forms, maintaining order, and providing a labor force. All of these are unpopular activities, difficult for the inmates to understand.

Unfortunately, the method of governing the camp is, in many ways, the same as it was under the Nazis. The American CO, Colonel Joyce, works with Haulot through the camp director, Rosenbloom. Orders are channelled from Rosenbloom to the camp senior, Mueller. The titles of the inmate leaders are the same as in the old days: *Lageraelteste, Blockaelteste, Stubenaelteste, Arbeitseinsatzfuehrer;* the secretarial hierarchy is the same; the inmate police force is still present—only many of the faces are different. Outside the gate, armed soldiers continue to patrol.

So, the grumbling increases: "Just a change in uniform for the guards." "The members of the IPC are Capos after special privileges. Just the same as it was before." "The sick people in Allach receive better care than the sick ones here." "The Flossenburg concentration camp has already been evacuated. Why do we still have to stay here?" "Poor management," say some of the inmates, who believe that the Americans are inefficient and bureaucratic. There are a few special darts aimed at Mueller being the camp senior; they do not approve of him because he is German. And there are many murmurs about the continued use of German as the language for camp communications.

This is aired at an IPC meeting:

> MICHELET: Firstly. French is the language that should dominate the IPC meeting. In San Francisco [where the formative sessions of the United Nations are taking place], English, Russian and French are official languages. German, for practical reasons, might be used as a fourth language.

Secondly. The chairmanship [of the IPC] should have been given to France because the French Army has battled side by side with the United States, Britain and Russia. France has been grieving over the deaths of uncounted men. Thirdly. It was most painful for the French at the reception for the American Ambassador to France: the French representative was not present! He was not invited! A rebuff!

HAULOT: As to the first point: up to now, all meetings have been in French, English and German. Point two: no comment—not my sphere of interest. Point three: the reception was held with the best of intentions. The second vice president and the secretary received the Ambassador at the gate; there was no expectation of any problem.

YOCARINIS: . . . My people understand nothing and hear nothing: they know only Greek and French. Communications should be in many languages, not just the voice of the majority. . . . Some delegates understand French only. German should be used if needed.

MICHELET: It was not right that the French delegate was not introduced.

KUCI: I only learned of the official reception the night before, in the circular. If Michelet sleeps while we sweat to get everything ready, let him be responsible for the consequences. If he has a better grasp of the conduct of affairs, let him take over now.

HAULOT: An unpleasant incident. Perhaps we are unconsciously guilty. Among the guests, we did not see the representative of the French, but only of the Americans. We did not think of all the consequences. If Michelet had spoken before the festivities, nobody would have opposed his wishes. But, we have more important things to do than waste time on details.

MICHELET: I have had to soothe humiliated feelings of my countrymen; this I did as a faithful member of the IPC. There will be no protest. But our disappointment was justified because the French are among the poorest people in the camp. They have nothing to wear. Others, who have been in the camp longer, have obtained the essentials. Therefore, it is remarkable that the only food in the camp after liberation came from the French. These 150 tons had been originally designated for French resistance, then for the French Army, and then for the French prisoners in the camp. The French Army considered it self-evident that the shipment should be divided among all camp inmates. The French inmates did not protest its dissemination to everyone in the camp. Consequently, the French received only a small fraction of it. The Americans had nothing to do with it.[3]

HAULOT: The French have suffered in the camp. Thousands died. Thanks to the generosity of the French, the food situation in the camp changed overnight. The claim of the French should be treated with consideration. The problem should be solved in a practical way. When O'Leary left, General Michailow automatically became president; I became the first vice president. The second vice presidency is vacant. This should be offered to the French delegate, and I hope he agrees to accept the position. This should solve the problem.

MUELLER: A resolution should be adopted to thank the French Army. There should be no conflicts. Let us solve national problems in national committees. Our concern is with order, discipline and improvements. The camp should be liquidated without dissension, quietly.

BLAHA: My country has never been mentioned in our meeting. We should be concerned with everyone's welfare. As IPC members we are linked with our national groups. But we must be equally concerned for all the inmates.

MICHAILOW: We must work. We can't consider such questions. It doesn't make any difference to me what language the meetings are conducted in because all are unfamiliar to me. I need a translator for complete comprehension. Let's talk about things that matter for the camp. Everyone should work for his people. If our meetings continue this way, we will never be repatriated. There have been many complaints about the French doctors, who, with their nationals, are more interested in politics than sick people. The most pressing need is to keep order in the camp, to care for the people who live under such shocking conditions. The question of the language used at the meeting is of no importance. If the majority understand French, then French should be spoken. But, in order to get the work done, Ger-

man would be most useful, the easiest to grasp—the Seniors speak German only. This will not hurt others who
don't speak German.

HAULOT: I agree . . . German is most practical. . . . The
second vice presidency should be offered to Michelet. For
the sake of friendship, let us terminate this painful discussion. . . . [Agreed unanimously.] It is requested that national questions not be brought up at an IPC meeting
again. . . .[4]

General Michailow is a good presiding officer. However, he
has not been able to attend all the meetings because he has not
been well. Formerly commander of an army corps, he was
captured by the Germans and sent to a POW camp. He escaped,
was recaptured, and was then imprisoned at the Flossenburg concentration camp where he was forced to labor in stone quarries
and where most of his fellow officers died. Early this year he
was taken to Dachau.

Haulot, too, is an effective chairman. He has the rare ability of
being able to reconcile people with divergent points of view. He
also has another talent: he can keep the main issue in sight, important when the IPC members stray down pathways of irrele-
vancies and trivia and the meetings are prolonged.

Each morning the executive committee of the IPC meets with
Rosenbloom. On May 10 it requests an extraordinary session
with the Americans. Colonel Bradford presides, and Colonel
Joyce attends, as does Major William Green, Executive Officer
of the 127th Evacuation Hospital. I am invited. Rosenbloom arrives with Haulot, Kuci, Malczewski, Mueller, Juranic, and
Kothbauer (an Austrian, head of a committee responsible for
the inmates' clothing and laundry and for the storage of their
personal effects).

Haulot, perhaps the youngest of them all, is their spokesman.
Tall and gaunt, he speaks with intensity:

Why are the inmates kept in the camp so long, when it is obvious that people are sneaking away daily? They desert by the
hundreds. Tomorrow they may desert by the thousands. What
is the sense in dusting people if they have to return to the same
filthy, overcrowded quarters? We understand the necessity for
the quarantine. We have repeatedly stressed its importance, but
many people do not understand, and others are becoming impa-

tient. At first they thought it would last only a few days, then a week. And now, how long? The people of the camp are becoming discouraged; many are refusing to work.

For ourselves, Haulot continues, we desire nothing. We will remain here until everyone leaves. We are grateful to the Americans for everything that has been done, but it is unlikely that we can control the survivors much longer. Our control comes from our personal influence, and this is being eroded by the lack of progress. We are no longer the masters of the situation. We reject responsibility for what may happen.

In the opinion of the IPC, says Haulot, the only answer is immediate evacuation.

There are many good reasons why it is impossible to comply with this request, says Colonel Joyce. There is nowhere to go. The transportation problems are insurmountable. A mass movement of the sort suggested requires an immense amount of planning and coordination. Many of the inmates have no place to go; their homes have been bombed out of existence. Furthermore, there is still an epidemic raging, and war criminals are still being sought.

We are doing all we can. We plan to restructure the camp along national lines. The inmates will be relocated into buildings outside of the prison area. There will be room for 4,800 healthy inmates in the outer compound. Furnishings and beds are still being sought because the contents of these buildings have been destroyed. We plan to fill each of the new buildings with 1,000 people, all of the same nationality. Their respective national committees will control each block. And, says the Colonel, despite the quarantine, major repatriation moves are being planned.

The meeting takes longer than expected. It has already lasted for an hour—translations are time-consuming. Everyone agrees that the projects mentioned by Colonel Joyce will be helpful. We also learn that occasional problems have been created by the well-meaning people of the visiting national missions, who have arrived at the camp to help their countrymen and escort them home. They have told some of the inmates that they would be out of the camp and homeward bound immediately—clearly impossible in view of the medical and security problems. The effect of these unfulfilled promises is that the jubilation of liberation has been replaced by unhappiness and frustration as confinement continues.

After more discussion, a suggestion is made—and promptly rejected—that national missions be refused permission to enter the camp! (On the other hand, the Yugoslavs and Hungarians feel forsaken because their national missions have not yet appeared.)

The meeting adjourns. Malczewski, the secretary of the IPC, has been taking notes, and will make his report to the IPC tonight.

There does not seem to be any positive approach to the problems created by the development of sectional and ethnic jealousies. People are beginning to recall old hatreds and long-forgotten ideologies. Partisan activity accelerates, prejudices return, tempers flare.

"Brotherhood and no politics," Dr. Kuci wrote in his bulletin. A laudable principle, but impossible to achieve. Not with the "grass is greener" attitude with which the internees regard each other. Not with the persistent overcrowding. Not with the overt dissatisfaction of the Poles. Not with the hostility of many of the Estonians and Lithuanians, dissatisfied because they are represented on the IPC by the Russian delegate. The Russians, mostly POWs, keep to themselves. Many seem to be suspicious of the other inmates, but if there is dissension in their ranks, they keep it hidden. But among the individualistic, outspoken French, there are no secrets. Devoted supporters noisily proclaim the virtues of Gaullism, and different socialist and Catholic-oriented political parties; the Communists seem to be in a minority. (The French in the camp are undoubtedly in bad straits physically: they were exposed to harsher treatment than most prisoners because of their inability to accept the tyranny of the Nazis, their impatience with trivial details, their rejection of what they considered to be stupid, and their individuality, often manifest as an inability to work with other inmates, and with members of their own group.) Among the Italians, proponents of socialist, Communist, Catholic, republican, and royalist parties argue vehemently with each other.

But I think that most of the intrigue emanates from the quarters of the Balkan nationals, particularly from the Albanians and the Yugoslavs. Perhaps because of my friendship with Kuci, I learn some details—perhaps stretched—of life in Albania. Most of the people are Moslems (two kinds); 25 percent are Eastern Orthodox; 15 percent are Roman Catholic. Minority groups consist of gypsies (two kinds) and Greeks. There are variations in customs and clothing. Come to Albania, says Kuci. Meet ignorant peasants and brave "eagles," the name given to the tough, predatory, violent mountaineers who leap from crag to crag, and who, regardless of religious beliefs, are ardent political conspirators, devoted gamblers, and possessed of fierce tribal loyalties and a talent for old-fashioned methods such as assassination. The people of Albania all prize their independence and are indifferent to the rest of the world. Recently they had been oppressed by the dictatorial government of King Zog, which, however, did make some improvements. Because of the poverty and corruption, many Albanians had migrated to Greece, Turkey, and Yugoslavia. Those who remained had fought enthusiastically against the occupying Italians and Germans. Even so, factionalism had developed with two powerful cliques vying for power—the Royalists and Communists.

Albania is a model of homogeneity when compared to Yugoslavia, which was molded at Versailles from many small countries previously independent or under Turkish, Hungarian, Austrian, or Italian rule. Language differences and religious hatreds led to wholesale massacres exceeded only by the extermination of Jews by the Germans. Serbs, the majority group, were slaughtered by Croatian Fascists (the Croats were the second largest population group); then Croats and Moslems were attacked and massacred by Serbian nationals, the Chetnicks. These were anti-Nazi guerrilla fighters led by Colonel Mihajlovic and supported by the Yugoslav government-in-exile in London, headed by King Peter, the son of the dictatorial King Alexander, who was assassinated in France in 1934. The other group is led by a Croat, the Moscow-trained Tito. His effective fighters are called the Partisans. Now, in mid-1945 a civil war is being fought in Yugoslavia, and probably Tito will emerge as top man, subservient to the USSR, according to my sources.

The Tito forces seem to dominate in the camp, judging from his large picture which hangs over the door of the building where many of the Yugoslavs live. I can pick out a few words from the surrounding signs: *Tito Marsal, Antifasist, Heroj.*

International rivalry is also becoming evident in other groups, surprisingly between the French and the Poles, and between the Dutch, Danes, and Norwegians on the one hand and the Belgians on the other. There is even some rivalry between the French and the Belgians—"We have always disliked each other," a Belgian tells me. The chronic animus between the Poles and the Russians has redeveloped. The Austrians have decided that they have no use for the Germans. There is also hostility between the foreign internees, the *Auslanders*, and some of the German inmates.

The episodes or expressions of dislike are mild, however, unaccompanied by violence except to known or suspected informers, probably because most of the inmates still lack energy and morale, and are still incapable of simple housekeeping duties. They shuffle through the camp, their backs stooped, sifting through piles of refuse, reminding me of the unemployed during the days of the Great Depression. They are irritable and still do not completely understand their continued internment. They have recovered moderately well now from their starvation, but their mental recovery lags.

Nevertheless, future turbulence seems inevitable.

23

GOOD NEWS AND BAD NEWS

At our regular Team meeting, Rosenbloom tells us the news that reached HQ only today, although it happened four or five days ago. The special prisoners everyone has been interested in were rescued on May 4 by a unit of the 42d Division, perhaps some of the same men who fought here and then headed south. The hostages were surrendered without a fight at an Alpine hotel situated on a picturesque lake on the Italian side of the Brenner Pass.

It was confirmed that the 137 prisoners had been forced to leave the bunker on April 27. Among them were the people we had heard of, Léon Blum, Kurt von Schuschnigg, Prince Xavier de Bourbon de Parme, and Martin Niemoller, the anti-Nazi Protestant pastor who had once been a U-boat commander. There were others we had not heard of, men, women, and children from twenty different countries, the "honorary" and "kin" prisoners of Dachau. They were political, military, and religious leaders, and members of their families; German generals and industrialists out of favor with Hitler; relatives of officers captured by the Russians during the battle for Stalingrad; and relatives of people of importance in the Allied nations.

Among the kin prisoners were Nicholas Horthy, Jr., a son of the former Hungarian Regent, Captain Peter Churchill, a distant relative of the Prime Minister, Prince Leopold of Prussia, a nephew of the Kaiser, Alexei Kokosen, a nephew of Molotov, the Russian foreign minister, and a son of Marshal Pietro Badoglio of Italy. Léon Blum's wife was in the group, as well as the wife and daughter of Kurt von Schuschnigg.

Stalin's son was not among the survivors. It was said that he had never been at Dachau.

Former Allied leaders included General Sante Garibaldi, an

Italian Partisan leader, Imrich Karvas, a member of the Czech cabinet, General Alexander Papagos, head of the Greek general staff, Nicholas von Kallay, former Premier of Hungary, Dr. J. C. van Dyck, the Netherlands minister of war, and Dr. Richard Schmitz, the former mayor of Vienna.

The German notables were Fritz Thyssen, an industrialist, General Georg Thomas, former head of the Office of War Economy, General Franz Halder, former chief of staff, and General Alexander von Falkenhausen, former military commander of Belgium.

What stories they must have to tell!

My own mental state improves with the receipt of four letters dated March 8, 9, 10, and 12. I am annoyed that it has taken them two months to get here, but I consider it a miracle that they arrived at all. Once a soldier is transferred on temporary or detached duty, especially overseas, the Army postal clerks seem to have immense difficulty forwarding his mail to the new location. Because of the poor mail service, I do not know if my wife has received her allotments for March and April, $81 and $85 respectively. Most likely Carol does not need the money because room and board are provided for her. But she might disagree with me: her monthly salary as a resident physician is a generous $30. My own economic situation is poor; I have not yet been paid for April, but this is not a hardship because there are at present no canteens, PXs, or restaurants in which to spend the money.

I hope my outgoing letters have been received. Lately I have been typing them on SS stationery, using a German typewriter that has one key with the harsh, angular, runic double-S symbol of the SS, and another with an umlaut. In my daily letter I mention that three more SS men have been captured. They have been hiding for almost a week and a half; their clothes are torn and muddy; they no longer look like supermen. There are now 130 of them locked up in the bunker.

Today, May 10, is an important day for the people of Belgium, Luxembourg, and Holland. Exactly five years ago, their countries were occupied by the Germans. At 2:45 P.M., in front of Blocks 26 and 28, they will hold a ceremony in memory of their dead. Everyone is invited.

Good news. There is more food available for the inmates, and now we can distribute more milk, eggs, fruit preserves, and meat. Also, the typhus epidemic is waning even though new cases continue to appear.

But no day is complete without bad news. One report concerns the disappearance of clothes, blankets, and other supplies from the warehouses, unfortunate because many of the people are still in need of these items. Howcroft finds an unauthorized inmate in our quarters, appraising our personal property, and turns him over to the IPC. Probably the looting is caused by wandering DPs and refugees, camp inhabitants, and some of our liaison people. Our French comrades are showing signs of restlessness, and Lieutenant Chaudon has his problems with them. Some of his men repeatedly request permission to travel elsewhere, but we are completely dependent on their trucks for hauling supplies, and we have to reject these requests. One man asks to visit his wife several hundred miles away. *Mais, non.* Then he asks for permission to visit his former CO in order to exchange his truck for a new one. But Chaudon says there is nothing wrong with the one he has.

So far, none of Chaudon's men has taken French leave.

A problem arises at the outer compound hospital, which is filled with 300 German soldiers and civilians and a few DPs. They are not getting enough to eat, according to one of the German doctors working there, a young, obese man born in Buffalo. I think the German patients should be sent to other hospitals where they can receive proper care. This would help us because we then could fill the vacated beds with our sick inmates. But if the German patients cannot be sent away, then we should feed them—we cannot let sick people go hungry. The camp CO decides to empty the hospital, and plans are made to fill it with our inmates and to staff it entirely with German physicians and nurses.

Another bit of intelligence circulates, that several internees have spoken out in behalf of the chief SS doctor during the Nazi rule. They say he was a decent man who did his best for the sick prisoners, although remembering the hospital conditions, the morbidity, and mortality when our Team first entered, I fail to understand these statements. I also hear that a few guards were not cruel.

But anyone who has had anything to do with a concentration

camp is now suspected of being a war criminal; judgment will be made later by military courts, when all the evidence is available. My feeling is that indifference or inaction by an SS trooper was interpreted by the prisoners as a sign of kindness or humanity. If the guard did not beat or overwork a prisoner, he was a friendly fellow, and the prisoner was overjoyed.

The prisoners conceived of good and evil as simple, uncomplicated states. Evil was anything that was life endangering. Good was anything that was not life endangering.

It is rumored that one of the beds in the outer compound hospital is occupied by a Frau Paulus, wife of the German Field Marshal who surrendered to the Russians at Stalingrad in 1943. According to the rumor, Hitler held the opinion that field marshals were not supposed to surrender, and he ordered Frau Paulus to be placed in Dachau as a hostage. This story, like many others that spread through the camp, was never confirmed.

As time passes, Lieutenant Junghertz and his fellow liaison officers talk a little more freely about their personal and political problems. Junghertz, whose English is the best, behaves like a man who has nothing but insoluble problems, and he may be right. He has trouble identifying some of his people. He cannot travel freely because of the quarantine. He worries constantly about the current issues, and he becomes more depressed each day. It is rumored that the land promised to the Poles at the Yalta Conference will not be given to them because of Stalin's rejection of the terms of that agreement. If so, Russia will incorporate a large chunk of Poland, and the border will not revert to the situation of January 1, 1939.

There are even more ominous tidings. Most of the liaison officers represent the Polish government-in-exile, which may become defunct. According to rumor, Stalin will not agree to a representative government in Warsaw, and that probably is the way it is going to be. Junghertz and others will be in the same position as many of the Poles in the camp who do not wish to be under Russia's domination—or anyone else's. They have encountered it in the past, including the two recent occupations, one following the Nazi-Soviet Pact of 1939, and the other as Russia fought back after the German invasion. They hear talk of the Katyn massacre in 1940, in which more than 10,000 Polish officers were machine-gunned by Russians. Stories are told about the decimation of the underground Polish army in 1944 after receiving orders from their own leaders and from the advancing Russians to rise up against the Germans in Warsaw. It did, and both Warsaw and the army were destroyed by the Germans while the Russians sat on the other side of the Vistula and waited.

So what does a Polish liaison officer tell his people? As time passes, Junghertz changes his mind about the English language. He can now fulminate as fluently as any American GI. Often Howcroft, Junghertz, and I stay up late at night talking. When I try to go to sleep, they won't let me, so I insult them scathingly, but they think my remarks are very humorous and complimentary, and the bull session continues.

The Americanization of Lieutenant Junghertz.

As roommates, Howcroft and I rarely have problems except in the selection of radio programs. His musical tastes are primitive. He is a boogie-woogie fan, and I like heavy, long-hair classics, so we shift from one station to another, neither satisfied, but any music is better than the constant babbling of German, Russian, or Polish that usually emanates. When he comes to visit, Rosenbloom complicates the situation. He dislikes both kinds of music. His preference is for semiclassics, and now there are three of us changing wavebands every few minutes.

Our quarters are agreeable. We have central heating, an electric stove, large, light rooms, comfortable beds, and unmilitary maple furniture in the kitchen. The only luxury we lack is running water, but despite its absence, we manage to keep well hydrated: we have plenty of beer, and, earlier this month, our resourceful French drivers brought us 6,000 bottles of white wine of 1939 and 1941 vintage. I have not been a wine drinker in the past, but now I find the wine pleasant, a worthwhile substitute for water, which is still of uncertain purity. Nevertheless, I try to be careful, being familiar with the possibility of acquiring cirrhosis of the liver, a malady not infrequently encountered among the occupants of American county hospitals, and, I am told, among the French. But, *c'est la guerre.* One must drink something.

We luxuriate in simple domestic pleasures—closets for our clothes, night tables, regular laundry service, and a clean, covered supper table on which our hired domestic employees always leave fresh flowers. One day I find three violet and two yellow orchids gracing the table. They must be from the experimental farm; orchids do not grow wild here—only in Mexico, I am told.

Everyone on the Team is well coated with DDT; no one has been able to bathe or shower since coming here. Today we are invited to use the showers in one of the buildings housing officers of one of the evacuation hospitals. My happiness is marred by finding a medical officer in the adjacent booth complaining loudly about having to do general medical work when he is trained in neuropsychiatry. His complaint is an old one in the Medical Corps. I have a specialty rating in radiology—not a high one, but enough so that I would probably have been working in my sphere of interest had I not had the misfortune of being under thirty-five years of age and free of disability, an unhappy combination which led to my being shipped out of a general hospital to an infantry division.

I find the ultimate luxury adjacent to the showers, thermostatically controlled footbaths, and I enjoy mine until I realize that a few weeks ago an SS guard, weary from his long day of beating, whipping, and killing prisoners, must have occupied this seat and been similarly soothed.

Our food has been dull since coming here. The French drivers have been too busy working, with little time for scavenging, and we are reduced to consuming government issue rations. As a result, Sergeant Aricer and Private Eastman have been the cooks, assisted by a variable number of Ukrainian, Polish, Hungarian, and French women, DPs whom we employ. Official policy requires that we offer them jobs before we try to recruit German civilians, which we do even without Army policy.

The women enjoy working with our men. They have developed their own method of communication. To them, the short, talkative Sergeant has become "Kleinbaby," and the tall, handsome Eastman is referred to as "Grossbaby."

Our meals are expected to improve in a few days. Aricer is negotiating for the purchase of a steer for 300 marks; we all look forward to a high-protein diet.

The enlisted men on the Team come to me for medical care. I

treat their cuts, bruises, bedbug bites, intestinal complaints, and other more personal disorders. I have become a doctor-father figure to them, and they address me as "Lieutenant" or "Doc" depending on their needs. Also, I have been treating the ailments of our DP employees; these efforts keep my medical muscles from becoming atrophied.

My reputation as a healer is enhanced by a major therapeutic triumph in a 45-year-old French washerwoman who has a long history of intermittent abdominal pain, backache, leg cramps, and innumerable other complaints. My French is fair, but not good enough to understand everything she says. I examine her briefly with my little wooden stethoscope, then treat her unscientifically with a special German compound which contains aspirin, magnesium sulphate (for the bowels), and phenobarbital. In two days all of her symptoms have vanished, but I do not know if the cure resulted from the medicine or from a few sympathetic words.

24

RESEARCH

In my spare time, I wander through the camp—there is always something to explore. On one of these walks, I enter a one-story building that contains laboratory counters and storage shelves. Almost everything in it has been smashed: I step over broken benches and drawers, twisted instruments and shattered glassware. In the debris, I am surprised to find a few specimen jars and bottles intact, filled with preserved human and insect tissues.

I am told that this is the malaria station where selected prisoners, used as experimental subjects without their consent, were either directly exposed to infected mosquitoes or were inoculated with infected blood. They were then treated with experimental drugs, some before they developed the symptoms of malaria, others afterward.

This was only one of the many medical investigations conducted at Dachau between 1941 and 1945; information about them is uncovered by a 7th Army investigating unit which prepares a special report about Dr. Klaus Karl Schilling, now an Allied prisoner. Formerly a professor of parasitology at the University of Berlin and a member of the Malaria Commission of the League of Nations, he was in charge of the malaria project at Dachau. Of 1,000 prisoners used in the test, 30 to 40 died of malaria and 300 to 400 from other diseases thought to be fatal because the prisoners' resistance had been depressed either by the malaria itself or the toxic effects of the drugs being studied. In many of the subjects severe pain and disability occurred. Nearly all of the Polish priests in the camp were forced to participate in the experiments.[1]

Three series of phlegmone (purulent infection) experiments were conducted at Dachau. Subjects were injected with pus and then treated with chemicals or antibiotics.

A Polish priest of the Capuchin Order, Father Stanislaw Wolak, sends me a copy of his description of one of the experiments. Twenty Polish, Dutch, and Czech priests were selected to perform their "duty for the welfare of mankind," he wrote. His ordeal began during the third year of his imprisonment, in November 1942. He thought he was picked because he was one of the few Polish priests considered to be relatively healthy. The subjects were taken to the hospital and superficially checked to be sure they were free of disease. Then they were divided into two groups, one to receive biochemicals, and the other to be treated with surgery and antibiotics. That night, about 3 cc. of pus were injected into each prisoners' leg; the pus was obtained from other prisoners with draining infections.

> The effect was immediate. Some of us had to be carried to bed because we could not stand on our legs. The pain was terrible, the temperature rose enormously. During the night I lost consciousness and regained it only a few times . . . during the next ten days. In those moments I saw by my side doctors examining my swollen leg . . . now three times normal [in size]. The tenth day when the swelling changed its color from red to whitish-yellow and when the whole thigh to the knee attained the form of a great sack of pus, I was taken to the operating room.

Father Wolak described the development of other sores on his back. The pain became "insupportable." He thought he was dying. He begged for amputation. His sight and memory were gone. He was in continuous agony. After four months, during which he was operated on seven times and received blood transfusions, he recovered to some extent.

He also observed other tortured patients. Of the twenty priests who received injections, seven died.

According to the 7th Army Counterintelligence Corps detachment, several incredible "mad" scientist projects were carried out, one to investigate the physiologic changes occuring in a parachutist falling at a tremendous speed from a high altitude to sea level. For this purpose, a mobile decompression chamber was placed next to Block 5, and, in a series of tests, was packed with Jews, Russian POWs, and Poles. Descent conditions were simulated. There were no survivors.

Two immersion experiments followed, one to record the reactions of prisoners forced to stay in icy water, the other to evaluate methods for warming chilled or frozen men. One of these methods required the services of prostitutes from the Ravensbrück concentration camp.[2]

Repeatedly we hear that the SS had developed a new material for making book covers, lamp shades, riding breeches, and saddles: human skin.

Dr. Blaha described this practice:

> Tatooed skin was especially valued by SS men. Russians, Poles and other inmates were used in this way, but it was forbidden to [remove] the skin of a German. This skin had to be from healthy prisoners and free of defects. Sometimes we did not have enough bodies with good skin and Rascher would say, "All right, you will get the bodies." The next day we would receive twenty or thirty bodies of young people. They would have been shot in the neck or struck on the head so that the skin would be uninjured. Also [frequent] requests for skulls or skeletons. . . . In the case of the skulls it was important to have a good set of teeth. . . . So, it was dangerous to have good skin or good teeth.[3]

Rascher, the SS officer who asked for the bodies with the uninjured skin, was the most infamous of the German doctors involved in the research projects at Dachau. As a protégé of the Reichsfuehrer SS, Rascher promoted and conducted the high altitude and "animal heat" experiments at Dachau. His fall from glory came about because he claimed that his wife had given birth to two children after she had passed the age of 48; Himmler believed that the babies had been kidnapped from orphanages. He had been lied to, the sacredness of German race and motherhood had been impugned! Frau Rascher was sent to the Ravensbruck concentration camp, where she was hanged. Rascher was locked into Cell 73 in the bunker at Dachau, and permitted to leave his cell to conduct sick call for the special prisoners. One of them, Captain S. Payne Best of the British Secret Service, said that Rascher claimed to be the inventor of the gas chamber. Himmler issued an order: Rascher was not to be taken alive by Allied soldiers. On April 26, an SS captain entered Rascher's solitary cell, placed his gun against the back of the prisoner's neck, and fired. It seems a singularly satisfying specimen of poetic justice for *Hauptsturmfuehrer* Rascher to meet his end in the same concentration camp as his victims.[4]

Only healthy prisoners could be transformed into lamp shades or be selected to serve as guinea pigs for medical "research." Psychotics and invalids were not eligible; for them the government had other plans. Periodically, teams of physicians visited Dachau to investigate the mental and physical condition of the prisoners. Those judged to be chronically ill were dispatched in small groups to euthanasia centers, particularly to the Hartheim Castle, near Linz. In 1944, a large transport of 2,000 invalids was disposed of in a small extermination camp in the Lublin district. And shortly before liberation, the camp had again been surveyed.

In practice, mental illness and invalidism were not clearly defined; euthanasic priority was given to "politically undesirable elements," particularly Jews.[5]

25

THE WAREHOUSES

As a result of the relocation of the inmates, nine different kitchens, all staffed almost entirely with Poles, are established: major ones in the prison area, the outer residential area, the satellite camp, the outer compound hospital, and the two American hospitals; small cooking units for administrative personnel. Each of the major kitchens is equipped with at least five 1,000-liter kettles, some of which operate on coal instead of steam or electricity.

The decentralization has produced special problems for the supply, maintenance, and labor offices, but, even so, I think it is easier for several kitchens to prepare meals for a few thousand each than for one kitchen to handle tens of thousands of persons.

It doesn't seem to make much difference in quality, however.

The hungry inmates are dependent on Howcroft's skill as the supply and mess officer, and on the competency of the IPC's food and labor committees. Howcroft is definitely the big man. He has been obtaining and issuing about thirty-five tons of food daily.

Now the foresight of someone in G-5 becomes apparent, because we would be helpless without Lieutenant Chaudon, his French drivers, and their fourteen trucks to procure, load, unload, and distribute the food, clothing, and other supplies needed here and at Allach.

When Howcroft discovers that he is going to be a grocer on an astronomic scale, he seizes the largest of the SS warehouses and tags it for food storage. Then he consults with the IPC's food subcommittee, headed by a Pole, Jan Marinkowski, and is rewarded with a Polish pearl, Mr. Farnik, whom he immediately appoints as supervisor.

The organization of space begins. Farnik bellows, and the labor office produces one hundred inmates, who sweep and clean. Groats are placed in one corner, dried beans in another, sugar elsewhere, flour somewhere else, potatoes in a special cellar, and eventually all of the floor space is covered except for one clear area, in the midst of which is a platform scale calibrated in kilograms.

Farnik is a big man with an infectious smile. Several times a day he circles the camp on his bicycle and shrewdly assesses the food supplies. After each tour, he submits helpful comments on shortages and surpluses. Soon we learn something of his statistical idiosyncracies.

When he enters our office with a disconsolate expression and announces that there is "nothing" in the warehouse, that means he has a one-day's supply. If he has "just something," it means that he has a three-day's supply. And a "good bit" indicates a two-week's supply.

Farnik is definitely the man for this job, decisive and resourceful. When there is a shortage of flour or potatoes, he conducts a mental search of the region and visualizes a certain storehouse in town or recalls hearing about a similar treasure trove in Munich; a call to MG invariably proves that his brain cells have not atrophied—the needed supplies soon appear.

One of Howcroft's most reliable helpers is the secretary of the food committee, a Pole whose last name begins with M, but is otherwise impossible for us to pronounce or spell. M, a small, thin, balding man in his mid-thirties who walks slowly and with great effort—a description that fits many other inmates—lacks the effusiveness of Farnik. M believes in a detailed, daily inventory. Farnik dislikes the thought of keeping books. To him, ledgers, vouchers, requisitions, receipts, and invoices are repugnant and unnecessary trivialities.

Often Farnik and M debate the importance of records:

M: Yesterday we receive 950 kilos [about one ton] of macaroni?
F: Well?
M: You give out 900 kilos today?
F: Yes.
M: Where are other 50 kilos?

F: So. Maybe some of sacks leak. Maybe Germans put in less macaroni than they tell you. You want I should weigh each piece macaroni?

M: This is no way to run business. You must have good scale and seven men to run books.

M and F then plunge into a colorful, heated discussion in Polish, but neither convinces the other. Later they come to see Howcroft and me, separately, and each explains his position in detail. Howcroft, of course, insists on detailed records. But Farnik is stubborn. He looks at Howcroft reproachfully, as though Howcroft were the foremost bureaucrat in the world.

A crisis arises when 5,575 packages arrive from the Geneva office of the International Committee of the Red Cross (ICRC). M insists that the contents be inventoried. Farnik sees no point in making this effort; he favors depositing a certain number in each block.

Angry words are exchanged. Howcroft orders them into their corners. M is forbidden in the warehouse. Farnik is banished from the food office. Forever! (This is one of Howcroft's peculiar expressions. When he says "forever," he means ten minutes; of course, Farnik and M know this.)

After consulting with the camp surgeon, certain members of the IPC, and Mr. Pires, the American Red Cross representative, Howcroft announces an order known as the Warehouse No. 112 Compromise. Certain items, such as the cocoa and chocolate, are reserved for the sick people of the inner compound hospital. The tobacco and cigarettes are removed; they are to be given to the 4,000 inmates who make up the regular labor force. The remainder: canned corned beef and sardines, Ovomaltine, condensed milk, margarine, artificial honey, and vitamin paste, goes to the main kitchen for distribution to all the inmates.

The Red Cross workers have been very busy. They are in the hospitals distributing playing cards and games, tobacco and toilet articles to the sick. Soon they hope to furnish patients with artificial limbs and orthopedic braces. Some of the workers are searching the countryside for clothes.

Wherever they are, these unassuming men wearing the American Red Cross uniform, with the symbol of hope on their caps and the civilian war relief patches on their arms, are welcome. (Except to the Nazis. At one time, most of the Yugoslav Red Cross workers were imprisoned in the camp. Eight Polish Red Cross workers were arrested in 1944 in nonoccupied France and interned here because they were Poles.)

Harry Pires probably knows more about the food situation in the camp than anyone, even Mr. Farnik with the redoubtable memory. Pires has information that settles the problem that arose at the recent IPC meeting: the origin of the supplies that Michelet was certain came from France. Rosenbloom and I were just as certain they came from American sources. Pires explains that the ICRC received packages totaling five tons of sugar and one ton of rice from the Jewish Committee in Geneva, and sent them along to the camp with another truckload of medical supplies. At the time of delivery, it was noted that most of the boxes and crates were stamped with the French Red Cross label. Because of this, said Pires, it was difficult to convince the French "that the packages were not for them alone but for the general use of the camp."

The French were right: the boxes had been labeled with the French Red Cross marker. We were right: other supplies had come from G-5. Everyone's honor was satisfied.

Another contribution made by the American Red Cross workers was the procurement of communication postcards. Only 1,500 could be obtained from G-5, so Pires arranged for 30,000 to be printed and distributed to the inmates. The CO had them flown from Augsberg to Paris, where they were put through postal channels when they were open. When this was not possible, the cards were taken to embassies and given to responsible government officials to be delivered to the families of the inmates.

Many of the cards reached their destinations. For the first time in many years—for some as long as seven years—contact was made by the inmates with their loved ones.

We think about these cards, delivered to small towns in France or Holland or Belgium. The postman knocks softly at the door. "Madame," he says, "sit down. I have a postcard for you. . . ."

Other local Red Cross workers are beginning to appear. Ambulances arrive from the French Red Cross, to be used to transport sick Frenchmen, Dutch, and Belgians—in anticipation of repatriation. Another truck drives in, labeled "Polish Red Cross Children's Relief Fund," bearing small quantities of chocolate and cigarettes for the Poles.[1]

Before liberation, Red Cross parcels had been received by Belgians, Dutch, French, Greeks, Italians, Yugoslavs, Spaniards, Poles, Norwegians, citizens of the Baltic states and a few other countries, and stateless Jews. The distribution of the parcels was uneven, some prisoners receiving none, others not sharing in the contents. I hear that none was sent to Russians because their country had not committed itself to the Geneva Convention of 1929 (for the humane treatment of POWs).

When an extra slice of bread meant survival for another day, it was not surprising to learn that the manna from Geneva tempted many inmates to violence, and others to change their nationality in order to become eligible for the packages. Some of the Capos demanded—and received—a share of the contents as the price for survival. I also heard that the SS men kept packages sent to deceased prisoners, and as many others as they could.

Howcroft has appointed as supervisor of the cold storage plant, where the eggs, meat, butter, and vegetables are stored, a 21-year-old Pole whom we know only as Joe for the same reasons that M is called M. Since liberation, Joe has acquired a large, ferocious police dog and a large, colorful wardrobe. One day he reports to work wearing a bright shirt, checked trousers, a yellow scarf, and a red fez.

I ask Joe where he found the fez, and he leads me to a warehouse in th administrative area which has thousands of gray and red fezzes, each with a similarly colored tassel, each carrying a skull-and-bones insignia. Someone says that these hats belonged to Turkish volunteers of the SS. (Foreigners were welcomed into the SS, provided they passed a physical examination and racial purity investigation.) The best guess is that these hats were used during SS ceremonies. Dachau had been a training camp for SS troops, and the skull-and-bones were part of the normal insignia worn by members of the Death's Head units (*Totenkopfverbande*); some of these special SS troops were used for concentration camp services. (The SS school at the Dachau concentration camp dated back to 1933. Two of its better known graduates were Rudolf Hoess, who became the commandant of the Auschwitz concentration camp, and Adolf Eichmann.)

The conscientious and diligent Joe guards his eggs like a mother hen, and his dog helps keep pilferers away. Joe has a reverent attitude toward requisitions; shortages disturb him. One day he receives and stores a large quantity of meat, 934 kilograms. Entries are recorded of the amounts sent to each kitchen. Joe's final tally shows that he has distributed only 891 kilograms. Considering a variation in scales, this should be acceptable, but not to Joe. Undecided as to whether the German butchers are cheating us or whether the French drivers have stolen some of his choice steaks, Joe embarks on a cloak-and-dagger mission to try to identify the beef thieves.

It is not easy for Joe to shadow anyone: his sartorial splendor prevents him from blending into the local scene, and, to make things worse, his faithful dog is never far away. But Joe tries. He tells us later, disconsolately, that he can find no evidence of theft or of a black market.

About this time, a visiting infantry officer who has been in the meat business in civilian life tells us that all meat shrinks when put into cold storage, and that our loss is not excessive.

Joe is not convinced; he still thinks someone is trying to take off with his beef.

Many of the inmates strong enough to work prefer assignments in warehouses to labor details. I am told that one of the more desirable positions is in a warehouse supervised by Alphons Kothbauer, an Austrian member of the IPC.

Here, theoretically, all clothing, shoes, bedding, blankets, towels, and other supplies are supposed to be stored until needed. But his facilities are frequently bypassed by inmates who, finding stockpiles of clothes, keep as much for themselves as they can and give what remains to their friends. This occurs after unofficial scouting parties return from their explorations of the countryside, and after members of labor details assigned to the outer compound spend their time scavenging instead of working.

A case in point is that of a Belgian officer who tried to divert all the available clothing to his own people. He would have succeeded had not Haulot, himself a Belgian, intervened.

The distribution of supplies is inequitable for another reason.

Requests from individuals and block leaders have been honored, but because of the lack of control over the requisitions and issue vouchers—in many cases, no records were made of disbursements—some inmates have more clothing than they need, many are still in rags, a large number have no linen, and others possess only a blanket.

At an IPC meeting, Malczewski expresses his indignation: "Interference by officers of different nations must be prohibited." He recommends that all unused and new supplies be deposited directly in Kothbauer's depot, where an immediate list can be drawn up. Malczewski is also in favor of rejecting requisitions signed by individuals and block leaders; he believes that only those submitted by recognized national committee members should be considered.

Something needs to be done. The matter is brought to Rosenbloom, who acts decisively. It has been said that man rises to an occasion. Rosenbloom's transformation from a plodding infantry officer to an effective administrator must be proof of the adage.

He quickly dictates regulations for the collection and distribution of supplies at Dachau and Allach. Members of work details returning to the inner compound are to be inspected at the gate; excess clothing and other goods found on their persons will be confiscated and brought to the depots. Scouting parties must be officially sanctioned; others will be refused permission to leave the camp. Requisitions must be approved by Kothbauer and countersigned by Howcroft or Rosenbloom.

After the regulations are enforced, all sorts of articles, including beds and mattresses, are properly stored. Thousands of American Army and SS uniforms are found and issued to those with the greatest needs. A thousand striped concentration camp uniforms gather dust in one of the warehouses—the inmates refuse to wear them.

Despite the improvement in the living conditions, special problems occasionally arise. A requisition for extraordinary supplies is brought to the attention of the IPC, whose speechless members shrug their shoulders. Arthur Haulot, presiding at the meeting, studies the request and neatly passes the buck. "Women," he says sagely, "want lots of things, and these will be taken care of by Lieutenant Rosenbloom."

THE RABBITS, THE PLANTAGE, THE CHAPEL, AND THE WOMEN

A few days ago an embarrassing situation was brought to the attention of the IPC at its meeting of May 7. The presiding officer, Arthur Haulot, explains the situation:

> French agitation in the camp . . . can no longer be tolerated. Yesterday, Sunday, a French officer came to Dr. Blaha and demanded that he take five sick Frenchmen to the hospital. This [was] impossible, the hospital being filled [and the admission officers] being off duty. Later he came again and demanded [that] more Frenchmen be [admitted].
>
> Once and for all, it must be stated that we, here in this camp, do not receive orders other than those issued by the camp authorities. The hospital [employees] are working with the utmost intensity. During only one week more than 2,000 sick have been taken to the hospital. Those who [take care of the patients] have scarcely time to sleep a few hours. Dr. Blaha states that the same thing happened again an hour ago. French officers arrived and demanded the acceptance of quite a number of Frenchmen into the hospital. He told a French doctor to examine them, but the doctor found only five of them sick. Thus, if they demand acceptance of healthy people into the hospital when there is no room for the sick, the French may build their own hospital where they can accept as many Frenchmen as they like. But as long as we have a common hospital, all nations must be on the same level.

Another incident occurred when the Red Cross packages arrived. Our French drivers, their trucks filled with the packages, stopped first at the barracks of their countrymen: Lieutenant Chaudon speedily halted this unauthorized dispensation.

Furthermore, a small number of French inmates have been spirited away from the camp by some of their "outside" representatives who seem unconcerned about the quarantine.

On reflection, I think that, proportionately, there are as many uncooperative Frenchmen as other nationals, but the French are more irritating because they feel their grievances more keenly and state them more colorfully and with greater frequency than the others. The increased demand for special privileges by all the groups seems to parallel their awareness of their new status —they are no longer wretched nonentities but citizens of important countries. There is one exception. I hear that the Dutch have made no demands, seemingly satisfied to bask in the sunshine of freedom. To express their gratitude, they bring flowers to our office every day. (For many years after the war, one of the Dutch internees regularly sent daffodil and tulip bulbs to Corporal Ferris.)

We are told of another side to the Gallic character. Before liberation, there were very few prisoners who shared the contents of their Red Cross packages with those who did not receive them. We hear that the few who did were some of the French, not only generous with their scraps of food, but with their quarters; despite the overcrowding, those with no place to eat could enter their barracks.

Because Hitler had repeatedly preached that the French were the natural unswerving enemies of the German people, they were singled out for particularly degrading treatment in the camps. The Nazi guards called them "Dogs." At other camps, they were required to wear the letters "HN," indicating that they came from a country of dogs.

In view of this, it seems inconceivable that when the worst conditions prevailed, the French were willing to help others. True generosity is an uncommon quality of the human spirit. I have decided that if I am ever in serious trouble, it would be comforting, and perhaps lifesaving, to have them nearby.

Today I have forgotten my resolution!

Periodically our quarters have been ransacked and personal property stolen. Today, when I return to my room, I find that my duffel bag is missing, taken some time in the afternoon, according to a French DP who works for us. A Frenchman with a moustache took it with him, she says. Perhaps one of the drivers. She elaborates a little, but no one is sure if he took it or if she has a grudge against him. Who knows? Coincidentally, some of our French associates left the camp at 2:00 P.M. for a visit to Austria.

My course seems clear. *Cherchez l'homme!* After obtaining passes, Mace fills a Mercedes convertible, one of our recently acquired vehicles, with gas, and late that night we pass through Salzburg. We know the destination of the French group, but when we arrive our quarry has not yet appeared. Early the next morning, Lieutenant Chaudon arrives with his convoy. He is surprised to see me, and distressed when I tell him the reason for my trip.

He orders a search of his vehicles and discovers my unopened bag; now he is even more distressed. Perhaps the bag was taken by mistake, he suggests.

Perhaps, but not likely. I tell Chaudon that I do not intend to press charges. But I think he will take action; he has to maintain discipline. If the culprit had not been in Chaudon's company, but an inmate of the camp, he would have been turned over to the IPC. Its court of justice handles such infractions, meeting six days a week.

We leave immediately. The return trip reveals the great natural beauty of this part of the world: spruce and pine forests, cool blue lakes and rich farming land, gentle grassy meadows with their flocks of sheep, and towering over them the dark brown Bavarian Alps, each proudly wearing its dazzling white hat. They remind me of the Grand Tetons. There are very few billboards along the road, and a dearth of filling stations. How did travelers fill their gasoline tanks in peacetime? We pass a large field with hundreds of planes, some damaged and others apparently intact, in all positions—nose down, tail down, upside down, wheels down, ready for takeoff—little planes and big planes. Nearby is an enclosure with thousands of German POWs. We are on one of the great autobahns. Most of the bridges are destroyed; even so, we save time, despite the gummy, mud-oozing detours.

The trip is worthwhile. I have my clothes back, letters from home, snapshots—evidence of the existence of the other world. Also the mementos that have accumulated since I came overseas; I am glad to have them back. A tourist guide to Edinburgh. An English camera. Books and pictures that I bought in Paris. A tarnished German sword.

We return in time for me to rush to a previously scheduled URGENT meeting. Our conscientious Team secretary, Arnold Jaeger, a French DP, routinely sent notification to the IPC secretary in German and a reminder to the Team members in English. I review the notice: "This afternoon at two o'clock an important meeting will take place at Lt. Smith, Medic Officer (Room No. 4). Arrange that representatives of the rubbish disposal system, latrine cleaning system, water purifying system, kitchen representative, disinfection representative report to Office No. 4 at Headquarters."

Reports are given, recommendations are made. I lecture on pest control and waste disposal. I have recently become so knowledgeable on these subjects that sometimes I dream about two to three foot trenches, garbage stands, tightly fitting lids, the cross trench, and old oil drums.

I know these details are important. Was it only a few hours ago that I was overpowered by the beauty of the Bavarian Alps?

May 12 is a momentous day. After a quiet ceremony, 450 rejoicing Belgians pass through the gate. Few look back. The move has been carried out without a hitch, with Rosenbloom as coordinator. Many units have been involved—the American command, the IPC, the Team, the Red Cross, and the Belgian Mission. The number leaving is small, but those remaining know that soon they will follow.

Top-level changes in the camp. Colonel Joyce is relieved as CO by Brigadier General Paul D. Adams, of the 45th Infantry Division. We are surprised by his arrival. A one-star officer! Are there political problems here about which we know nothing? Or are there serious difficulties in the war crimes investigation? Our speculations are unanswered.

Colonel Oral B. Bolibaugh, an experienced medical officer, becomes the camp surgeon. His Executive Officer is Colonel

Roy B. Cohn, a superbly trained physician formerly a Rockefeller trainee in India.

As a result of the administrative shake-up, I am no longer the sole occupant of my luxurious, sunny office. In fact, I am deprived of my desk, retaining only a half-interest in a drawer. I am beginning to feel like a lieutenant.

One of the new officers, Lieutenant Bang, the camp adjutant, accidentally shoots himself. Such incidents have become more frequent since V-E Day.

The entrance to the camp remains heavily guarded by GIs who scrutinize minutely everyone's pass. The guard units have changed three times; each time different officers have been authorized to sign passes. For a few days, the 45th Division supplied the guards. Then an antiaircraft detachment took over. Now an MP outfit has the job; its men are said to be the most unbending in the performance of their duties.

I discover this truth for myself when I reach the gate and find our usually good-natured Sergeant Aricer trying to induce one of the guards to let him out of the inner compound. The louder Aricer expostulates, the colder the MP becomes. Your pass is void, says the obdurate MP—that's the way it is. Are all your buttons buttoned? asks the MP.

Aricer is happy to see me, pointing out the ridiculous situation of his pass having become void between the time he entered the inner compound and now. I express my displeasure with the situation, but the guard is unmoved. In order to effect Aricer's release, I have to return to the adjutant's office and have him issue a new pass.

As the gate opens for Aricer, he chokingly thanks the guard for his courtesy and heads back to quarters muttering Louisiana imprecations as the MP watches him suspiciously.

Our Team is responsible for issuing passes to the inmates, using different forms from those for Army personnel. We adopt a two-tone red and white card, valid only for specified times and places. Corporal Ferris spends most of his time interviewing applicants for these permits. Because of the quarantine, our policy is to deny as many as possible, but there are many requests that Ferris cannot reject, such as that of an inmate whose relatives have arrived and are in a nearby town. Ferris is sympathetic, and finds it difficult to be negative. Perhaps too many authorizations are issued. At least, this is the word that comes down to us.

Now Howcroft becomes the passer of passes—in addition to being the mess, supply, and transportation officer. His experience in detecting attempted pilferage in food supplies has made him very distrustful of people. He can say no in sixteen languages.

Both the energy and the patience of our small staff are drained by the incessant barrage of complaints and demands. We feel an overwhelming compulsion to spend the time on issues related to the basic requirements of life, and find other subjects distracting and irrelevant to our purpose. We are exasperated by the frequent requests for special privileges, forgetting that many of the prisoners who survived did so by learning how to obtain or trade favors; it may be that this technique is indelibly stamped on their personalities.

So, when some of the inmates ask for extra food for the rabbits, we suspiciously and peremptorily turn them down. "Rabbits!" shouts Howcroft. "We need all the food we can get for human beings. If there are rabbits here, cook them. *Hasenpfeffer* is healthy—full of protein."

The concerned inmates sadly agree that this is a wise answer, and dejectedly leave the office.

During the next few days, additional requests to consider the rabbits flood our desks. We pigeonhole them. We do not worry about rabbits. But the inmates do. Delegations visit us several times a day to request food for them. There must be unwanted spinach or lettuce somewhere. Can we find grass? Soap and scrubbing brushes for the cages? They write letters to all the officers, including General Adams, but no one has the time to bother with the bunnies.

Finally we visit them. There are about 2,000 clean, pink-eyed, fluffy white Angora rabbits in hutches in the rear of the prison compound. For years their needs were attended to by Dutch and Polish prisoners, who still continue to administer tender care to them. Nobody had the heart to carry out the original order, and now, almost ten days later, the bunnies are still scurrying about their little cages, clean and plump; they have been well fed and maintained all this time. No one cares to change the situation now.

I find the behavior of the inmates inexplicable. Why weren't the rabbits killed at the time of liberation? I would have expected them to be devoured by the inmates. Would killing the rabbits bring back gruesome memories of mass slaughters perpetrated by the Nazis? Had the internees seen enough of death? Did they identify with creatures in a cage? Is the SS order to keep the cages spotless still obeyed, like a posthypnotic suggestion? Or does the relatively undisturbed existence of the rabbits bring back to the inmates a dimly remembered time when they too lived without anxiety?

I cannot obtain a satisfactory explanation. One of the internees tells me that he likes the rabbits because they are pretty. Perhaps it is as simple as this.

Dietrich Bonhoeffer, the brilliant German theologian who was hanged at the Flossenburg concentration camp in April 1945, commented in one of his letters that "prison life brings home to a man how nature carries on its quiet, care-free life quite unconcerned, and makes one feel almost sentimental toward animals and plant life—except for flies." [1]

Why were the rabbits there? Not for their fur, said one of the inmates, but so that the SS commandant could boast about the camp's enlightened rehabilitative methods to the Nazi Party members and SS dignitaries who frequently inspected the camp. After watching the prisoners feed the rabbits, the visitors toured the "chapel" for incarcerated priests, then the prison area brothel, the assembly area, and finally the experimental farm, the *Plantage*. When the Reichsfuehrer SS inspected, he seemed particularly interested in the *Plantage*, discoursing enthusiastically on the medicinal value of herbs.

When I first heard about the rabbits, I paid no attention to them; there were too many important things to think about. I react the same way when I am told about the *Plantage*. Stories about it reach us from the military investigators and inmates: that it was the brainchild of the Reichsfuehrer SS, that it was operated by the Institute for the Study of Medical and Alimentary Plants, an SS research organization, that German scientists, particularly physicians, botanists, and chemists, supervised the research, that political prisoners who had been scientists in the past were permitted to contribute their talents to the program in return for the privilege of staying alive.

We hear that many ambitious projects were undertaken, such as the production of artificial pepper, the evaluation of seasoning mixtures, the extraction of Vitamin C from gladioli and other flowers, the potentiation of plant growth by hormone-enriched manure, and, of most importance to Germany, the development of synthetic fertilizer.

As a profitable sideline, garlic, malva, and other medicinal plants, and vegetable seeds, were cultivated by the prisoners and then sold; the profits went to the SS.

The SS kept the results of the research projects secret. The inmates seemed to think that the experiments were nonsense, a Swiftian endeavor, a lifetime struggle devoted to extracting moonbeams from cucumbers. They knew that the grisly medical experiments were without value. Knowing that the Reichsfuehrer SS was a fanatic, they believed that everything he promoted was mad.

Elderly prisoners, some of them priests, were assigned to work in the *Plantage*. Despite their age, they were forced to labor at the same frenzied pace as younger prisoners. Army investigators hear that internees believed to be too sick to work were marched into a lake near the *Plantage*, at any time of year, and compelled to stay there until they drowned.

At liberation, there were 1,400 clergymen and priests imprisoned in the camp, 975 of them in Block 26, the "Priest's Block." The companion building, Block 28, had originally housed non-German priests; at the end of April it was packed with 1,528 prisoners, some of them clergymen. According to Pope Pius XII, there were 816 priests in the camp when it was freed; 326 were German. A total of 2,800 "ecclesiastics and religious" had been interned at Dachau; 1,800 had been subjected to special abuse because they were Poles. Polish priests were a special target of the Nazis: by the beginning of 1941, 7,000 had been liquidated.[2]

Peter van Gestel, a Dutch Jesuit priest from Maastricht, sends me a copy of his account of the life of the persecuted priests. They came from twenty-four countries. On entering the camp, they were greeted:

> "Ha! Another pope. Why are you here?" Beating and kicking. "Not married? How many wives did you have? A servant maid? How many illegitimate children?" . . . One

of us, carting gravel, had a barbed wire crown put on his head by an SS private, who sneered: "Tell me who wore a crown like that?" And the Jews present were forced to give a rehearsal of the gospel scene, Christ being crowned with thorns. So crowned, our comrades had to parade along the main street of the camp.

A crucifix at the roadside was the only consolation in our daily fatiguing march to the agricultural works. An SS notices that one of us greets the crucifix. The culprit was beaten and slashed in his face with fists and bludgeon and had to stand on his feet for two days without anything to eat or drink. . . .

On Holy Days, special treatment was provided:

On a Good Friday the SS guards proclaimed, "All you popes climb on top of the lockers and sing a religious song." . . . On Good Friday in 1942 they pretended to have found on one of us a sum of American money. Without exception all of us were stripped naked in public several times and had to march in line day after day in pouring rain and cold, without decent shoes and without food or drink.

Every religious utterance, every ministerial help to a fellow-prisoner was most severely forbidden. We did what we could in secret always under the permanent danger of being denounced by the Communists, who were on this point willing instruments of the SS.

Visitors were told that the priests did only light work. Accordingly, they were not part of any recognized work group and did not receive the extra bread allowance.

But three times a day we had to carry the huge kitchen buckets with food from the kitchen to all the blocks. It frequently happened that the weaker and older priests stumbled, spilling the contents, causing the priests to have one pot less. Heaven only knows for how many of us this was the cause of death. But the SS propaganda could broadcast: "The priests of Dachau are having a holiday. They have their chapel and need not work."

The depth of their misery was reached in the summer of 1942 when they were forced to participate in the medical experiments. Despite this, there was a bright moment:

In the autumn of 1942 we were allowed to receive food parcels. The world demonstrated its sympathy for us in a most touching way. So many parcels came that they had to be carted to the priests' block. But this was a painful thorn in the eyes of the SS. They jeered: "Here are living the full-fed popes with their rich parcels, but don't expect them to give anything away." As a matter of fact, thousands of loaves of bread and great quantities of sugar, sweets and medicines were put at the disposal of the hospital and the starving. The SS leader of the camp meeting a poor Russian boy, who is eating a piece of bread given him by a priest, orders at once: "Block 26 is to get no bread for a fortnight."

Periodically, protests had been lodged with Berlin about the treatment of the priests, but little had been accomplished for them. According to Father van Gestel, the Archbishop of Paderborn renewed his pleas in 1943 to have the priests released, but his request was rejected:

> "We are sorry, but the prisoners concerned did not behave well in the camp . . . every priest has a bed for himself and the priests have more to eat than your people in Paderborn." In reality . . . we slept with three men in two beds and later with two in one bed. . . .

The Nazis granted permission to the priests to have a place of worship. Father van Gestel described this "so-called privilege":

> The Chapel, i.e. a room with a table, was only for the priests, and for a long time, till the end of 1942, only for the German priests. The priests' block was isolated: forbidden ground for the whole camp. In these long tiring days of heavy manual labor from 6 A.M. to 7 P.M. we could only find time for a Mass or a religious service by rising earlier still than the camp, i.e. at 4 o'clock. We gladly did this. On Sundays just the shortest possible form of a High Mass was possible, because this "free" day was devoted to a general cleaning of the block. . . . Very soon the Chapel privilege was taken away from all non-German priests. But bear in mind: the Chapel remains for the purpose of SS propaganda and to show visitors. Any person of significance visiting the camp was always led to the Chapel and from the Chapel to the brothel.

Certain inmates were jealous of the priests because of the gifts sent to them; others were resentful because the priests prevented them from worshiping in the Chapel. The SS regulation specified that those who disobeyed were to be shot. So, many prisoners knelt and prayed outside the Chapel near a sign in Gothic letters: "Here, God is Adolf Hitler." The ultimate degradation, said Malraux many years later, after talking with Michelet and other survivors: with the SS order, the concentration camp system had reached its zenith.[3]

The priests aided in the care of the sick:

> In the winter of 1942–43 the camp was gripped by typhus, and nurses were urgently needed for the numerous sick. An appeal was made to Block 26 for help. We were told that this was a chance to volunteer for a duty of honor. Priests entered the hospital as nurses willingly to assist as we could with the sick and dying, and to administer to them spiritually as opportunity arose. And in the winter of 1944–45, priests volunteered again for the blocks where typhoid fever took a toll. . . . All of those priests contracted the disease and many died. . . .
>
> A last frustrated attempt—there were a good number —to deprive us of the Chapel was made in the summer of 1944. Room was wanted for the thousands of newcomers from France and other places and we were asked to give up our Chapel of our own free will. But this was quite a different matter from being asked to voluntarily nurse the sick typhus patients! We answered firmly: "First that it was not in our power to give up a privilege obtained for us by the Vatican; Second that it was not our duty to create room for newcomers in the camp; Third that the Temple of the true God was of more importance than the temple of Venus, the brothel, which could afford more space than the Chapel ever could."

So ends Peter van Gestel's story, appropriately titled *The Church in the Bonds of Dachau.*

Some of the priests had a different point of view. They described their feelings as they helplessly watched their friends and parishioners removed from life because it suited German policy. In the mad stagnant world of stumbling bodies, they did not consider impartiality a virtue. Why had the Vatican adopted a wartime policy of neutrality? Were the intentions of the Nazis known only to the priests of Dachau? We knew that they meant to destroy the Roman Catholic Church, said one of the priests. Apparently the neutrals did not believe this.

Block 31, the brothel, has been converted to quarters for honorary prisoners. The inmates whom I talk with have little to say about it, except to mention that it probably dated back to 1942 or 1943 when an incentive system was established in order to improve the output of working prisoners. The hardest working prisoners were promised special privileges, such as extra money, tobacco or food, or authorization to visit the brothel. Few prisoners took advantage of the opportunity, probably because of their weakened sex drive. The incentive system was a failure, said one of the inmates; physical persuasion continued as the accepted method of increasing performance of the slave laborers.

The subject of the brothel was considered at the IPC meeting of May 9, when a suggestion was made that Block 31 could be transformed into comfortable quarters for high-ranking Russian officers, and so further relieve the congestion in the inner compound. The proposal was rejected: the building was judged to be inappropriate for such a purpose because of its past history. At this meeting, it was mentioned that the women inmates were scheduled to leave the inner compound the next day. A special building in the camp outskirts, formerly used to house SS enlisted men, had been cleared for them.

The exodus of the women is in line with American policy, clearly stated by Rosenbloom to the members of the IPC at one of its earlier meetings:

> I am happy to have been placed here by the American government in order to cooperate with you, the IPC. Of course, the difficulties are enormous. The American government cannot provide for everything needed in the camp. The cooperation of the prisoners, represented by the IPC, is therefore most needed. We are counting on your active cooperation. You no longer work for the Nazis, but for yourselves. We shall do all that is possible and necessary. But first we must provide for the sick, who will be in

four hospitals. Then we shall take care of the women and children. After this, it will be the turn of the others.

The move of the women into their new quarters is uneventful. I hear that the building is off limits to the inmates, and that some complaints are arriving because of this.

Not all the women are in the new dwelling. Fifty-six, some with children, are patients in the American hospital. Three have fled to the camp at Allach.

27

COMPLAINT DEPARTMENT

Most of the French, some of the Romanians, Germans, and Austrians, and small numbers of people from other countries have been able to move into newly furnished quarters in the outer compound. The relocation began on May 11. Eventually 5,000 people will be living here. We are happy to see this migration. Perhaps the pleasant new environment—the fresh beds and the clean rooms—will help them to forget the horrors of their past.

I wonder what they thought in their old blocks, as they looked for the last time at the slats of the beds above them, at the bleak faces of their neighbors. *Who died in these beds? There I was beaten. Here I hunted for lice nightly. The Capo slept in that corner. Through that door the SS guard entered. . . .*

Despite the move, the prison barracks still are badly congested. After studying the problems of the camp, General Adams acts decisively to relieve the overcrowding. A satellite camp will be established at a large *Kaserne* (German military barracks) between Dachau and Munich. The operation will begin on May 15. Inmates selected for relocation will bathe, be disinfected, and receive clean clothes. Trucks will be ready to pick them up at 8:00 A.M. On the first day, 1,000 will leave, then 1,500 on the second and subsequent days until 10,000 have departed. First to go will be the leaders of a national group; next, the people selected by them for the work details in the new facility; following them will be the nonworking members of that group.

Rosenbloom presents the plan to the IPC at its meeting of May 14:

ROSENBLOOM: . . . We have been waiting a long time for this step to be taken. It will be a great boon for the people of Dachau. . . .

MALCZEWSKI: The order comes from the new American General who is interested in the well-being of the camp residents. . . . The projected move will reduce the population of each barrack to only 500. . . . The inmates in the new camp will stay for fourteen days, then be released for repatriation. . . . Who will go?

DOMAGALA (the camp registrar): Among those in the inner camp are 1,100 Germans, 2,200 Italians, 3,100 Yugoslavs, 9,000 Poles, 4,500 Russians and 1,600 Czechs. A total of 21,500.

KUCI: No problem. The Poles should be transferred. This will solve the problem.

HAULOT: There are not enough healthy Poles. But, we could send them and add the Italians. . . .

MICHELET: The Poles are the *doyens du camp*, the most experienced men. They occupy the most crucial positions here. Without them, the camp would collapse.

KUCI: Only those who are indispensible should remain here.

HAULOT: This is not possible. Either none or all. I agree with Michelet. If we send 4,500 Russians, 3,100 Yugoslavs, 1,600 Czechs and 1,100 Germans, the new camp will be filled with 10,300 people.

MICHAILOW: I am opposed to the transfer of Russians to the new camp. In our group there are many feeble people who have recently arrived from Buchenwald and Flossenburg. They cannot reorganize their lives. I will have to inform my government. By the way, there are only 3,500 Russians here, not 4,500; only 2,500 are transportable. Furthermore, it is very difficult to fill out lists in English—the lists are not ready; it will take time to fill them out.

MELODIA: In the Italian group are many criminals who will not work. We contribute very little to camp life. Therefore, it will be better if we remain here.

MUELLER: Do not count on sending the Germans to the new camp because their transfer to the quarters in the periphery of the Dachau camp is already underway.

HAULOT: Under the circumstances, we have no choice but

to figure out a percentage for each national group and move these people into the new area.

ROSENBLOOM: That is what will be done. There is no need for further discussion.

HAULOT: There is no point in moving the Czechs—they are going home in the next few days. Only Russians, Poles, and Yugoslavs will remain.

JURANIC: Within our ranks are 1,000 POWs. We Yugoslavs have already been badly treated. And, now when a percentage is determined, we will be split again. Once more, we are not treated as well as the French or other small national groups, who have been moved into the new buildings in the outer compound.

KOKOSZKA: The same is true for the Poles. We have been here the longest and have made the greatest sacrifices.

MALCZEWSKI: If we cannot solve this ourselves, then the American authorities will have to make the decision. The Yugoslavs are opposed to a percentage evacuation of national groups. But if we do not resort to this, there is no solution to the problem.

ROSENBLOOM: It is better to send out national groups as a whole. The new camp has no barracks, but large buildings made of bricks.

MICHAILOW: It is impossible to permit completely exhausted people to leave the camp in their condition. It is best to leave the decision to the Americans.

YOCARINIS (Greece): I also speak for the Spanish. We will go to the new camp. We have complete faith in the Americans.

MELODIA: I agree. The Italians will go.

MALCZEWSKI: A uniform percentage for all nationalities will be figured. But, working personnel remains here. In the new camp, new residents shall create another work force.

ROSENBLOOM: In the near future, liaison officers are expected, hence it is recommended that a national group should be moved as a whole.

MALCZEWSKI: Our liaison officers are already here and have moved into an office. It is best if we stay here.

MASETKIN (Poland): The Americans need some basis for selecting one, rather than another group to be moved. We

Poles were the first ones here. Many of us have been here since 1940. We have supplied the life-supporting activities in the camp. We have worked as translators for the Americans, as requested by them. Now our liaison officers are here. Everyone knows that the Polish question has not been decided. We have two governments: therefore it will be easier for us to stay here. In that case, in addition to the Poles, only a few smaller groups will remain. As a result, the camp operation will be simplified from the point of view of nationalities. This will be a great advantage.

ROSENBLOOM (leaves to talk on the telephone, then returns): Tomorrow, 1,000 Russians will depart. The others to leave will not be decided now, but from day to day. Colonel Joyce says that those who move into the new camp will be repatriated before those who remain here. It will be best to transfer one-quarter of each group.

KUCI: I know the new place. It is a well-furnished building with comparatively better facilities than Dachau.

JURANIC: On the basis of the latest information from Kuci and Lieutenant Rosenbloom: the speedup in repatriation and the improved living conditions, and, as representative of my people, I am ready for the transfer of the Yugoslavs.

MALCZEWSKI: If possible, a committee should be formed to inspect the new place.

MICHAILOW: I do not want to say anything because I have the deepest faith in the Americans. I have stated our opposition, but if we are transferred, we have faith. We have not picked the new building, or agreed to go there. Hence inspection is useless.

A Pole, a Yugoslav, and an Italian are appointed to a committee to visit the new site. The meeting adjourns at 11:30 P.M. The minutes are signed by *Schriftfuehrer* (secretary) Zdenko Knez.

Early in the morning, the investigating committee members examine and approve the new lodgings. Immediately, Russians begin to move into them at a high rate of speed. Almost as rapidly, complaints from them are received at HQ, and Rosenbloom and I are sent off as troubleshooters; this will be my first visit to the *Kaserne*.

The new quarters comprise three immense, clean buildings with good kitchens and adequate recreation space. Large sleeping rooms are filled with single and double-decker beds; each person sleeps alone. The beds, mattresses, and pillows are acceptable, the blankets poor, but useful, the space between the beds insufficient. It does not take long to find the reasons for the complaints: there is no water, and in some parts of the buildings electricity is lacking. Sabotage?

The newly transplanted residents are angry. Particularly incensed is a Russian major-general who, I hear, likes to drink his tea scalding hot. It is possible that Moscow may be informed about this situation.

We return to our office. Ferris rapidly types our report, which recommends that transfers to the new dwellings should be halted, and the new tenants returned to the old quarters until the utilities are functioning—unless repairs can be effected immediately. The report is rushed to camp HQ.

Now another general is incensed—this one, our own. We hear that he is annoyed and angered, an anxiety-producing combination. Even we company grade officers know that hell hath no fury greater than a general seething with such emotions.

The telephone lines hum, couriers rush about, experts are located, but even so it will take time to repair the faulty water mains and electrical circuits. (Almost two weeks pass before the *Kaserne* is fully occupied. When I visit again, I find the residents happy. A little happiness is like a communicable disease; spreading rapidly from person to person, it causes those overcome to disregard minor discomforts: the tenants in the comfortable buildings no longer notice that their bunks are too close together. Even the Russians are happy. Perhaps our general has given their general a samovar.)

We are into the third week of May. Case-finding teams are still uncovering patients with typhus fever, who still show the classic symptoms of fever, a fine rash, and a painful headache. Fortunately, the course of the disease in these patients turns out to be mild. The inmates have all been immunized—more or less. Here, 13,500 inoculations were administered on May 9 and 10, and 18,400 on May 15 and 16. At Allach, 14,000 injections were completed on May 14. Despite the attempt to keep accurate records, there was confusion as to who received the inoculations. Some inmates say they were vaccinated on two successive days; a few say they received more than two injections; many thought that they had none.

The epidemic at Allach is different from the one here because it began much later: the first case appeared there on April 22, 1945; the patients are not as sick, I am told. Now, almost a month later, there are more than 1,200 patients hospitalized in the Allach camp hospital, and in wards established by the 66th Field Hospital.

Intestinal complaints persist. In very few patients could a bacterial or parasitic origin be demonstrated, so it is assumed that their symptoms of enteritis were caused by overeating.

One of the inmate doctors is being questioned about the prevalence of castration operations, and I am called to help in the investigation. The testimony is being recorded. The doctor is a poor witness—his memory is bad. Vaguely, he recalls that a Gypsy had voluntarily requested such a procedure years ago because he wanted to marry an Aryan and the intermixture of his blood with that of an Aryan was officially prohibited.

Colonel Joyce, now the executive officer of the permanent camp staff, asks me to survey the food situation and recommend a uniform diet for both healthy and sick people. Although I understand the importance of the assignment, I do not look forward to spending most of my time on the dull calculations that are part of the job. But there is a fringe benefit: I will be able to leave the camp and see more of the countryside in the next few days while searching for sources of food.

Step number one is to inspect the available provisions. There are obvious shortages of eggs, milk, and cereals; certain other foods are still difficult to obtain. Step number two is to watch the distribution of the rations from the warehouses to the different kitchens, and then watch food preparation in each of them. Individual differences are noticeable but not necessarily undesirable, except in one of the hospitals where the patients are not receiving enough to eat.

The only surplus is in the number of complaints. The increased quantity and improved quality of the food, occasionally leading to intestinal complaints, have been reasons for grumbling; many of these complaints have been leveled at Dr. Blaha, the hardworking head of the IPC food committee. When the rich food is restricted, complaints arrive that rations are insufficiently nutritious. Or the sick receive too much and the healthy not enough, or vice versa. Sometimes distribution falters as with the *Breikost*, a cereal-milk soup sent only to blocks with sick people. Sometimes it arrives for breakfast but not for dinner. One morning, every person in Block 8 receives ten small cakes for breakfast, but the inhabitants of Block 2 are given only four cakes apiece.

The inmates grouse, and so do the members of the IPC, the mess officers of the American hospitals who have not adjusted to German supplies, the people at Allach who procure all their rations from us, and the camp surgeon who wants the healthy people to be given 2,400 calories a day and the sick 2,500. (A good idea. I think that 2,000 calories a day is insufficient for an adult. And those performing heavy labor should receive about 4,500 calories.) Probably even the general complains, but we do not hear him, fortunately.

Unexpectedly, an innocent remark by an American Red Cross worker contributes to our difficulties. A new wonder drug has been discovered, she says, that enables a starved person to eat normally in seventy-two hours, without any harmful effects. Now we are visited by delegations from the barracks, urging us to obtain the drug. If it existed, we say, the Army would supply it just as it is doing with DDT and penicillin. It is remarkable how many people will seize on any rumor, newspaper article, advertisement, or shabby "guarantee" by a charlatan for a quick "cure" rather than submit to established methods.

After completing the survey, I arrange to meet with Howcroft and an assistant to the camp surgeon, Major John Brown, in order to begin the juggling of calories, minerals, proteins, carbohydrates, fats, and vitamins. Striving for a balanced diet, we work late into the night using the weight of available food in grams per person per day as a basic unit—except for eggs, where the unit is a "piece." Weight is converted into calories, then ounces per person per day, then kilograms per 100 persons per day and finally per week. We have to alter the figures for different kinds of diets, and provide additional bread (250 grams) and meat (100 grams) for working inmates. The regular diet is a monotonous succession of potatoes, butter, fats, vegetables, cereals (rice, macaroni, groats), milk, and the mainstay, a heavy dark bread. Meat is limited to 120 grams a day.

Our planning session is constantly interrupted by inmates with special requests and by our own enlisted men with messages: Can I take my uncle home? Can so-and-so go to Munich? What happened to the requisition from the Italian committee? Telephone calls. Ten German POWs armed with mops and pails invade the office in which we are working; they have their orders to clean the room now, and orders are orders. Major Brown has to pull rank to get rid of them. Signs of strain appear. Howcroft must be cracking. He makes his first joke— someone is pulling his legume. Major Brown replies that he must have rapid pulses.

The job is complicated, requiring many contacts. We see ourselves as the hub of a giant wheel with spokes radiating in all directions for hundreds of miles.

We work closely with a Lieutenant Haynes, a resourceful MG supply officer who scours the district diligently. I visit an MG major in Munich almost daily, and while there call on the harried district food administrator, who has to provide food for several hundred thousand DPs and POWs and all the German civilians. Supplies on hand may last one or two weeks. Planting has been late this spring, perhaps too late. The "imported" foreign agricultural workers no longer care to contribute to the German economy. Transportation is hopeless. Somebody is going to have to pay for everything, and a German banking and monetary system has yet to be established.

Everyone has problems. I concentrate on mine, the procurement of specific foods. I often sit with the district administrator until midnight, mesmerized by his lamentations. I am rewarded by his promise to circulate through other districts to get us what we need.

Cooperation increases. From a dump at Furstenfeldbrook we receive sixty gallons of eggnog daily, and one of the hard-to-get items, chocolate. Dehydrated eggs arrive from Munich. Milk, fresh eggs, and other perishables begin arriving daily from a number of cities—we consume 15,000 liters of milk daily. Regular deliveries of flour enable our bakers to turn out 20,000 loaves of bread a day. We receive forty cases of vitamins— 384,000 capsules.

The style of cooking is Continental, but only because of location; no gourmet would approve. Nevertheless, there are few complaints about the cooking, except in obvious situations: when the eggs are spoiled and the potatoes rotten. The poor quality of the beans is not noted, nor is the mediocrity of the flour discussed. We receive *Brotmehl*, a white flour made of rye and corn, and another made of wheat. Despite the quality, many inmates demand more bread. They have been receiving 375 grams (932 calories), but they want this amount doubled. To do so would unbalance the diet. Still, bread has strong psychological significance here; the prisoners often survived because of a few extra mouthfuls. We will recommend 500 grams a day.

The job of food supervision keeps us busy. There are consultations with the butcher, the baker, the chief cooks in the different kitchens, and the warehouse keepers. Garbage disposal. Milk and vegetable routes. Soft diets. Special food for those going home. Emergency rations. A broken kettle. Lettuce for the rabbits. Spinach crates. Maggi soup mixes. Ersatz coffee and tea —made from acorns, I believe. Requisitions. Security of the warehouses, kitchens, potato cellar, and delivering trucks. French drivers. Labor problems. Visiting colonels.

Howcroft is becoming more irritable, and I wish I were a medical doctor again.

My old pen has happily reappeared, and I sit down to write to my wife about my achievements. I tell her that I have become a magician. I can convert a gram to a calorie—a great accomplishment for a medical officer. I also tell her about the bread controversy—that the amount we have recommended will probably not satisfy the inmates, that we will have to increase it to 750 grams.

The Army has said that we can now write about our overseas trip. Up to this time we have not been permitted to do so.

So I tell her about that cold, unpleasant foggy afternoon in Boston, the POE (port of embarkation), where I was given a cup of hot coffee and a doughnut by a pleasant Red Cross worker. Then I donned my helmet, shouldered my gas mask and duffel bag, marched slowly up the gangplank, and sailed away on the great luxury liner, the *America*, now renamed the *West Point*. Traveling a zigzag course across the south Atlantic, we eventually reached Liverpool. I was told that these evasive tactics were ordered to avoid hostile submarines, but I secretly suspected that they were planned to save the government money because, as a result of the maneuvering, almost no one ate. The only men in our general hospital unit who were not seasick were the Catholic chaplain, Father Paolucci, and me. Misery loves company, I discovered for myself. Despite our selfless devotion to the physical and spiritual needs of our suffering comrades, they resented our continued interest in food.

In the letter I describe some of the youngsters in the camp, handsome, mature Poles about 15 or 16 years old, all willing workers; we use them for odd jobs; one becomes our office boy. Another is from Cracow; he has not heard from his parents since 1939.

An industrious 18-year-old Pole takes over the two-chair SS barber shop. It has been more than a month since my last visit with a barber, so I decide to try Stanislaw. His charges are modest: a haircut is one mark, a shave free. Excessively careful, perhaps fearful of men in uniform, he takes an hour to do what should take fifteen minutes. During this time I learn that he has been a prisoner here for three years and does not know why he was sent here.

More satisfying is the arrival of thirty letters postmarked between February 27 and April 25. I read, among other news, that the lilacs are blooming in Chicago. Here in the countryside, they are profuse; the ground is also dotted with lupines, and pansies and azaleas grow abundantly.

Overcome by nostalgia, I decide to visit 63rd Division HQ, now in Bad Mergentheim, in order to find out what is being rumored about our immediate future. Furthermore, I would like to retrieve the personal property that we left behind a long time ago, when HQ was in Saargemeines; everyone asks me to bring back his barracks bag. Finally, it would be pleasant to be paid.

When I arrive, I find the Division's subdivisions are dispersed over such a wide area that I cannot visit all of the units to which our men belonged, so I settle for being paid $34 in marks, all that remains of my salary after deductions for room and board and the allotment to my wife. (We pay for K rations or three meals a day whether we eat them or not—one of the privileges of being an officer. However, we receive an allotment that more than covers the disbursements.)

At my former collecting company, I find only one of my old friends; the other medical officer is away at school in Paris. We talk of the days that have passed, and I learn that our battalion earned a citation and that everyone in it, including me, is entitled to wear a gold-braided laurel wreath on his left shoulder. I notice, however, that no one is wearing the decoration: no gold braid is available. Now, everyone in the battalion is sitting, waiting for something to happen; the inertia is tiresome. Gone are the days of informal dress, jam sessions, and togetherness; now everyone is neatly and correctly attired. Buttons are buttoned. Military courtesy abounds. Time has slowed down again. I see that no one has the slightest intimation of the future of our collecting company, or can think of gossip to transmit, an unusual situation. My friends promise to remind Division of our stored personal property. Sadly, I say goodbye again, and my driver and I return to Dachau.

May 19. Mail censorship ends. I am glad it is over; no longer need our men be inhibited by it. Now I have thirty more minutes of free time each day.

Communiqué No. 19 is issued from the Central Press Bureau, an arm of the IPC Division of Information and Culture. Ali Kuci first mentions the distribution of three different kinds of communication postcards made possible by the efforts of Harry Pires. Then other news:

> All the national committees are asked to compile a list in four copies of all the members of their national groups. In these lists should be written the names and home addresses of everyone. The Secretary of the Camp has been charged to gather them. It is the duty of everyone to help in handling them as quickly as possible. In the next days we are going to reveal the purpose for which this work is [intended].
>
> After many times we repeat again: no one will be repatriated before the lists for the CIC are completed and handed into that office. These lists are necessary in order to make it possible for the people to be repatriated.
>
> For the evacuation of different nationalities outside the compound the American Medical Authorities have constructed in the same zone showers that were immediately placed at the disposal of the groups. Later they placed there a great quantity of soap. Now we are informed that no one is using these showers. It is a great pity. . . .

About this time we move out of our previous quarters into a two-story gray stone house nearer the camp. There is a good piano here and the previous occupant must have been a competent performer, judging from the musical scores here— Beethoven Sonatas and Liszt Rhapsodies. I look but of course do not find anything by the *verboten* composers Mendelssohn and Hindemith.

A large garden, unfortunately filled with debris, is located in the rear of the house. We will have the debris cleared and then it should be pleasant beneath the tall, cool trees when the weather gets warmer. The only trouble with our new home is that the main switch and fuse box have been smashed: we will have to use candles for a while.

Military police occupy the two houses on either side of ours, which gives us a feeling of security. But the feeling is illusory, for on the second day we are visited by thieves and vandals. The contents of our duffel bags are strewn through the rooms and my rolls of film are opened and thrown around. Nothing important has been taken, however, and later I solve Howcroft's dental problem when I find his missing tooth powder in my bag.

We do not have sufficient personnel to keep someone in the house all the time. During the day DPs are present, but not at night. Perhaps we can obtain a special guard.

These houses were previously occupied by Nazi officers and their families. In our house is a photograph album with many pictures of a small child, arranged chronologically, some showing candid, playful attitudes, others more formally posed. The prison environment seems to have had no effect on the boy's appearance; he is revealed as a light-haired, handsome child in a picture that hangs on a wall in an upstairs bedroom. Even the mother in the album looks chic and content. I suppose I expected to see horns.

I wonder about these people. Who were they? This boy— this woman?

This time I find out a little about them.

One day a tall, thin dark woman, about forty, walks wearily into the house and claims to be the last tenant. She bears a resemblance to the woman in the picture, but is no longer so chic. Her recently deceased husband was an SS officer, she says listlessly; he was killed when the Americans took the camp. She wears a stark black dress as if to confirm her status of widowhood. Otherwise, she has little to say and displays an authorization permitting her to remove any of her property that remains. But little is left except the piano and a few teacups. She arranges to have the piano moved, and, taking the teacups, the photograph album, and the picture of her son, she trudges out the front door without looking back.

Life must go on.

But one of the Army investigators disagrees.

When I tell him about the incident he says that there is no proof that her husband is dead—the Army is looking for him. He knows nothing about the boy. The wives of SS officers will not give out information, he adds. He and the other members of his unit are forbidden to beat the SS women.

"Too bad," he mutters. "They are cold, savage egotists and sadists, and the world would be better off without them."

28

HOMEWARD BOUND

Communiqué No. 30, dated May 21, is two pages long. Dr. Kuci again cautions the people to be patient, saying that if they had been permitted to return home immediately after liberation, 80 percent of them would have died. Then the big news:

> The Czechoslovakians are leaving tomorrow . . . returning to their country. A delegation of their Government is here to receive and accompany them home.
>
> The Czechoslovakians are among the oldest inmates of this camp. Some of them came here about seven years ago. Many of their people were murdered and many others died in Germany. Few survived to tell their brave nation the story of these years. Now their country is free. The normal life in Czechoslovakia has begun. Its future will be constructed on a new and sound basis of life. That we know because these people have always given impulsive signs of vitality.
>
> Here in the camp at Dachau they were always good and fine comrades. They helped whenever they could and did everything possible to ease the hard life in the concentration camp, for their friends and fellowmen. They worked seriously, for seriousness is characteristic of these people.
>
> We, their old friends, wish them the best of luck for the future and hope that all may return to their homes, wives and children.

The census report for May 21 arrives from the IPC and shows a total of 26,813 inmates remaining; of these only 17,648 are still in the prison compound. Compared to the original figures, about 10 percent of the Poles and 25 percent of the French are gone: some have died, some have fled, and some of the Poles have adopted a new country. A small number of Luxembourgers has been repatriated. The Hungarian population has doubled. Only 60 percent of the Belgians remain, and about 30 percent of the Dutch. Most of those who have returned home are western Europeans. But the large national groups that predominated originally—the Poles, Russians, French, and Yugoslavs—are still here.

Today there are 64 deaths, 467 legal departures, and 246 missing. The outer compound hospitals house 3,390 patients and the camp hospital holds another 4,024; there are an additional 820 sick in their quarters.

Imprisoned in the bunker—the "dungeon-house"—are 162 men.

Leaving today are 137 Luxembourgers, 95 French, 72 Poles, 62 Russians, and a handful of Belgians, Czechs, Dutch, Hungarians, and Yugoslavs.

During our infantry days we measured time as the distance between rivers. Now we use as a measurement the number of days between the repatriation of large national groups.

May 24. This should be a memorable day. The French are the first large group to leave the camp. After their departure, the Dutch, Belgians, and Norwegians are scheduled, then the Italians, Yugoslavs, and some of the Russians. The return of the Poles and most of the Russians is delayed.

For the internees, these are days of great excitement and impatience. For us, they are days of great labor and even greater paperwork. Despite the tumult and agitation, the movements are usually trouble free, except for occasional bickering, such as who is to ride in the first convoy, who is to wait for the second. Sometimes people of one country smuggle themselves into a convoy of another country, and the appropriate liaison officers have to eject them—if they are discovered. More often, some are inadvertently left behind. The homeward move is for the healthy and the ambulatory sick. Even so, all citizens of the specific country scheduled for departure are rechecked from a medical and security point of view.

For the French, the first part of the journey is by truck, with each vehicle holding thirty people and some luggage. At the appointed time, thousands of crying and laughing Frenchmen line up with unaccustomed obedience and march to their trucks to the cheers of the noisy spectators; some need to be assisted by their countrymen. As the dust rises behind the disappearing trucks, we see tears in the eyes of those who must still wait.

The tears dry quickly. The crowd disperses. It is time to plan for tomorrow.

Now living in the new satellite camp are about 3,000 Russians, hundreds of Italians, Albanians, and Hungarians, and a sprinkling of others. By arrangement, the Russians have cooked for everyone living there. But today, they announce that they will cook only for their own people. This is very awkward because there is only one kitchen in this area.

Rumor has it that their action is a reprisal, that yesterday their request for special quarters for their officers was rejected and now they are retaliating. If so, it is another annoying example of a food stoppage threat being used to obtain special privileges. But annoyance is not a constructive reaction; it will not fill empty stomachs.

After lengthy, restrained negotiations, their spokesman, a towering, irascible man from Kaunas, Lithuania, again agrees to permit his people to cook for all the residents of the new complex. I am told that there was no deal consummated, that the major consideration was administrative—the smooth operation of the kitchen. Now the food requisitions are signed, but almost immediately a barrage of complaints arrives, unfavorable allegations about the food, particularly the potatoes. I do not wish the agreement to founder in a sea of putrid potatoes, so I rush to the cold cellar where I find the potatoes to be in sound condition. But to no avail. A few hours later, the Russians have changed their position again: they will cook only for themselves, and this is final and irrevocable, says their leader. If so, about two thousand non-Russians will have nothing to eat tomorrow.

I report the new development to Rosenbloom. Fortunately, he has minutes of a meeting with a Russian general that say that his countrymen will be responsible for the operation of the kitchen. Rosenbloom handles the situation smoothly. The agreement is ratified for the third time, which makes it binding according to *Alice in Wonderland*—"What I tell you three times is true." Late that afternoon, the food rations are on their way to the new camp.

Almost immediately, another crisis erupts.

The French return, in a somber mood. Their air transport has been called off, their departure postponed. Perhaps it will be on again tomorrow. In the meantime, we are to feed and house them. We cannot return them to the buildings they occupied last night, because, as soon as they left, word had filtered down to us to move the Yugoslavs into these better quarters. Simultaneously, Poles, and some Russians living near the desirable properties reached the same conclusion and decided to move into them. These decisions, made independently of Army orders or IPC recommendations, indicated that many of the inmates were now able to think for themselves. The result of these two migrations into the empty barracks was considerable damage to the barracks and to many heads before order was restored.

So, where should the French go? To the new complex? Where will they eat? When this is discussed with the Russian leader, his reply is not unexpected: his agreement is to cook for those residents who are living there at this moment. Not for a single other person. The thousands of French and any others can take a flying leap into the Seine, as far as he is concerned. A short discussion is then held with the disconsolate French. Would they cook for themselves? Yes. But not for a small number of Spaniards and Poles returning with them.

I remember a young couple and their baby daughter, who, in those distant civilian days, lived in a tiny apartment, sharing one bedroom with their child while the other bedroom was occupied by the two mothers-in-law. My friend said that the bedroom situation was harmonious, but the three women of the house required separate kitchens.

After further discussion of the French quarters, an order is given to oust the Poles, Yugoslavs, and a few Russians, and move the French back to where they had been, a decision accepted with bad grace by all concerned. There is no satisfactory solution to the problem, but this way, at least, it is easier to establish culinary tranquility.

Edmond Michelet, the leader of the French, is heartbroken at the failure of the air transport. A tall, square-faced man, usually intense despite his poor health, he spends the remainder of the day grumbling. It has been years since he has seen his wife and seven children. Such intelligence comes to me from an unusually unreliable source, one of his enemies, who suggests that Michelet was elected chief of the French contingent not because of his able leadership or his talent at dynamiting German trains during the occupation, but because of the number of his progeny, considered a patriotic achievement.

The next day the cheering is subdued as Michelet leads his people out of the camp. This time they do not return.

The Russians are not quite as content as I thought they were; they are still simmering about cooking for others. We try to make them happy; we even acquiesce to a special request they submit for extra eggs and butter for a sick Russian general. Still, we wonder whether they did complain about the premature move into the new quarters, or about minor things like the group kitchen.

It may be that Rosenbloom's resourcefulness in handling angry hordes of inmates has reduced the number of complaints. Recently he has developed a new technique—he takes extensive notes. Evidently the power of watching the pen write is greater than the power of the pen, at least in our efforts at international mediation.

Fortunately for Howcroft's sanity—and mine—a special Army unit appeared on May 21 to take over the procurement and distribution of food. Now, after five days of study, the new team of twenty men takes over. Operating on the quartermaster system, it is headed by a major, and has two captains, several lieutenants, and many enlisted men. From now on I will only check diet lists for balance and quantity.

We completed our duties yesterday after finding a welder to fix a broken kettle and finishing a report on our food activities —a long report with charts and tables. Last night I dropped it into the camp surgeon's office and found him still at work. He poured us some bourbon, and we chatted for a while. I realized that in the daytime he is an indefatigable, bristling bear of a man, all business, but off duty he is an interesting, observant gentleman. Amazing metamorphosis.

From the office of the camp commander I receive a copy of a large sheet of paper, with the contemplated administrative structure of the camp in the weeks to come on one side and the projected personnel requirements on the other. Army services are recorded in small rectangles: twenty-three are labeled and placed directly under the box of the camp CO. Whoever drew this chart was uncertain of the position of our DP team and finally placed it in a separate box to the left of the CO.

The projection calls for 54 officers and 591 enlisted men to remain, and for three hospitals with 4,000 beds to be kept in operation. German POWs will be used for labor needs—750 men and 15 officers. Medical needs will be taken care of by other Germans—120 doctors, 400 male nurses, and 400 female nurses.

Sunday, May 27. Church services. Some of the German inmates are marching into town to attend them.

The work continues in the camp. The Italians depart, but after they have gone small groups begin to appear. At least 135 have missed the trucks, and they are unhappy, but less so than the sick Italians in the hospitals who loudly voice their grievances: the other Italians should not have left without them, the food and medicines they receive are inferior to those given patients of other nationalities, and so on. In the past when I had to listen to these complaints I reacted with provincial, self-righteous indignation: we are giving these people the best of medical care and they respond by bellyaching about everything when, instead, they should be expressing their gratitude. But now, after a few weeks in the camp, I am beginning to think that distrust and hostility are part of their sickness—a result of camp life.

A major catastrophe. One of our two remaining sedans disappears after the CO leaves it parked on a street in Dachau. He is left with the keys. We desperately need more vehicles.

A minor personal victory: the fountain pen about which I worried several months ago has unexpectedly stopped leaking, a change of life I attribute to the customary causes—the altitude or lack of altitude. I never did drill a hole in its cap. Now the pen writes beautifully and is the envy of the inmates. With bulging, wondering eyes, they watch me sign my name, ask if they can try it, and then write carefully, gingerly, a few words with the great American instrument and exclaim, "*Prima!*"

29

THE TOWNSPEOPLE

Dr. Kuci once said it was no coincidence that Hitler committed suicide on April 30. He believed that the act inevitably followed the liberation of the camp the day before, just as the opening of the camp twelve years earlier had immediately followed Hitler's assumption of power. One could not exist without the other. The camp was the symbol of the dictator's philosophy. Kuci, as well as many of the inmates, considered "Hitler" and "Dachau" synonymous.

The purpose of the camp was to deter anyone from opposing the Fuehrer, hence news of the punishments and deaths in the camp was deliberately spread throughout Germany: the fate of those who even thought of resisting the Nazis. Have no illusions about the residents of the town of Dachau, said Kuci; they knew about the camp's activities. Malczewski agrees.

Many inmates talk about the townspeople. Some say they were sympathetic to the prisoners, that they offered food to them but the SS guards were hostile. However, in recent months this attitude changed to some extent—the guards sometimes permitted the prisoners to accept gifts from the residents. We are glad to hear about these offerings because everyone in the camp has hardened in his attitude toward the Germans. The evidence of Nazi cruelties is so tangible and the causes so unfathomable that we seem to have no alternative but to react emotionally with condemnation of all things German. Perhaps this is unfair, but we are soldiers, men of action, not philosophers, and it will be a time before sufficient detachment and perspective develop so that we can distinguish between Nazis and Germans.

We wonder about the people in town, living so close to the ovens. What do they have to say? We do not know; our few relations with them continue to be nonfraternizing, businesslike.

However, members of a Press World Bureau Section of 7th Army have been interviewing German civilians, and have published their material in *Dachau*, a G-2 publication. The investigators believe they have identified three distinct civilian groups.

Within the first group were people who found it profitable to associate with the SS. They admitted that they had occasionally seen prisoners passing through the town under guard and had noted brutal treatment of townspeople by the SS guards. They usually stated that the Nazis had lied to them about everything. And they seem surprised to learn of the large number of deaths in the camp. They denied seeing the boxcars pass through the town, jammed with starved and dying people. The transports passed through at night, they said; the doors to the cars were sealed. They presumed that the cars were filled with loot from the occupied countries.

A second group consisted of people who claimed to be anti-Nazi, whose attitude was expressed by the question, "What could we do?" They resented the SS men because they misbehaved toward the civilian population and prevented them from helping the prisoners. These people were too terrified to say or do anything; they were frightened by the horrible things going on in the camp; they were afraid to watch the arriving transports.

The investigators decided that the most outspoken anti-Nazis were those whose income did not depend on contact with the SS.

A third group was limited to a few people who had protested for many years, who believed that most of their neighbors had profited from "the blood of innocent human beings" by doing business with the SS. They had seen the transports rolling through the streets, their gruesome cargoes evident. One person described the increase in the number of boxcars entering the camp. After 1938, they arrived by the thousands: the Jews, then the French, their bodies decaying, and later the Poles: when the car doors opened, those still alive scrambled out and "ate grass and drank out of puddles."

One of the men in this group, a person who had defied the Nazis, refused to join with them, and survived, said that the German people were cowards and had only themselves to blame. "They didn't want to risk anything, and they lost everything, and that is the way it is through Germany," he said. Another man with the same convictions opposed the Nazis, but, as the years passed, secluded himself for fear he might talk too freely.

The investigators were aware of the problem faced by the residents of Dachau. "Before judging the city," they said, "remember the fearsome shadow that hangs over everyone in a state in which crime has been incorporated and called the government."

It is refreshing to hear stories of heroism in behalf of the Jews. These are related by the surviving Jews themselves, particularly those from France, Belgium, Holland, Italy, and Norway. They were hidden in private homes, Catholic schools, barns, and even ships, despite the penalty for helping a Jew—hanging. We hear that the Nazi occupation forces in Denmark were able to round up very few Jews.

It was rare for the Jews who came from the eastern occupied countries to tell such stories; apparently, the tradition of anti-Semitism had prevented many Jews from being saved. Despite this prevalent attitude, some of the Jewish inmates told about efforts made by individuals on their behalf, or for people they knew. Two Jews from Romania were hidden by their neighbors for one year, until they were all caught and sent to the camp. A Polish storekeeper was executed for feeding Jewish children. There were many tales of brave, compassionate Poles, who were deported or shot because of their heroic actions.

In Poland, the people were shocked by the slaughter. They began to understand that racism was a contagious disease, and that they, too, were to be enslaved or exterminated. A major effort to help the Jews was made by the Polish resistance forces.

But it came too late.

Unfortunately, racism dies hard—if at all. It is not consumed in the flames generated by its own senseless passions.

When conditions permitted, the prisoners in the camp tried to save each other. In his account, *The Last Days of Dachau*, Kuci tells about one such incident involving the survivors of the Buchenwald convoy:

> . . . . The scenes that afternoon were the most macabre that the human imagination [could ever conceive]. Skeletons [lying] on the ground and longing for help. . . . Never

had we seen such a spectacle! Two cases were the most pitiable: a young lad of 15 years had a deep wound in his right shoulder, and an old man with a . . . hole in his head from which his brains could be seen. They were beaten on the way. . . . The first and only help we could give was some hundreds of liters of soup that we stole from the kitchen with the help of the Poles who were working there.

There were other stories of assistance given the Jewish prisoners, related not as evidence of heroism but as everyday occurrences—when they were feasible. The inmates did not consider such acts unusual; they were part of their ordinary life. At the third IPC meeting, devoted almost entirely to a discussion of the inmates' questionnaires, an incident of this sort was mentioned casually.

Captain Agather had explained that the forms were to be signed by the inmates. A question arose:

> PARRA (the Spanish representative on the IPC): Two of my countrymen are Jews who have changed their names during their arrest. One of them called himself Alexander, being really named Isaak.
>
> CAPTAIN AGATHER: The proper name should be mentioned. In such case, Isaak. The name adopted for prison purposes should be mentioned in brackets. . . .

VACATION

An Army dietician arrives on May 28, and I am so overjoyed to be relieved of food planning that I work with her until 9:00 P.M. on menus and large-scale recipes. I see that she is more flexible than I was, and more generous in the use of milk and eggs, but this is only possible because, by this time, the supplies have increased. There are now one million frozen eggs under guard—enough for forty days—and large quantities of frozen peas, asparagus, cauliflower, carrots, and beans.

One of my remaining jobs is to make certain that each kitchen receives its fair share of the food. Another is to persuade the people to eat what we give them. The complaints these days are different from those we used to receive: I am told that the meals are monotonous, and that certain items are unpalatable, particularly the spinach. Furthermore, in the DP-operated inner compound hospital, I find that many patients are not receiving an adequate diet because one of their doctors, a Romanian, is opposed to meat and vegetables. I hear that I have hurt his feelings by asking him, "*Wo sind die Proteine?*" I wonder if I will hear from Bucharest about this.

When I talk further with the Romanian, I discover some of his unusual views. He dispenses a large variety of herbs for medicinal purposes, and he diagnoses his patients' disorders solely from a study of their eyes. He divides each eye into four quadrants, and after looking at each segment carefully, he claims that he can tell if the patient has diabetes, pneumonia, or other illness solely on the basis of special configurations. If I had met this doctor in civilian life, I would have recommended that his credentials be investigated, but here no one has credentials.

So I give my opinion to higher Army authorities—who are also meat-and-vegetable advocates—and they promise to look into the matter.

On May 30 I visit the hospital again, literally to see what is cooking. Again I find many patients who are not receiving a high-protein diet. Their meals continue to be unbalanced: they receive cereal three times a day, supplemented with black bread and milk. (While I am there, the doctor lodges a complaint with me: his patients have to eat the coarse black bread because someone hijacked the white bread!)

Again I consult with the permanent camp officials, and now our dietician thinks she can solve the problem. She goes to work, and the next day her concoction, a soup-like mixture containing all necessary nutrients, is served to the patients and to the residents of the living quarters and is well received.

When I make rounds, I notice that the patients seem to look better. In the quarters, people are sitting contentedly in the sun. There is evidence of much industry, with electricians, carpenters, and tailors whistling occasionally as they work. Tempers seem equable. The Russians greet me as *Tovarich*. Everywhere I have to taste the soup de jour, and it is good. The dominant flavor comes from the thousands of onions that our dietician has cleverly used to conceal the proteins from the Romanian doctor.

Garlic is also popular. Our records show that in twenty days we have used about sixty pounds. Some of the people believe it has curative powers.

As I wander through the camp I note that the plans previously made to bring in German POWs as camp laborers are operative. They are beginning to replace inmate labor forces. Also, many German doctors, nurses, and orderlies have been arriving to help alleviate the medical manpower shortage. Eventually they will take over all patient care and will also operate a long-term tuberculosis hospital.

The daily report for May 30 shows that there are still 1,900 patients with typhus fever in the camp. Patients are still dying, but the death rate is fewer than 20 a day.

Stars and Stripes, the Army newspaper that carries on its front page a recommendation: "PAPER IS SCARCE! Pass this S & S On to Another Soldier Up Front," and a slogan: "Everything for the Front," announces that the last western Europeans have been moved out of the camp. But the reporter who wrote this forgot to look in the hospitals.

Recreational facilities at the two American hospitals are open to the Team, and I have seen two movies, one an exciting bandit-hunt through the jungles of Brazil, and the other a *Dr. Kildare* feature: it is refreshing to see the handsome young intern, Lew Ayres, outsmart the wily, lovable old doctor, Lionel Barrymore. This never happened to me when I was an intern, but then none of my overseers was either old or lovable.

In one of the hospitals I meet two friends, Warren A. Lapp and Ralph Schwartz. We talk briefly, then resume a poker game that started long ago, when we were all interns. They relieve me of forty marks in the next hour. Things are now the way they used to be: my understanding of the game has not improved. Another medical officer, a specialist in grousing, cuts into the game. From him, I learn that this is the first time his hospital has been situated indoors since coming overseas. But he is still unhappy. No one is comfortable. He has to sleep on a cot. The CO is a son of a bitch. There is no place to go for excitement.

Still another officer stationed nearby, whose chief interest is in unleashing his sex drive at every opportunity, has been visiting occasionally. The situation is no longer favorable for him at his present post. Now he appraises the women inmates and nurses, making crude and unkind remarks. Perturbed, Rosenbloom consults with Howcroft and me. We agree that the visitor should be ejected, which Rosenbloom does in his forthright, laconic way. Everyone gives Rosenbloom a vote of thanks.

I spend part of the afternoon of May 31 with a new barber in the camp, an American soldier. It feels good to have a cool, close Army-style haircut. The young Pole who tried to cut my hair earlier is still here. He has become a protégé of the GI. Some day he will be a good barber, I am told.

New regulations arrive reminding us to refrain from careless demeanor and dress, to observe the curfew, and to emphasize military courtesy. Everyone complains about the restrictions now that the war is over. But there is no question which is better—combat conditions or polished shoes and snappy salutes.

Having nothing better to do, I visit with the supply officer of the permanent camp staff, Major Louis A. Nolfo, a tough New Yorker whose job is to inventory all the German goods here.

According to one of his officers, this is an impossible task because there are not enough goddamn filing cards in the world to list the new items being found constantly. Only yesterday, says the major, a warehouse was discovered crammed with hundreds of thousands of prisms, lenses, fine adjustments, telescopic sights, and other kinds of optical equipment. Last week an immense supply of French perfumes was found. There is a building packed with skis and ski equipment, another with uniforms and insignia. The major proudly shows me his files. I note that he is very thorough: one of the cards reads "Automobile, Building 28, without motor."

Later Lieutenant Vandermuhl, an MG officer, visits me. I had met him in Pappenheim late in April. Now he is stationed at Hitler's former headquarters in Berchtesgaden where the only treasures he can find are bottles of wine. He drops in not only to inspect the camp but because rumors of the fabulous warehouses of Dachau have spread throughout the American zone and someone has told him that one building is stuffed with flutes. We consult the major's files, but there is no mention of flutes, fifes, flageolets, recorders, music, or instruments— orchestral, wind, and brass.

Nothing. A great disappointment to the lieutenant.

This morning, June 2, I pass a weird scene. Although I have observed it before, it continues to transmit to me a feeling of uneasiness, as though I were watching explorers in a shadowy land participating in strange and ominous rites.

Not too far from one of the hospitals is a large, barren field, partly grassy, partly burned over. Beyond is an empty swimming pool, crevices in its sides. Nearby is a small olive drab tent marked with red crosses. In front of the tent are several slender metal tables, on each a corpse. Water buckets are on the ground, and three gloved, masked, and aproned laboratory corpsmen regularly pour the tepid contents of the buckets over the bodies as an Army pathologist hurries through his examinations, sweat pouring from his face mask onto his soiled white gown. Near this primitive morgue, with its stinking odors of decomposition and formalin, is a German tank, its black crosses still visible. In the neighboring field are Russians in groups of ten, practicing American-style close-order drill.

The autopsy findings are about as expected: malnutrition and emaciation in all cases, tuberculosis in a third. Patients with typhus fever died from complicating pneumonias and toxemias. A minor surprise was the discovery of unsuspected heart disease in several patients thought to be recovering. Evidence of infections and fractures—including head injuries—was found in many patients.

Tonight Ali Kuci drops in with his Polish secretary, and, for a while, Rosenbloom joins us for a rubber of bridge, Howcroft noisily kibitzing. Leon Malczewski arrives in time for the party. From my secret cache I contribute cans of blue cheese and shrimp, Rosenbloom produces a box of peanut brittle, Howcroft a can of hard candy, and Kuci the champagne.

Suddenly, as in similar previous social situations, the gaiety dies. One of our guests remembers. His hands shake, his pupils widen, his face is ashen—he has returned to the nightmare world where he is reliving an episode of terror or humiliation. In a choked voice he tells the story; he recalls the time of day, the date, the weather. Now our other guests reenter the world of darkness. Accounts of brutality and degradation pour forth: the flogging, hanging, or shooting of spiritless, starved men, the terrible wounds inflicted on the prisoners by the dogs, the search for safety in the herd of silent prisoners.

Kuci's stories are more dramatic. In them, the victims fought for the survival of their personalities.

He tells about an incident that occurred on March 16, 1944. Ten prisoners, two of them women, were selected for execution. "What manner of death would you prefer?" asked the SS captain. Shooting, they said. The men died instantly, but not the women. One staggered to her feet and cried, "Long live Poland!" She received another bullet. The other woman cursed the SS officer. He pistol-whipped her until her skull split in two.

Kuci describes another incident that happened in Augsburg, when 420 Jews were rounded up and taken to the roof of a tall building, where they could admire the towers and steeples of the city's beautiful churches. Each Jew was given a cigarette to smoke, then forced to jump while the SS men laughed. All were killed except one man, who stood up, climbed the stairs again voluntarily, smoked another cigarette, and leaped. . . .

We cannot bear to listen to these appalling stories—

perhaps embellished by Kuci—but it is difficult to stop our friends from telling them. Eventually we turn the conversation from the past to the future, and for Kuci and Malczewski, the frightening shadows disappear—for the moment.

Kuci thinks the war in the Pacific will be over in a few months, but the rest of us believe it will take years of hard fighting to defeat the Japanese. Even Malczewski, a very wise man, holds this opinion. Kuci is very astute. I am not sure of his background because he has told me so many things, but Ferris, a favorite of Kuci's—they are both poets, and talk with each other for hours; I know Ferris has been reading some of his poems to Kuci, who has listened eagerly, and then recited his own, sometimes in Italian—says he has been a former minister of state under King Zog; Kuci has entertained Ferris with accounts of lavish, bacchanalian state banquets lasting as long as eight hours, tales that sound like the *Arabian Nights*.

After we finish the champagne, our visitors leave. I sit down to write my regular evening letter, but the impact of their dreadful stories is so strong that I cannot get beyond the salutation. After brooding for a while, I go outside, walk briskly for thirty minutes, return, and, with difficulty, complete the letter. I do not mention the incidents related by our guests. Writing home helps the memory—but there are some things I would like to forget.

A one-day vacation on Sunday, June 3, with Mr. Pires, who is in great need of a holiday. He has been overworking, but finds so much to do that he hates to leave the camp for even a few hours.

After Corporal Hollis repairs one of the tires, we head south in our BMW six-cylinder convertible and soon reach the Brenner Pass where we are permitted to look at Italy but not to step over the border. I am surprised that the altitude is only 4,511 feet. The drive through the pass is easy, with only a few minor curves, and the road on the Italian side looks just as smooth as the one from Innsbruck.

The town of Brenner is very small. I can see about forty houses near the road, none with visible damage. This is resort country; every house has a sign, *Badezimmer und Essen*. Many of the houses are old and dilapidated, some are old and pretty, a few are modern. Most of them are two-story wooden buildings with attics, a thin balcony circling the upper floor, religious murals painted on their sides. Others have intricate ironwork lattices. Many are painted pink.

The Bavarians are handsomely attired, especially the women, who are attractive in their great white shawls and wide, dark, festooned skirts covered with white or dark blue satin aprons. There are more women than men, the sad situation of all countries at war. I do not think that nonfraternization will last long here.

The men wear short white shirts, knee-length leather breeches, and silver-studded leather suspenders with many buckles. Large white plumes (goatsbeard or eagles' feathers) spring out of their felt hats.

We look up and see the wrinkled Alps covered with pine, spruce, and fir trees, and, above the timberline, deeply cleft gray ridges and glistening snow fields. I think about Hannibal, who marched his great army through a western pass in these mountains. About the other conquerors: the Huns and Goths, and Napoleon, who built roads across some of these mountains. About Hitler, the most cruel tyrant of all time, whose mountain retreat in Berchtesgaden is not far away. About Mussolini, executed by Italian partisans a month ago in Como. Even for a moment, I cannot forget the blood and tears.

A magnificent sight. There is no evidence here of the ravages of war. For hours we look at the hills and peaks, watch the colors change, the running rivulets turn into lustrous rivers and lakes. The brooks are pale jade-green. A world of valleys, ridges, glaciers, and flowers, and man-made ski runs at a low level.

Man-made! The spell cast by nature's wonders is broken as I think of the evil created by man.

I light a cigar. I am now smoking German *Zigarren*, cigars about two-thirds the size of American five-cent ones, but only because it is difficult to obtain American cigarettes; most of the time I have been smoking "Waldorf-Astoria" cigarettes, made in Hamburg from Turkish tobacco.

It is time to return to the camp. Mr. Pires agrees.

On the trip back, I learn a little more about the contributions made to the camp by the American Red Cross. A total of 12,000 parcels was received in May; many of the parcels were sent directly to the patients in the inner compound hospital, where the need was great. The clothing requested from the Red Cross finally arrived on May 26. In the shipment were 500 women's dresses, which were immediately distributed. They had been made by Red Cross sewing groups in America—the first package to be opened had come from South Bend, Indiana. "The day I visited the women's barracks," said the proud Mr. Pires, "the women were attractively clad in bright cotton dresses and the narrow streets were gay with laundry hung on outside lines." Other clothes arrived: socks, pants, underwear. Nevertheless, the situation was still desperate until General Adams decided to use Army sources for essential supplies not otherwise obtainable. For example, he persuaded someone in the quartermaster department to contribute 7,000 suits of underwear to the inmates. The general has also worked closely with the Red Cross organizations and has been a source of continuing encouragement to Harry Pires.

Pires has been unable to establish a small clothing factory in the camp, but he has not given up. He is still trying to find competent workmen; the inmates who had labored under the SS were exhausted. (In June, his effort succeeds. German workers are recruited, supervised by Poles.[1])

Waiting for me at the camp is another package postmarked April 28, Chicago, overflowing with chocolates, cheeses, crackers, honey, a genuine Cuban cigar, an old *New Yorker*, and a book by Sumner Welles. For security reasons, I bury the chocolates in my footlocker, where they join other selected foods earmarked for festive occasions or periods of deprivation. Much as I enjoy the attractively packaged gifts my wife sends, I know that the institutional meals she receives in Chicago must be dull, and furthermore, food for civilians is rationed. I intend to ask her not to send me any more packages. Here we get more than we need, even though it may be unpalatable. We average 3,300 calories a day, mostly from C rations.

In her last letter, Carol wrote that the war tax on the new purse she bought was higher than expected: $2.31. This convinces me to try to have a purse made for her by one of the Poles, a gifted craftsman who has been working with some of the beautiful blue leather that fills one of the warehouses. If he will do this, the handbag will be an interesting gift to commemorate our fourth wedding anniversary.

After supper, I sit quietly in my room and smoke my gift cigar (now a little stale). Then it is letter-writing time. I have a supply of new writing paper. Each sheet has a thin red border. On the left is printed *Waffen-SS, Konzentrationslager Dachau, Kommandantur;* on the right, *Dachau;* and in the middle, *Schnellbrief.*

What happened today? Sergeant Aricer liberated a small quantity of powdered milk, which he served at supper. It tasted better than we thought it would. Everyone congratulated him on his new refreshing beverage.

Carol, I write, thank you for the fine cigar. Its good, heavy smoke is floating out of the window into the darkness. I can see lighted houses for miles, rivaling the stars in the skies, an unusual sight after a year of blackouts. A sign of peace.

Then I describe the trip to the Brenner Pass, the majesty of the Alps.

My mind wanders. I think about tyrants, and the evils created by man.

And the number of people who have died in this camp.

Everyone would like to know this figure, but it is difficult to obtain accurate data about what happened here. Particularly deaths, because the Nazis deliberately camouflaged or destroyed their records, or kept none. An inmate says that in the official prison register—no longer in existence—the prisoners' names were written in pencil. The inmates try to be helpful; they describe what they have seen, but their memories are personal, and often unreliable. Their estimates are uncertain and contradictory; their guesses as to the number of deaths range from fifty thousand to as much as hundreds of thousands.

Apparently the most reliable information is for the beginning of this year, obtained by the 7th Army CIC Detachment: 14,700 deaths occurring during the first quarter, a reasonable figure when compared to the present daily death rate.

The SS attributed these deaths to "natural" causes. A prisoner who was shot or beaten to death, or died as the result of some other violent means, was reported as having died from a "natural" cause such as a "heart attack." However, it is likely that most of the deaths occurring from January through April 1945 were the result of sickness and starvation.

The published report of the Detachment said that 16,717 German prisoners from foreign countries were executed between 1940 and 1945, and that during five months in 1944 a total of 29,138 Jews were brought to Dachau from other concentration camps and executed.

In its report is an estimate that 229,000 prisoners had been processed at Dachau since its inception in 1933; this included about 7,000 who arrived during the last three weeks of April.[2] However, Rosenbloom says that the camp registrar thinks there were about 202,000.

How could anyone be sure? Nobody knows the number of prisoners who died in death marches leaving the camp. A large number of Soviet POWs were killed in the shooting range, but no one even tries to estimate the size of this group.

Despite the extent of the present investigation, it seems likely that the true figures will never be known.

A diary was found in the camp, the *Diary of E. K.* Portions of it followed the CIC report. An entry dated December 8, 1942 said that about ten prisoners died each day. The writer's guess was that one-third of the detentees would die during the year. (The population of the camp that year must have been about 10,000.)

However, E. K. believed that Dachau was a much healthier prison than others, such as the one at Mauthesen. "In spite of everything," he wrote, "Dachau is a golden camp!"[3]

An incredible statement, which I did not understand for many years, until I discovered that in official SS circles, Dachau was designated as a Grade Ia concentration camp for prisoners "in need of consideration." Elderly persons who could not work were to be assigned to the herb garden. The camp was also for "prisoners with good records who are definitely capable of improving," and for "special cases and solitary confinement."

Mauthausen, the camp that the prisoners of Dachau feared most, was a Grade III camp for "those who cannot be reeducated."

A Grade II camp was "for those likely to benefit from education and reform." Auschwitz, where millions died and extermination was a science, was in this category.[4]

DEPARTURE

Sergeant Louis Thompson of Crookston, Minnesota replaces Sergeant Morivant as the operations NCO; Morivant is ordered back to Division. The new arrival is distinguished by his good habits: he neither smokes nor swears. Corporal Norman Cady of Bakersfield, California reports for service as a driver; he has been sent to us from a disbanded DP team, arriving with the news that we are one of the more permanent teams because of our fine record. With our customary cynicism, we interpret this to mean that we will probably be recalled tomorrow.

Two hours later Rosenbloom receives orders to report back to the 63rd Division for reassignment!

HQ is stirring and we speculate on what may happen. Obviously, combat DP teams are no longer needed; civilian United Nations Relief and Rehabilitation Administration units are well qualified for most jobs, except perhaps for a few special installations like the one here. If we are shipped out, will we be returned to our old outfits? Or sent to new ones? Or redeployed to the Pacific theater where the fighting against the Japanese continues unabated? Or assigned to occupation duty in Germany? There is unanimity on the need for occupying Germany: everyone here agrees that it should be policed for a long time. Everyone also agrees that it would be very nice if someone else did the occupying.

Another possibility is that we might be sent home!

And discharged!

We prefer to dwell on this delightful contingency.

Now, to give us something concrete to discuss and to improve our arithmetic, the Army announces that 400,000 men are going home, to be selected on a point system. Points will be awarded to each soldier—one for each month of service, six for overseas duty, five for each battle campaign, and others for children and decorations. Almost immediately an odious officer I know cables his wife to adopt two children.

Rosenbloom packs rapidly—orders still carry a note of urgency. Handshaking, quiet farewells, and he is gone.

Some of the Army medical officers on the "permanent" camp staff are also leaving, including my poker-playing companions, which means I will have more money available. A young infantry officer from New York, Lieutenant Edwin Smolen, arrives to replace Rosenbloom, but because he has not previously worked with DPs, I am appointed to be acting head of internal administration. And special orders arrive for me, announcing my promotion. I am now a captain. (This has nothing to do with my temporary assumption of command.) I am happy to receive this, for it is overdue, although nobody's fault because I have been placed on temporary duty several times, once for six months, and such assignments interfere with seniority. Major Green finds a set of captain's bars for me from one of the officers who has just received his majority; they are not very shiny, but I like them. Then the telephone begins to ring—friends asking for Captain Smith, social calls to accustom me to being addressed properly.

Communiqué No. 32, dated June 6, from the Central Press Bureau takes full note of these changes.

> A full meeting of the IPC was held this morning. First Lieutenant Charles Rosenbloom, camp commanding officer . . . is going away. . . . [He] came here on the first days of our liberation. The situation he found was tragic . . . the IPC was in difficult [straits because it had not] yet established contact with American authorities. Great problems needed solving. This work was immediately taken in hand by Mr. Charles Rosenbloom and he came through with great success.
>
> Charles has a great capacity of recognizing the people and a greater psychological ability of penetrating into the masses. We collaborated with him on a spirit of friendship and brotherhood. We found him everywhere and at all times. Night and day this son of the noble and generous country of the United States was ready to help us. . . . We

regret his departure. It seems that we have known him for many years. . . . But other work calls him and he must leave. We all wish him a happy journey. . . .

Captain Smith and Lieutenant Smolen have already taken over his work. They were present at the IPC meeting and introduced. We know well Captain Smith. He is from the "old stuff." . . .

The German Committee calls witnesses to give evidence against . . . to the Minister of Justice, dungeon house, or to the German Committee, barracks No. 241.

I have mingled emotions about being called "old stuff," but I begin to feel old soon after I take over the new job. Rosenbloom had been scurrying around the camp from dawn to midnight, but I knew nothing of the numerous details that kept him busy. Not even when I take over his plush office, sit behind his massive desk, admire the many easy chairs and small tables and the push buttons communicating with four surrounding rooms where interpreters, secretaries, and office assistants are deployed. I press all the buttons and am overjoyed to find that two of them light up *Eintritt Verboten* signs; others are for an interphone system: I can listen to everyone's conversation.

The soft life, I think. So this is what Rosenbloom has been doing while I have been working myself to death, saving lives. But the thought quickly fades as an avalanche of requests, memoranda, orders, appointments, meeting notices, and assorted administrative-looking papers pour onto the desk.

Requests for passes that have already been denied, but the first rejection had been appealed. A Pole wants to go to Munich to visit his dentist; he asks for a five-day leave. Another for sixty Russians to picnic near the river. An Albanian wants a car to visit a dying aunt. A Yugoslav wants to visit his wife for a week.

Some of the notices are about the utilization of the efficient, hard-working German POWs now in the camp. Their housing is in the inner compound, where they are building a barbed wire fence around their quarters.

Barbed wire within barbed wire.

There is a shortage of transportation. This information arrives with an order to cancel the planned departure of some Russians to the new satellite camp, scheduled for this afternoon. Now there are other offices to notify, in turn. Messages are delivered relating to the evacuation of 750 more Poles to the *Kaserne:* they are supposed to leave tomorrow at 1:00 P.M., and their showers, disinfection, and medical examinations must be arranged and coordinated with their personnel and ours. Medical and census forms must be duplicated. Similar details will be required for the repatriation of the Yugoslavs on June 8 at the unspeakable hour of 5:00 A.M. This movement has already been scheduled twice but cancelled both times.

Other communications concern plans for the liquidation of the inmates' canteen, now unnecessary, and for meetings of the IPC and its subcommittees. Then conferences with the minister of justice and the police chief.

There is also a major Team problem. We now have only four vehicles; two are not authorized. One is a truck in its death throes. I need a car badly and have my eye on a cream-colored convertible, which I will try to promote. If this is possible, I plan to have large red crosses painted on each door.

Lieutenant Smolen has been sitting and listening to everything. I guess it will take him a while to learn this business. He seems worried about the location of this office—it is next door to General Adams. I agree that this is worrisome. I have not yet met the general, which I consider prudent.

I begin to long for the simple days when I was taking care of food and water.

This thought passes through my mind the following day when the 750 Poles appear at the collecting point, ready to be driven to the new satellite camp. Two hundred of them are invalids, but many seem exceedingly healthy as they hoist large loads onto the trucks. An inspection of their property reveals chairs, tables, beds, mimeograph machines, bags of cement—anything portable. We confiscate some of the items that are clearly designated as belonging to the United States Army. This annoys some of the Poles, who expected us to be more generous.

The entire move has been unpleasant because we have had to coax some of the Poles to leave. Most of them depart in a sullen mood. We are angry, and troubled by our own impatience, which led to a show of force.

It is the morning of June 8. The first thousand of 3,200 Yugoslavs are supposed to be ready to go home. Yesterday, plans were completed, watches synchronized, medical and security details arranged, and food packed into vehicles for the one-day trip. (Some of the food has been provided by the Red Cross.) Repeated roll calls were made during the day: at 9:00 A.M. 978 responded, three hours later 860, in the afternoon 800, and in the evening 920.

Now, at 5:00 A.M., the time scheduled for departure, there are 300 more Yugoslavs present than provided for. We find out that they are not camp inhabitants, but Yugoslavs who have been living near Dachau and want to go home with the others. The Yugoslav leader, a very tall, stooped man, knows these people and agrees to take them. After consultation it is decided to include them. In order to do this, we have to put about 38 people into each truck, instead of 30. They know that people of other countries have departed with only 30 in each truck, so someone lodges a complaint of discrimination.

But there is no alternative. If they want to leave now they will have to tolerate the overloaded vehicles. They decide to go. Their route is from Dachau to the Brenner Pass and into their own country. I hope the trucks can make it.

A dawn run is planned for another thousand Yugoslavs for June 9. This move will include the personal property of all the Yugoslavs, including the effects of those who have died in the camp. These are now in paper sacks, under guard by a detail of Yugoslav police. It is estimated that 700 sacks could be placed on one truck and four additional trucks would be needed for all the baggage; anything left over could be put with the packages. Everything is set; the preparations are completed; clean clothes are distributed.

At the last minute, a request arrives for an extra truck, not because it is needed, but because it is a very special three-ton Lancia of sentimental value. The unique nature of the truck was first recognized several weeks ago by one of the Yugoslav inmates who accidentally noted the star of Tito on the bottom of the engine. Later, several others identified it as one they had stolen from the Italians in 1941 or 1942 and had used to transport ammunition and evacuate the wounded during their guerrilla war against the occupying Italians and Germans. History had been made by this vehicle—the inmates could not bear to see the truck remain on German soil.

Because of my innate skepticism, I automatically reject this request, but the leader appeals to a higher echelon and permission is granted for the release of the Lancia.

The June 9 move begins at 3:45 A.M. The first truck serves as a jail for fourteen prisoners, who are escorted to the truck from the dungeon by armed guards. Long lines of men carrying bundles move slowly, flickering shadows, an eerie procession as the darkness begins to fade, a strange moment.

A last-minute count shows only 860 people; 1,000 were scheduled. After a rapid search for Army property, the vehicles move out—no bands playing at this hour—but there are Yugoslav and American flags on the trucks, and banners reading "Hurrah for the Allies: America, Russia, England," and "Hurrah for the Soviet Union," and "Long Live Tito."

I circle the debris, past the empty carts and wheelbarrows, and drive over to something that looks like a pile of rags: it twitches. Here is a weeping Polish boy. Disguised as a sack, this 14-year-old had tried to stow away with the Yugoslavs, but was discovered and cast overboard. He even has a star of Tito embroidered on his jacket. I bring the unhappy boy to our quarters for breakfast, after which he will be sent back to his own people.

What happened to the missing 140 Yugoslavs? I inspect the barracks and discover that they are still there, in bed: they had suddenly become acutely ill last night.

Obviously some sort of mysterious Royalist epidemic disease.

In my opinion the Yugoslav move was efficient and trouble free, but Colonel Joyce does not agree. He scolds me for not counting the sacks of "personal" property as they were loaded onto the trucks. Now I realize that I will never be a good administrator. Little things are important. At 4:00 A.M. the thought of counting the bags never occurred to me.

Loss of American property is becoming serious, and an order is circulated that nothing may be removed from the camp without authorization. Shortly afterward, the efficient Farnik, manager of the food warehouse, comes to see me. Although a Pole, he has been granted permission to leave with the Czechs who are still in the camp, after which he will find his own way home.

Has his work been good? he inquires. It is excellent, and I

dictate a letter attesting to his industry and honesty, and to his contributions to the camp. Can I do him a slight favor? he asks hesitantly. There is something he would like to take back to Warsaw.

Was he aware of the general's order? I ask.

Of course he was, but, perhaps, because we are close friends, I might be able to help him. Besides, as a farewell present, he has brought me a box of strawberries, pretty, red, delicious berries, um, very tasty, I agree. I'll be glad to help him, if I can, I reply to the strawberries.

What he wants is to take home an urn filled with the ashes of some of the dead Poles.

I am touched. I thought he might ask for a railroad car, an Army tank, or one of the buildings. The request moves up the ladder and, of course, is granted.

Perhaps we are all unstable now: tears come more easily than in the early days. Some time ago the mainspring of my wristwatch became unsprung. I borrowed a pocket watch from one of our men, giving him my treasured Nazi hunting knife as security, and turned my watch over to a bald little Pole reputed to be a good watchmaker. Today he returns the watch and then shows us a picture of his tiny shop in Warsaw. Nobody asks questions because we know what happened there. I pass the picture around and there is moistness in everyone's eyes—except the Pole's. He seems devoid of emotion.

Our 12-year-old Jewish office boy, Arnold Unger, weeps copiously. He too is Polish, no family left, no place to go. It has been one of the few pleasures here to watch his starved face fill out, his hair begin to glisten, his smile return, his eyes become bright with gladness and joy. He would do anything for us, for all Americans.

These were the deadly enemies of the Third Reich: the Polish Jews.

I strap on my rejuvenated wristwatch and return the borrowed one, and reclaim my knife.

The enlisted men have not been paid for months. I am the only member of the Team who has been reimbursed—I took care of this during the trip to Division HQ last month. As a consequence, I have spent $30 for the men at a nearby PX for extra rations and personal necessities. This is one of the morale-boosting responsibilities of an officer.

Even more important than being paid is receiving mail. Everyone in the unit has complained bitterly about the poor service. Division HQ, also interested in the state of our morale, has initiated a regular courier service for us. Now mail from home arrives rapidly.

One of my letters contains a clipping from a Chicago newspaper, which says that 75 percent of the students in a classroom at Northwestern University believed that the stories from the Dachau and Buchenwald concentration camps were propaganda. I read the story aloud and it is greeted with the derision it deserves. Private Eastman, about the same age as the undergraduates, says that the students should be flown here right now. He would be glad to show them around.

Arriving with the letter is another package from my favorite package sender. In it is Carl Sandburg's *The American Songbag*. After supper in our quarters, Howcroft, Sergeant Thompson, and I pick out some of the songs. An *Apologia* at the beginning of the book says that it is intended "for sinners, and for lovers of humanity. . . ." An appropriate environment—Sandburg would undoubtedly be pleased to know that his book circulated through the Team and was well received.

Ali Kuci drops in and eagerly studies the book; some of the tunes remind him of Albanian melodies. He has read Sandburg's poems, and approves of his style.

The evening is not over. Our last guest is Major Brown, who complains for ninety minutes about the camp surgeon. He is a martinet, a workhorse, a slave driver. In thirty months he has never spoken favorably of anyone. (Such complaints are standard. In the Marine Corps it is said that "a good soldier beefs all the time.")

Both the camp surgeon and Major Brown were in a general hospital before coming here. That unit, now located fifty miles away, is the site of a celebration tonight to commemorate their thirteenth month overseas. The colonel won't permit any of their former staff who are stationed here to return for the festivities.

The Old Man is strictly business, a member of the duty-comes-first school, and that is the way it is. Major Brown knows this and so do I; both of us share this view despite the major's wine-supported lamentations.

Our last Sunday at Dachau. A tall German civilian is sent to my office. Can we help? he asks. He has been imprisoned at five concentration camps since 1933 for anti-Nazi activities. Somehow he has survived, and, after waiting all these years, he was married on June 6 and has decided to live in the city of Dachau. Was there a possibility that he could requisition blankets, pots, pans, and other household wares? He had been afraid to be married in the past because he believed that his chances of remaining alive were poor. His resources are depleted; he can use some assistance. A security check confirms his story, and his wedding present is from the warehouses of Dachau with the blessings of the United States Army.

An unusual story. All of us hope that there are more people like him in Germany.

The remainder of the day is without incident, but at 11:00 P.M. Sergeant Thompson wakes me, excitedly saying that fifty Russians are marching through the streets with bayonets fixed, shouting. He tried to find out what had happened, but it is not very clear. He thinks that one of their men has been murdered, and the marchers are out for vengeance. They are searching for the killer, an SS man supposedly disguised in an American Army uniform. (Such deceptions were known to have happened during the war, particularly during the Ardennes offensive.)

Howcroft digs out his P-38, Thompson his carbine, I find my Mauser, and we head toward the security office, although we agree that we would probably be safer if we hid in a closet. Later the security officers tell us that by the time they reached the scene only three intoxicated Russians could be found and these were easily persuaded to go back to bed.

Nobody had been murdered.

Monday morning, June 11. On my desk is the population report of June 9, which shows 12,166 inmates remaining. Of these, 4,146 are still in the hospitals and 115 in the bunker. During the twenty-four hours covered by the report, 6 inmates disappeared, 92 who had fled earlier returned, and 11 died. The Russians constitute 4,071 of the total number, the Poles 3,303, and the Yugoslavs 1,649. There are small numbers from twenty-four other countries, and a handful of stateless individuals.

Other figures show that 9,435 patients were admitted to all of the Dachau hospitals between May 9 and June 9. Of these, 1,598 died (17.1 percent). Those with typhus fever accounted for about a third of the admissions—3,497, but only for a fifth of the deaths—320.

The enormousness of the operation is suddenly too staggering to contemplate.

One item of business pertains to the repatriation of the remaining Yugoslavs. The preparations for this move will begin at 4:00 P.M., with their departure set for the following 3:30 A.M. My calendar shows three conferences with members of the IPC, Mr. Ipswichi, chief of guards, and Mr. Dortheimer, minister of justice; they are to begin in an hour.

Then orders arrive. Everyone on the Team is to leave the next day: we are through at Dachau. This means that a detailed report about our activities must be written today. It is begun. Captain Deal, my successor, takes over the office. I turn over all the unfinished business to him, brief him on everything I can think of, attempt to clean up the desk, a hopeless job, and leave him in great confusion.

I visit the hospitals for the last time. It has been sad to watch the critically ill patients die, but it has been an exciting experience to observe the steady physical and mental improvement of most of the patients. As I talk with some of them, I realize that their conversations are different from what they were six weeks ago. Then they could talk only about food. Now they mention their families, their homes, their plans for the future.

In the X-ray department of one of the hospitals I look at the chest films of some of the inmates with tuberculosis—at the immense cavities. How can they still be alive? I wonder.

Because of good care. I am suddenly proud of the superb job performed by the Army Medical Corps.

At our quarters I find a friend waiting—the Polish leatherworker. He has heard the news about our departure, and has rushed over with the handbag I asked him to make. I thank him for his effort and thoughtfulness, and wish him well.

I now have a worthwhile present for Carol, a gratifying thought. As I look at it, the pleasure fades when I remember the stories of the purses made of human skin ordered by SS men for their ladies. Were they fashioned by the same craftsman? I think I will always make this association.

Several other gifts arrive. Drawings—I am never able to trace the artist—of the emotionally drained, half-dead prisoners of Dachau on the back of cheap, lined white paper with the imprint "PARAGON." Two old maps of Germany. My friends on the IPC have not forgotten me. An album filled with photographs of the camp and covered by the blue-white cloth used by the prisoners as uniforms is a present from the Yugoslavian delegation. In it I find an envelope from the Czechoslovaks, pictures of Prague.

I pack the mementos in my footlocker, then set my alarm clock for 3:00 A.M. in order to observe the evacuation of the last of the Yugoslavs—except for those in the hospitals. I don't have to be there, but it might help Captain Deal, who undoubtedly will have many questions. But despite the alarm I sleep until 7:00 A.M. This upsets me but does not prevent me from dozing another five minutes. I rush out to find that the Yugoslavs are gone.

I hope someone counted the sacks.

Seeing us off is Ali Kuci, who again invites me to visit him in Albania, and perhaps I will, although I intend to stay home for a long time after the war ends. Kuci has brought Arnold, the office boy, who would like to come with us even to the far Pacific. Some of our Polish friends, Farnik, Malczewski, and Joe, and our French comrades say goodbye. The Ukrainian and Hungarian women who have worked in our quarters rub their eyes. A few hospital doctors, General Adams, whom I have finally met, Colonel Bolibaugh, Colonel Joyce, Major Brown, and Harry Pires are sorry to see us leave, but envious, I think. Major Brown says that if he does not receive his orders soon he is certain his tic will return.

I have conflicting emotions about leaving. It is strange to think that in the six weeks we have been here I have met people whom I would cherish as lifelong friends under other circumstances. It is unlikely that we will meet again. We will move to other places, work, raise children, age, and forget these awful days when men struggled to be recalled to life. The sadness of departure lies in the bitter foreknowledge of the permanence of separation and the frailty of memory.

I am also happy to be leaving; my burdens have been lifted; I feel like a person fleeing from Hell. But there are several minor regrets: I would have preferred to stay to witness the exodus of the Russians, find out what will happen to the Poles, and watch the hospitals close down after the last patient recovers—or dies.

We circle the inner compound for the last time, salute the waving inmates, then on, past the watchtowers, the crematorium, the improvised morgue, the *Plantage* where vegetables now bask serenely under the hot sun. We cross the railroad tracks—the boxcars are gone. We stop momentarily at the burial grounds.

Then away.

AFTERWORD

Our next assignment took us to a Russian repatriation center in Heidelberg located at the *Grenadier Kaserne,* formerly a German military post. We worked with a French-Belgian United Nations Relief and Rehabilitation Administration team, two French Army doctors, an American Army nurse, and four liaison officers at this shipping and receiving plant for human cargo. Each day we registered, screened, examined, disinfected, and sent home thousands of Soviet citizens in boxcars decorated with pictures of Stalin. By June 22, ten days after our arrival, 20,000 Russians had come and gone, and the *Kaserne* became home for 6,000 Poles who were undecided about where to go or what to do.

One evening, having nothing else to do, Howcroft and I and Mace, our driver, headed for Heidelberg's famous castle in our distinctive Mercedes-Benz convertible, acquired a month before.[1] We roared up a curved steep road, past woodlands, vineyards, gardens, granite columns, and ruined buildings, to a hotel where we found a roomful of GIs—the castle was occupied by an American regiment—sitting on the floor listening to a heavy, gray-haired woman with alert brown eyes and a deeply lined face. She wore a gray skirt, cotton stockings, and low, flat oxfords. She fingered a set of wings pinned to her blue blouse. Gertrude Stein, said one of the soldiers. We sat and listened, engaged by her warmth.

An American major, probably her escort, said, "Of all the people in Europe, I have the most respect for the Germans because they do what we tell them to do."

Miss Stein reacted; her thoughts poured forth, her meaning clear, her voice firm.

"We are flattered by the Germans," she replied. "We should not be deceived by their attitudes of subservience, docility, and rectitude. These are the only bad features of the Germans, who, unfortunately for themselves and the rest of the world, are obedient. When you have a nation of obedient people, that country is bound to do the wrong thing. History proves that a man will come along and take an obedient people into places where they do not want to go. He will make them do things they should not. It is better for people to be skeptical.

"Germans have always believed everything they were told. There was never a revolution in Germany as there was in the United States and France. The Germans must learn to ask questions; they must be taught *disobedience*."

I thought of the German people who had lived to serve the state, convinced that it was supreme, divinely empowered to govern the world. Of their slogans: "Heil Hitler," "Deutschland ueber Alles," and "My Fatherland, Right or Wrong." It was unnecessary for them to think. A Nazi booklet in my office at Dachau simplified decision-making for its readers: "The Fuehrer is always right. Right is what serves the movement and thus Germany, which means the nation."

During the five years of the German occupation of France, Miss Stein was on their wanted list. All this time she lived in a small French village. Hundreds of German soldiers were billeted in the house where she was a guest. Every French person in the town knew who she was, but she was not caught because *no one told the Nazis she was there.* One enemy officer, an Italian, discovered her identity but kept silent. The Gestapo was effective, she said, only when its agents received tips from informers.

She rented rooms in Paris. German law required the registration of all dwellings. Her landlord listed her apartment as a place for "French refugees, empty." It was never inspected.

She recalled another story. Aliens and Jews were required to register. A Jewish woman came to the proper office.

"Can you prove you are Jewish?" the French clerk asked her rudely.

"Why, no," stammered the woman.

"Well, get out of here and don't bother me until you can!"

Miss Stein talked about her French friends, honest and individualistic, people who accepted you as you were.

Then it was time to go.

We fell into weeks of routine. There were many frustrations. The camp was overcrowded; the residents inequitably distributed. It was difficult to maintain elementary standards of cleanliness. Some of the Polish officers tried to avoid working with their countrymen. Often the Poles were moody, unaccountably violent. They remembered the years of persecution and slavery; they were forced now to watch Germans stroll through the streets while they had to beg for passes in order to leave the camp. Believing that everyone was against them, they found support for this in the attitude of some Military Government officials: "troublemakers," one officer called them; "Why don't you take them out and shoot them?" The Poles knew they had been treated badly. Their surly indifference may have been because they found life to be without meaning. When we were angered by their behavior, they seemed puzzled by our reactions and resentful of our decisions. They were weary of the past. The present was nothing. There was no future.

We were responsible for the "Buchenwald Hotel," a nearby building housing sixty survivors of that concentration camp. Conditions at Buchenwald were worse than at Dachau, but the stories of hunger, sores, lice, cruelty, degradation, disability, and death were the same. On my periodic visits I took them gifts from our personal supplies.

July 4 was a legal holiday for all American soldiers. The DPs attended the observance at an amphitheater. Toward the end of the ceremony a resident of the Buchenwald Hotel said a few words and everyone wiped his eyes. Finally, a Polish leader expressed his gratitude to the United States and its brave soldiers. There was more weeping as he talked about the suffering of his people: how the Nazis deprived the people of their citizenship, and banned their books and newspapers; how those with higher education were deported or killed; how Jews were forced into extermination camps and millions of Poles into slave camps; how it felt to listen to the sounds made by Nazi firing squads in the quiet days and nights.

As he talked, I began to understand. It was not surprising that some Poles were unstable, hostile, difficult to deal with. What was amazing was that so many were stable, friendly, cooperative, people like Malczewski, Farnik, Joe, the warehouse supervisor, Arnold, our office boy, and many others, perhaps an indication of the resilience of the human spirit.

Gentlemen, I thought, may you soon have your day of independence!

On July 16 an order arrived to evacuate all DPs in the next two days. We sent them to other camps. On July 18 the Army took over the *Grenadier Kaserne* for its own use. We were sent to Karlsruhe where we assisted in the operation of a Russian repatriation center and coordinated certain activities in four other DP camps.

August 7. We listened to Danny Kaye's friendly voice from Radio Luxembourg, followed by Yehudi Menuhin performing a violin concerto. Trapped in the middle of a cadenza by a faulty record, Menuhin was saved by a news bulletin: Yesterday an atomic bomb was dropped, one with the destructive power of 20,000 tons of TNT! The next day more information came: 4.7 square miles in Japan had been leveled by the blast. It gave us something to talk about.

Does it really matter how one dies? Is it more acceptable to be killed by an exploding grenade than by lethal atoms? No aesthetic method of destroying an enemy has yet been devised. One of the men said, "We shouldn't mess with something we don't understand." Most believed that the new weapon should be used until the Japanese surrendered.

August 8. Russia declared war on Japan. Two days later, our long-awaited order arrived. We wrote letters of recommendation for our fourteen staff DPs, then drove each to a city or camp of his choice. Three days later we arrived at Bad Mergentheim and reported to Division Headquarters. We turned in our dilapidated vehicles and DP Team 115 was officially dissolved.

We returned to our original units in the 63rd Division. The next day, August 14, Japan surrendered.

On August 16 I left for a new post in France. Soon I would be going home to cities that I knew still stood; to people who I knew still waited for me.

I looked at the handsome German countryside for the last time and saw a DP carrying a battered suitcase down the road.

APPENDIX A

Loose Ends

It took many years for the greatest human tidal wave in history to come to an end: 60 million Europeans had been set adrift by the events preceding and culminating in World War II. After assisting in the repatriation of nearly 7 million DPs, the United Nations Relief and Rehabilitation Administration (UNRRA) ceased to exist in 1947, at which time more than 1.5 million DPs still languished in European camps. The International Refugee Organization, a temporary United Nations agency, succeeded UNRRA. During the next four years it resettled more than 1 million persons in overseas countries; only 73,000 chose to return to their native lands. In 1951, an Intergovernmental Committee for European Migration was established; through June 1957 it had assisted 600,000 more to relocate overseas.[1]

In 1945, the repatriation of Soviet nationals from the western zones of Germany had proceeded with such great rapidity that, in four and a half months, 2 million Russians were returned to their zone. During this time, among the numerous complaints received by the western Allies from Moscow was one that said that Soviet citizens had been unnecessarily held in the Dachau and Allach camps, and were mistreated by an unspecified Army unit. On investigation it was shown that these particular Russians had been sent home two months before the incident was alleged to have happened.

The complaints were without basis, their purpose to silence Allied complaints about Soviet noncompliance with the terms of the Yalta agreement that related to British and American POWs.[2]

I have not been able to find evidence of other complaints about the treatment of camp inmates.

At Dachau, we often wondered how the inmates were greeted on their return home. Andrus has described one reception.[3]

In May 1945, in the small resort town of Mondorf, Luxembourg, the Palace Hotel was being converted into a secret prison for suspected high-ranking Nazis; the prison's Allied code name was ASHCAN. Security was tight. Constantly patroling American soldiers cordoned off the area with barbed wire.

As activities at the Hotel increased, a convoy carrying 160 Luxembourgers, former prisoners at Dachau, reached the town and wound through the narrow streets. During the sad trip, Prince Felix and the 14-year-old Prince Charles had helped nurse and feed their sick people, and had watched some of them die.

News of the procession spread. The townspeople rushed to welcome the party. Shocked by the "yellowish, parchment skin and hollow, sunken eyes" of their countrymen, some of whom needed help to walk, the spectators began to weep. Soon they were sobbing loudly as some in the crowd identified and then embraced their parents or children, relatives long thought of as dead.

An ominous moment. Whispers, then shouts. The Nazi criminals in the hotel! Murderers! Vengeance!

Allied soldiers began to consider what action to take should the incensed townspeople storm the fences and barbed wire.

Prince Felix, who had served as a brigadier with the British Army, stepped down and talked to his people at length, and as the convoy continued on its way, the crowd dispersed.

So did some of the survivors of Dachau return home. No triumphal entry. No exultant celebration. No brass band.

During the first week of liberation of the camp at Dachau, it seemed important to many inmates to establish the identity of the first American to enter the camp, but nobody was certain.

The front-page dispatch in the *New York Times* of May 1, 1945, told about the battle to take the camp, and the killing of Nazi guards. "One of the infantry officers, Lieutenant Colonel Will Cowling of Leavenworth, Kansas, opened the main gate and was all but mobbed by the prisoners. . . ."

In his diary, one of the inmates wrote a brief account of the day of liberation. The battle over, an American soldier walked slowly into the prison hospital, chewing gum. "Hello, Boys!" he says. He looks like a giant, the inmate thinks. But he does not know his name. Later he hears that an American soldier of Polish extraction mounted a Polish flag—he had been carrying it for four months—on the main watchtower. Another American jumped on the tin roof of a bicycle shed and gave his gun to a prisoner. The soldier wanted to be the first one in the camp; he was a German-American Jew from Cologne; his father had died in the camp. No names.[4]

In an account of the activities of the 222d Infantry Regiment of the 42d Infantry Division, reference is made to a small advance force of officers and men who were the first to reach the camp. This task force consisted of Brigadier General Henning Linden, Major Herman L. Avery, Captain John L. McLaughlin, T/5 Robert H. Wilcox, and Pfc. Robert C. Nash. A few moments later they were joined by "two representatives of the *Stars and Stripes*, Miss Peggy Higgins, a representative of a Chicago newspaper, and a photographer from the Belgium government."

The report of a 7th Army CIC detachment mentions the first American to reach the camp, a "dark-complexioned, calm American soldier, an American Pole, pistol in hand. . . . A few shots . . . the guards were taken care of. . . . Then a jeep arrived. . . . The first American was hoisted into the air and two others, a 19-year-old farmer from the West, and a 19-year-old university student, were dragged out of the jeep and carried around the grounds on the internees' shoulders. A blond journalist in uniform was also in the jeep, and she climbed the tower by the gate with a young officer. . . ."[5]

Was Marguerite Higgins the first, or one of the first, to enter the camp? Yes. The eyewitness accounts agree.

The *New York Herald Tribune* of May 1 carried her dispatch:

> . . . . The liberation was a frenzied scene. This correspondent and Peter Furst, of the Army newspaper *Stars and Stripes*, were the first two Americans to enter the inclosure at Dachau. . . . While a United States 45th Infantry Division patrol was still fighting a way down through SS barracks to the north, our jeep and two others from the 42nd

Infantry drove into the camp inclosure through the southern entrance. As men of the patrol busied themselves accepting an SS man's surrender, we impressed a soldier into service and drove with him to the prisoners' barracks. There he opened the gate after pushing the body of a prisoner shot last night while attempting to go out to meet the Americans.

There was not a soul in the yard when the gate was opened. As we learned later, the prisoners themselves had taken over control of the inclosure the night before. . . . But the moment the two of us entered a jangled barrage of 'Are you American?'. . . came from the barracks. . . . An affirmative nod caused pandemonium.

Tattered, emaciated men weeping, yelling and shouting 'Long live America' swept toward the gate in a mob. . . . In the confusion they were so hysterically happy they took the SS man for an American. During a wild five minutes he was patted on the back, paraded on the shoulders and embraced enthusiastically by prisoners. The arrival of the American soldiers soon straightened out the situation.

Ali Kuci confirmed the story in *The Last Days of Dachau:* April 29. "5:31 P.M. Three American soldiers and a woman descend [from a military vehicle]. They keep their guns ready. We cry loudly in English. They understand and come in our direction. The door is opened and the young lady, I think it was the correspondent of the *New York Herald Tribune*, is the first to be among us. Then the three soldiers. . . . We kiss our guests and try to explain something. No one is able."

Miss Higgins may be remembered in history as a woman liberator. But, in fact, the first outsider to enter the camp was a Swiss, Victor Maurer, the representative of the International Committee of the Red Cross (ICRC). Some of the inmates had said so, and so do the records of the 222d Infantry Regiment of the 42d Infantry Division. Maurer's report was sent to me by the Geneva office of the ICRC; he arrived at the camp on April 27 with a column of trucks:

At the camp, I told a sentry that I wished to speak to the camp commandant. A little later I was received by the adjutant, Lt. Otto, in the commandant's office. I asked for permission to circulate freely through the area where the prisoners were kept. The commandant said that it was not possible to issue such authorization, that only General Kaltenbrunner could grant such permission, and that he was in the vicinity of Linz. The telephone and telegraph being out of order, the affair had become considerably complicated.

The Germans were very happy to know about the arrival of the food parcels. The commandant acquainted me with his desire for the immediate repatriation of 17,500 prisoners in a good state of health. These were mostly French and Polish; German, Jewish and Bulgarian inmates could not be released. I replied that I had to contact my district commander as soon as possible, but I could not do this until the next day. Lastly, the commandant asked me to quickly transport a cargo of food parcels to a depot in the Tyrols.

We said good-bye. I was permitted to personally distribute parcels to the prisoners. Lt. Otto accompanied me to the prison courtyard while a column of prisoners were led into the courtyard. Naturally, a very great joy prevailed among the prisoners because this was the first time a delegate of the ICRC has had access to the camp. Because some SS officers were always around, it was with great difficulty that I learned that, since January 1, 1945, 15,000 prisoners had died of typhus, and that in a transport of 5,000 prisoners from Buchenwald, about 2,700 were dead on arrival at Dachau. I further learned that M. Blum, Schuschnigg, and others, were taken away a few days ago at the same time as 6,000 others. In my opinion, this happened because the combat front had drawn nearer. Some of the prisoners (trustees) emptied the trucks and signed the accompanying receipts. I spent the night in Barrack 203, Room 3. This was not in the prison camp.

During the night there was a loud uproar on account of the closeness of the battle. Also, in nearby barracks, many SS soldiers were probably getting ready to fight, or had been given other tasks to accomplish. But I only learned that on Sunday morning. The atmosphere was strange: wherever one looked there were signs that made you think that the troops that had been in the barracks had fled. Furthermore, the roar of battle was closer. Arriving at the front gate about 10:30 A.M., I met the soldiers who were guarding the camp;

a white flag now floated from one of the principal towers. Most of the officers, soldiers and employees had left the camp during the night.

I remained with a German lieutenant until the camp was delivered to the Americans. He and his soldiers had intended to abandon this large camp containing 35 to 40,000 prisoners, and it was only after lengthy negotiations that I persuaded him to change his mind, but with the following conditions:

1. Sentries should remain in the towers in order to keep the prisoners under control, to prevent them from escaping.

2. The soldiers who were not on guard were to remain in the courtyard, unarmed.

3. A guarantee should be made that the remaining members of the German garrison would be allowed to retreat to their own battle line.

These conditions were most happily accepted, for otherwise there would have been a catastrophe: if the thousands of prisoners, motivated by their desire for vengeance, had been allowed to escape, the people in the bordering region would have suffered; it was impossible to predict the damage that might have resulted from the epidemic.

The sound of the battle became unbearable, and I noticed that the fighting was now in front of the gate. I then decided to take the following action: I found a broomstick and hung a white towel from it. I asked a German officer to accompany me, and we walked through the main gate. The bullets whistled about us. A little later, I saw an American motorized column which I attracted by waving the white flag. Soon we were surrounded by American military vehicles. I introduced myself. At first, the American general asked me to have the German officer take photographs of a train filled with cadavers. As I learned later, the train had arrived from Buchenwald; within it were 500 cadavers. In my opinion, many of them had been killed, others died of hunger. I then met Major Every [Major Herman L. Avery, of the 42d Division], and I told him about the plan to turn the camp over to the Americans, and I asked him to transmit this information to the General.

We reentered the prison courtyard in the Major's vehicle; by this time some Americans were there. Thousands of prisoners were beside themselves with the joy of freedom. The guards in the towers had already been replaced by

Americans. In a small exterior courtyard, a few shots were still being fired; some soldiers were killed on both sides. I personally contacted the American general and told him about the plan to deliver the camp, and received his consent.

The happiness of the prisoners knew no bounds. Many were milling around us, ready to avenge themselves against the Germans. Those carrying arms were immediately disarmed. Many in the crowd succeeded in tearing down the barbed wire, and some took advantage of the disorder to run away, while others embraced the Americans. . . . By 10:00 P.M. the camp had calmed down, but many shots were still heard that night.

At midnight, I finally returned to my lodging at the German commandant's house, where I occupied his room. I noticed that my trunks had been forced, and many things were missing including the sum of 200 French sous.

The ICRC representative spends two more days in the camp. He requests a list of the prisoners. Soon he is ready to leave:

The Americans asked me to deliver as quickly as possible great quantities of food and medications. The officer responsible for supplies expressed his gratitude for our efforts. I returned to my room in the afternoon. Unhappily I must report that I had been robbed a second time.[6]

Long before Maurer arrived, parcels had been received at Dachau, apparently contrary to Red Cross policy—parcels were to be sent only to prisons permitting inspection by Red Cross men. The remarkable story of how these packages found their way to the inmates is found in a report buried in ICRC files.

At the Geneva Convention of 1929, many countries had committed themselves to the humane treatment of POWs; Russia and Japan had not. The ICRC, staffed by Swiss nationals who prided themselves on their absolute impartiality, became the guardian of POWs. Once a month food parcels were sent to German prison camps and once or twice a year kits containing razor blades, soap, a comb, toothbrushes, and toothpaste. By the end of the war, ICRC workers had made 11,000 trips to inspect POW compounds and supervise the distribution of parcels, of which more than 7 million were for Frenchmen, 2 million for Yugoslavs, and 1 million for Poles.[7]

Despite the absence of an international agreement to protect civilian prisoners in time of war, the ICRC believed that something should be done to alleviate their suffering, but the German government refused to permit ICRC representatives into concentration camps. Because of this, the Allies would not permit supplies intended for camp prisoners to pass through their blockade of the continent. Undeterred, the ICRC continued their pressure. These dedicated men—half the Committee members served without pay—persisted in their efforts, despite the monotonous rejection of their requests by the German Foreign Office.

In August 1942, the German position softened very slightly. A Foreign Office representative announced that alien prisoners at the Oranienberg and Dachau camps could receive small food parcels from their relatives, provided that the contents could be eaten rapidly. Immediately, the Committee pressed to extend this benefit to German and Alsatian prisoners. This was granted in February 1943, unless the detentees had committed political crimes or had imperiled the security of the regime or the occupation authorities.

In March, after additional pleas, the Foreign Office made another concession: parcels could now be sent to alien prisoners in concentration camps, provided that their names and addresses were known to the ICRC. However, this did not apply if the prisoners had been guilty of crimes against the German government or armed forces. The number of parcels that could be sent was unlimited, but no prisoner could receive more than he needed. If so, the remainder would be distributed to other detentees.

In practice, the concession was trivial—the Geneva office of the ICRC had on file the names and addresses of only sixty civilian prisoners known to be imprisoned in Germany! But now the office began to collect such information from private and secret sources. In June 1943, the same month as the Allied invasion of Normandy, a few supplies began to reach the designated prisoners. News of the arrival of the parcels spread through the camps, and inmates permitted to write home mentioned the change in regulations. As a result, many requests for parcels to be sent to inmates arrived from their relatives. Names were added to the file. Furthermore, because the prisoners receiving parcels often signed receipts for them, the names of Belgian, Dutch, Spanish, Yugoslav, Czech, French, Norwegian, and Polish prisoners were added to the file.

In order to procure more supplies, the ICRC tried to persuade the Allied authorities to open a passage in the blockade just large enough to permit overseas parcels to reach the concentration camps. The request was rejected. Additionally denied for relief purposes was a request to use funds brought to London from occupied countries. Not possible, said the Allies, not until the Germans permit agents of the ICRC to inspect the camps and supervise the distribution of supplies. The Nazis refused to budge. No right of inspection, not even if it meant bringing food, clothing, and medications into the camp. Not possible, droned the Nazis.

But, if the blockade were not lifted, where would the supplies come from? A severe food shortage was widespread in Europe; people in many of the occupied countries, particularly in Holland, were close to starvation. Undeterred, the representatives of the ICRC, with an almost religious fervor, hunted throughout Europe for foodstuffs, finally locating large quantities of canned meat, biscuits, jams, sugar, and other essentials in the Balkan states, particularly Romania, Hungary, and Czechoslovakia. These were purchased with money provided by foreign governments, Red Cross societies, and relief organizations, then taken to Geneva for packaging.

The ICRC could never be certain that the parcels were received by the designated inmates, but they sent them anyhow, hoping that many prisoners would survive because of them. When instances of confiscation of packages became known, further shipments to these camps were temporarily suspended. The Swiss learned about the fate of the parcels from letters written by inmates, and from escaped convicts.

What could be done to help prisoners whose names were unknown? Nobody knew the identities of the *Nacht und Nebel* —night and fog—prisoners. They had suddenly disappeared from their homes; their families did not know what had happened to them, were not even informed if the prisoner died in a concentration camp. To help such detentees, the ICRC, in spite of German opposition, decided in the summer of 1944 to send collective parcels to the camps earmarked for groups of nameless prisoners. Now the Allied governments approved; there was increasing concern for the inmates, known to be in poor condition. The Allies also wanted relief supplies increased, despite the absence of ICRC supervision. In order for this to succeed, the blockade had to be relaxed, and this was accomplished after the acceptance of a recommendation to this effect by the War Refugee Board, an agency established by President Roosevelt in 1944.

Toward the end of 1944, larger quantities of supplies began to arrive at the concentration camps. The camp commandants had the authority to decide whether or not prisoners would be allowed to sign receipts for the Red Cross parcels; in Dachau they could. The receipts, some carrying as many as fifteen signatures, were sent back to Switzerland. On the basis of these returns, the Geneva office developed a unique form of arithmetic: if seven Poles in a particular camp shared one package, then the number of Poles in that camp was seven times greater than the number of parcels sent out!

Next, the ICRC sent out medical parcels containing vitamins, stimulants, disinfectants, and cotton wool. Clothing was difficult to obtain; all that could be bought were artificial woolen underclothes. These were sent, as well as woolen garments donated by the Belgian government.

Occasionally, surprise packages were dispatched: cases of communion wine to French chaplains, and Bibles and New Testaments to French and Norwegian prisoners.

In February 1945, the shortage of food in Germany became so acute that many camps received no food at all, and the suddenly concerned German government asked the ICRC to send individual and collective packages to French and Belgian prisoners! Then, in March 1945, SS General Kaltenbrunner granted the five-year-old request of the ICRC: one ICRC representative would be permitted into each concentration camp provided that he remain there for the duration of the war.

The staff of the ICRC began to work around the clock; as many as 9,000 parcels a day were prepared. (Between January 1, 1945 and April 15, 1945, more than 300,000 parcels were put together.) But, now that permission had been granted, it was almost impossible for the parcels to reach their destinations, so thoroughly had the German transportation system been ravaged. There was only one thing to do. The ICRC sent out columns of its own trucks, each with large red crosses painted against a white field, the only sign of humanity in a pitiless world. When able to do so, the Swiss distributed supplies to prisoners within the camps, at other times to escaped prisoners.

Some camps received no parcels, their very existence unknown to the ICRC until after the war.

When the trucks were empty, they headed back to Switzerland, filled with DPs and escapees—women, children, the old and infirm.

Final figures from the ICRC showed that 1,112,000 parcels were sent to the prisoners in the concentration camps between the autumn of 1943 and May 1945; their total weight was 4,500 tons.[8]

A new Geneva Convention was adopted in 1949, intended to protect civilians in times of war. No longer would representatives of the ICRC be denied access to prisons filled with civilians, provided that these prisons were located in countries whose governments were signatories of this important Convention.[9]

In 1948, Paul Mueller, a chemist working for the J. R. Geigy Company in Basle, Switzerland, was awarded the Nobel Prize for being the first to appreciate the properties of DDT. Mueller had learned that DDT was a remarkable insecticide, lethal in a few minutes, and effective for about two to six weeks when applied to clothing, skin, walls, or blankets. He had tested the chemical on the Colorado potato beetle, which had shown its aggressive character by traveling to Europe and attacking the Swiss potatoes. The crop was saved. A small amount of the original product was given to the United States, where at the Orlando, Florida laboratory of the Department of Agriculture, the active component was isolated and synthesized by the end of 1942.

Subsequently, DDT became indispensible in the battle against other diseases of man, such as malaria, and against a variety of crippling plant diseases.

As the years passed, reports began to appear about the resistance of certain insects to DDT, and its harmful effects on certain species of birds, fish, amphibians, and mammals.[10]

But in 1945, we had no inkling of adverse effects. We used DDT by the ton; it coated our clothes, food, and air, and the results achieved by it in the control of the typhus fever epidemic were spectacular.

Historians showed that many German doctors who had participated in the medical experiments at Dachau were motivated by their desire for status and material gains, such as promotion in the SS. Others, concerned about the possibility of being considered disloyal, tried to prove that they were good citizens. One such was Dr. Karl Gebhardt, professor of surgery at the University of Berlin, who injected bacteria into the legs of test persons at the Ravensbrück concentration camp, ostensibly to clear himself of complicity in the death of the hated Gestapo leader, SS General Heydrich (the "Hangman").[11]

As a consequence of totalitarian rule, professional and educational standards deteriorated. The spokesmen for the State made it clear that a doctor was to be "an alert biological soldier [whose] foremost task [was] to defend the State and his people against asocial elements," his first duty to carry out the racial policies of the State.[12]

A doctor in the Third Reich worked for the benefit of the State. But he had once taken the Hippocratic Oath. He had pledged himself to work "for the benefit of the sick," and he had promised not to administer "deadly medicine to anyone if asked, nor suggest such counsel. . . ." Could he reconcile the differences? He watched the liquidation of his colleagues who had protested or resisted; by the end of the thirties the medical profession had been purged of anti-Nazi or potential anti-Nazi elements. He listened to his Leaders.

The result was inevitable. Individuality died. Once again, the eternal conflict between the conscience of an individual and the authority of government was resolved in favor of the government.

The judges at the Military Tribunal at Nuremberg decided that the actions of the German doctors were "consistent with an ideology and racial philosophy, to use Himmler's own words, which regarded human beings as lice and offal." [13] (Himmler had once described concentration camp inmates as "the offal of criminals and freaks, for the most part, slave-like souls" who were "taught to wash themselves twice daily, and to use the toothbrush, with which most of them have been unfamiliar. Hardly another nation would be as humane as we are." [14])

As a consequence of the concentration camp experiments, a ten-point Nuremberg Code was proposed in 1947 to protect persons used as test subjects in research projects. A prerequisite should be the informed, voluntary consent of the subject. The physician proposing the investigation should be certain that the desired information could not be obtained by other means. The results hoped for should justify the risks assumed. The test should not be conducted if the subject might be disabled or die, except, perhaps, if "the experimental physicians also serve as subjects." Efforts should be made to minimize the risk to the subject—a qualified person should direct the project, provisions should be made for ending the experiment.

Many of these recommendations were adopted by the United Nations, the World Medical Association, and the French National Academy of Medicine. The American Medical Association endorsed the Code, and recommended an additional safeguard: a pilot study using laboratory animals prior to the exposure of human subjects.[15]

A revision of the Hippocratic Oath, the first in 2,200 years, was presented by the World Medical Association as the Geneva Code: ". . . . I will maintain the utmost respect for human life from the time of conception. Even under threat I will not use my knowledge contrary to the laws of humanity."[16]

At the war crimes trials an important principle was under investigation: are individuals responsible for the actions that they take in order to carry out the policies of their government—actions taken with the approval and/or direction of that government? Offered as evidence at some of the trials were the inhuman acts which had taken place at Dachau.

MILITARY GOVERNMENT COURT
CHARGE SHEET

Dachau, Germany
2 November 1945

NAMES OF THE ACCUSED:

[Forty men, named] are hereby charged with the following offenses:

FIRST CHARGE: Violation of the Laws and Usages of War. Particulars: In that [the accused] acting in pursuance of a common design to commit the acts hereinafter alleged, and as members of Dachau Concentration Camp and camps subsidiary thereto, did, at, or in the vicinity of Dachau and Landsberg, Germany, between about 1 January 1942 and about 29 April 1945, willfully, deliberately and wrongfully encourage, aid, abet and participate in the subjection of civilian nationals of nations then at war with the then German Reich to cruelties and mistreatment, including killings, beatings, tortures, starvation, abuses, and indignities, the exact names and numbers of such civilian nationals being unknown but aggregating many thousands who were then and there in the custody of the German Reich. . . .

SECOND CHARGE: Violation of the Laws and Usages of War. Particulars: In that [the accused] acting in pursuance of a common design to commit the acts hereinafter alleged, and as members of the staff of Dachau Concentration Camp, did . . . willfully, deliberately and wrongfully encourage, aid, abet and participate in the subjection of members of the armed forces then at war with the German Reich, who were then and there surrendered and unarmed prisoners of war in the custody of the then German Reich, to cruelties and mistreatments, including killings, beatings, tortures, starvation, abuses and indignities, the exact names and numbers of such prisoners of war being unknown but aggregating many hundreds.[17]

All sentences required agreement by two-thirds of the members of the court. In December 1945 the findings of the court were announced. Thirty-six of the defendants, including Dr. Schilling, who had directed the malaria experiments, were sentenced to death by hanging. The other prisoners received prison terms ranging from ten years to life. (Eventually 420 Germans were executed at Dachau.[18])

In the summation, the president of the court said that the inmates of the concentration camps were subjected

> to killings, beatings, tortures, indignities and starvation to an extent and to a degree that necessitates an indictment of everyone, high and low, who had anything to do with conducting and operating the camps. . . . when a sovereign state sets itself up above reasonably recognized and constituted international law or is willing to transcend readily recognizable civilized customs of humane and decent treat-

ment of persons, the individuals effecting such policies of their state must be held responsible. . . .[19]

In the soft, warm evenings at Dachau, the members of DP Team 115 would sip wine and talk of many things. A favorite subject was survival. We believed that the inmates would recover from their mistreatments, basing this on the behavior of Kuci, Malczewski, and others, who were rational and productive. Since that time, hundreds of reports have appeared in medical journals of many countries attesting to the prevalence of a pattern of severe and often permanent personality and character changes leading to impaired working capacity and intellectual deterioration in many concentration camp survivors. "Persecution-connected personality changes," "concentration camp pathology," and "concentration camp syndrome" were the names applied to this disorder.[20]

Another popular topic in 1945 concerned the pressures applied to the prisoners of Dachau, forcing many to collaborate. How would we have fared if we had been subjected to the same stresses? Better, some of the men thought. But nobody could be sure.

Until a report appeared on the "DDD Syndrome," another name for the pattern seen in concentration camp survivors, and now reported in American POWs returning from North Korean prison camps. "DDD" referred to the factors responsible for the syndrome: *debility*, the result of starvation, exhaustion, and illness; *dependency*, from lack of sleep and food; and *dread*, of the real possibilities of torture, crippling disability, permanent incarceration, and death.

The techniques used by the North Koreans and Chinese Communists to brainwash the captured soldiers were essentially the same as those used by the Nazis. Of 7,190 American POWs, only 4,428 returned; most of the others died in POW compounds. Fifteen percent of the American POWs collaborated, and 70 percent "confessed" to "crimes." [21]

There was no reason to think that we would have behaved differently.

APPENDIX B

The Special Prisoners

One of the best known of the special prisoners of Dachau was Pastor Martin Niemoller, whose opposition to the Nazification of the Protestant churches, as well as his forthright rejection of anti-Semitism, led to his imprisonment in a Berlin jail in 1937. After eight months, he was taken before one of the Fuehrer's Special Courts, established to pass judgment on persons accused of antigovernment attitudes and activities. In the opinion of the three judges, all reliable Nazi Party members, the pastor was guilty of "abuse of the pulpit." He was fined 2,000 marks and sentenced to seven months in jail, but because he had already served eight months, he was released.

For a few minutes. Outside the court, he was arrested again and taken to the concentration camp at Sachsenhausen where, for two years, he paced back and forth in a cell seven steps long and four steps wide.[1] In 1941, he was transferred to Dachau, given a new red triangle, a new number, 26,679, a cell in the bunker, and a convicted murderer to act as his orderly. The food was adequate; he was permitted to write, and read books and magazines; his wife visited every two weeks. The door to his cell was open to that he could visit the occupants of adjacent cells, two Roman Catholic priests. Together they spent the mornings in prayer and the early afternoon hours in Bible studies; in the evenings they played cards.

The years passed slowly. In 1944, another concession was granted to Dr. Niemoller—he was permitted to preach. On Christmas Day of 1944, in his cell, he addressed his congregation of six prisoners: a British Army colonel, two Norwegian shipowners, a Yugoslav diplomat, a Greek journalist, and Dr. van Dyck, a Dutch cabinet minister. Subsequently, he was allowed to preach five more times, for the same audience, and in the same location.

In a sense, Dr. Niemoller was lucky. He had been sentenced to death by the State, but the sentence had not been carried out, probably because of his popularity. Despite the efforts of Nazis, he remained a German hero.[2]

While exercising in the bunker courtyard, the pastor was able to talk briefly with another special prisoner, Major Richard H. Stevens, a British military intelligence officer who occupied a comfortable cell where he painted and listened to his radio. Permitted to wear civilian clothes, he occasionally shopped in Munich. In the camp, he was in solitary confinement, like most of the honorary prisoners. The pastor believed that Stevens had been falsely accused of participation in a plot to kill the Fuehrer (the Venlo Incident), a plot that had been rigged by the Nazis for political reasons.[3]

Elsewhere in the bunker was a British Secret Service officer, Captain S. Payne Best, imprisoned for the same reason as Stevens. Their story dates back to 1939, when a Gestapo agent, Walter Schellenberg, using an alias, contacted Stevens and Best with a strange story: certain German generals were thinking about kidnapping Hitler. If this happened, could the new government in Germany be assured of fair treatment by the English?

While exploratory contacts were under way, a bomb exploded in the famous Munich Beer Hall on November 8, 1939, twelve minutes after Hitler had completed a scheduled speech and had left the premises. Schellenberg was ordered to kidnap Best and Stevens. He accomplished this the next day on Dutch soil. (This occurred before the invasion of Holland.) One Dutch officer was killed during the foray.

Best and Stevens denied all knowledge of the bombing, but the Nazis proclaimed their guilt, saying that they had hired a German Communist, a carpenter named Georg Elser, to construct and detonate the bomb. The two Englishmen were taken to a concentration camp where they spent two years in solitary confinement wearing heavy chains night and day. Elser was interned in the Flossenberg concentration camp where he was permitted to work in a shop and play his zither; an SS guard was posted outside his cell. Despite the guard, he managed to tell Best that the Nazis had commissioned him to construct the bomb. Eventually, all were taken to Dachau, Best and Stevens in 1941, and Elser in 1945—his second internment there; the first had been in 1937.

Schellenberg became an SS general. Elser was liquidated at Dachau; the order dated April 1, 1945, was signed by the Reichsfuehrer SS. Stevens and Best were among those liberated with Niemoller.[4]

Kurt von Schuschnigg, the former Austrian chancellor, had been a prisoner of the Nazis since March 1938. At first he had been under house arrest. Later he was locked into a room in the servants' quarters of the Hotel Metropole, Gestapo headquarters in Vienna. He was transferred to a cell in a Gestapo prison in Munich in 1939, and, two years later, sent to the Sachsenhausen concentration camp; in 1942, his wife and daughter were given permission to stay with him.

Early in 1945, Schuschnigg, accompanied by his wife and daughter, moved to the Flossenberg concentration camp. They did not stay there long. On April 8, they moved again. In the prison van he had his first opportunity to talk at length with other prisoners. Sitting next to him was Dr. Hjalmar Schacht, the former German Minister of Economics and Plenipotentiary for War Economics, jailed for conspiring against the Fuehrer. Other occupants of the van were General Georg Thomas, former head of the Office of War Economy, and General Franz Halder, former Chief of Staff. Both had been involved in a plot against Hitler; General Thomas had also made the mistake of advising Hitler against the invasion of Poland. Another member of the German General Staff, Colonel Bogislaw von Bunin, was sitting nearby. He had been arrested after his superior had ordered him to sign an operational order—Hitler had disagreed with the order.

At a brief stop, others joined the convoy: General Alexander von Falkenhausen, former military commander of Belgium, arrested in 1944 because he opposed the SS; Fritz Thyssen, the noted German industrialist; the former French premier, 72-year-old Léon Blum, suffering from lumbago and bronchitis, and his wife; the Bishop of Munich; and many others.

That night they arrived in Dachau and were assigned to the bunker. Schuschnigg's cell contained two metal beds, stools, a water basin, and a table. The food was passable, although later it deteriorated to the same watery soup given to the ordinary prisoners. Communication with the prisoners outside of the bunker was forbidden, but Schuschnigg talked with one of them, a former circus clown who worked in the courtyard.

In the middle of the walled-in courtyard was an air raid shelter. Because alarms were almost continuous, the special prisoners spent much time underground conversing with each other, their words pouring forth like water from a broken dam. Literature. From memory they recited the *Iliad*, in Greek, then tried to recall Virgil and Goethe. (Did they weep when Aeneas passed through the River of Hell?) They talked of the future, their chances of survival, their hopes for their countries. Then politics. What might have been. Why the nations of the world had failed. The German officers were violently hostile to Hitler and his entourage. In Schuschnigg's opinion they were "as decent and responsible men as one could wish to meet." Nevertheless, he believed their thinking was "mechanical. For instance, they were in favor of acquiring Austria because the Inn Valley made a better defense line than their former border. Not a thought of how this would affect the people in Austria. . . ."[5]

They talked and talked. As the days passed, they acquired new hope.[6]

Another prisoner in the bunker was the German physician, Dr. Sigmund Rascher. Each morning he asked after the health of the others, then returned to his cell. He did not leave in the convoy. Later, the liberated prisoners learned about his participation in the medical experiments at Dachau.[7]

Attending Dr. Rascher's sick call was the French general, Charles Delestraint, another prisoner who did not leave in the convoy. We had learned about him from some of the inmates. Now I was able to find out more about him in the memoirs of Charles de Gaulle. Probably Delestraint's fate was inevitable after General de Gaulle, sitting in his London office in 1942, decided that the Resistance forces in France were fragmented, that a unified command was needed. To head the secret army, he chose General Delestraint, formerly an inspector of tanks, a "steadfast soldier, not too well prepared for his mission."[8]

A short, rigidly erect man, diplomatic when necessary, he succeeded in becoming head of the Armée Secrète, the fighting force welded together from the military units of most of the underground groups. Like many in the Resistance, Delestraint did not last long. In 1943 he was arrested by the Germans, after being betrayed by another captured underground fighter. Apparently the Nazis were not aware of his eminence. He was first imprisoned in Paris, then sent to Dachau where he was quartered with other French prisoners.

Perhaps he would have survived if he had remained unnoticed. For him, this was impossible. One day while being interrogated by an SS officer, he proudly announced that he was a "general of the French Army now serving under General de Gaulle, who once served under me!" [9] The Germans realized that they had netted a big fish. They removed him from his crowded block and put him into solitary confinement in the bunker. His food was better. He was allowed to wear his uniform. Toward the end of April 1945, as the rumbling sounds of American artillery were heard, he was ordered out of his cell, marched to a spot near the crematorium, then forced to dig his own grave. Here he was shot.[10]

April 27, 1945, a day long remembered by the special prisoners of Dachau, the day they were forced to leave the camp, the day they would probably die. No notice was given. They had time only to pick up a suitcase or bundle of clothes. Schuschnigg described their departure:

> . . . . Mothers took their children by the hand and our sad little group began to walk toward the buses. When we arrived at the large square at the central camp, we halted involuntarily: a sea of emaciated figures, in blue and white striped prison garb, moved slowly in complete silence along the camp walls toward the exits. . . . A narrow aisle was being kept open by the guards, through which we were to go. Suddenly, as we passed, a worn-out hand stretched from the mass. Here someone called, there a familiar face smiled tiredly. . . . Hands were raised in salute. . . . They are our friends—human beings. . . .[11]

The special prisoners were pushed into buses by carefully picked SS guards. They were reinforced with Gestapo agents from Munich who carried written death sentences for the prisoners.[12]

"Shoot them all! Shoot them all!" had been Hitler's last words on their disposition.[13]

Several days later, Captain Best and General Thomas arranged to have a Wehrmacht detachment replace the SS and Gestapo guards. Best had notified the Gestapo leaders that he was taking command. "A magnificent bluff . . . to his surprise, this worked," according to the story in the *New York Times* of May 8, 1945.

When the American patrol arrived at the hotel on the picturesque lake high in the southern Tyrol mountains, there was no bloodshed.

Others in the same party rescued by the American patrol were Karl Bruno Kuhl, a Catholic priest; Jacob Koos, a former Center Party leader (the Catholic party that dissolved after Hitler came to power); Johann Neuhasler, a Catholic canon from Munich; Fabian von Schlabrendorff, a young German officer deeply involved in the 1944 bomb plot against Hitler—one of the few who survived Hitler's vengeance; Prince Philip of Hesse, the son-in-law of King Victor Emmanual of Italy, whose wife, Princess Mafalda, died in a German concentration camp despite the Prince having become a Fascist and German general (at one time he was known as "Hitler's mailman" because he used to fly messages to Mussolini). In 1943, the Prince was arrested after Allied forces invaded southern Italy. After his liberation with the other special prisoners, Prince Philip of Hesse was taken to the interrogation center in Mondorf, Luxembourg. Among the kin prisoners known to be in the group of hostages was Countess Elizabeth von Stauffenberg, wife of the German officer who was one of the leaders in the conspiracy against Hitler, their children, and members of his family.[14]

These were some of the special prisoners of Dachau about whom we know something only because they survived. There were hundreds of others about whom nothing is known, not even their names. Did they spend their days of hopelessness pacing back and forth in their cheerless, windowless cells? Did they try to leave a message on the dark concrete walls? No one will ever know.

Until 1969, the bunker served as a stockade for the United States Army units patrolling the camp. Perhaps an American soldier convicted for stealing Army property was locked into Cell 34, where Dr. Niemoller preached his Christmas sermon.

Perhaps another soldier, court-martialed for drunken driving, was confined in Cell 73 where he slept on the same cot on which Dr. Rascher once dreamed about his days of glory as an SS research scientist.

Neither dreams nor nightmares now. After thirty-six years, the bunker is empty, closed by the Army after reports of beatings of GI prisoners by guards.[15]

Postscript: 1972

Where are they now? I sent out many letters requesting information about some of the former inmates of Dachau. There were only a few responses. From Ruth Jakusch, a staff member of the Dachau concentration camp, now a memorial site. From the International Tracing Service at Arolsen, Germany, an arm of the International Research Service, in turn a department of the International Committee of the Red Cross. From the Secretary General of the Comité International de Dachau, Georges-Valery Walraeve, "en 1945 à Dachau Kapo de la Desinfection Kommando Revier" (in 1945, a Dachau Capo assigned to supervise the disinfection crew working in the inner compound hospital).

At the time of this writing, Albert Guérisse (Patrick O'Leary) is a general in the Belgian Army, and holds the office of Executive President of the Comité International de Dachau, an appropriate position for the man who was the first president of the International Prisoners' Committee. General Nikolai Michailow, who succeeded Guérisse as president of the IPC, lives in Moscow, and Arthur Haulot, the IPC vice-president, in Belgium.

A little information is available about certain members of the IPC. Dr. Franz Blaha resides in Czechoslovakia, and Pim Boellaerd in Holland (in our records of 1945 he was listed as Willem Boellaard). I have not been able to confirm a report that Ali Kuci became a United Nations delegate, and later died in a New York sanitarium of the disease he contracted at Dachau. Oskar Mueller became a Minister of Hessen; he died as a result of an accident in 1970.[1] George Pallavicini, the Hungarian member of the IPC, is said to have died in a Siberian concentration camp in 1948.[2] For Edmond Michelet, the leader of the

French, death came in 1970 at the age of 70; he left behind his widow, seven children, and forty grandchildren. We know more about him than the others because he had become a public figure.

The son of a wholesale grocer, he became a businessman, but it was in the Catholic Trade movement that he was able to devote himself to social work. A fervent Gaullist, he helped found "Combat," one of the earliest Resistance movements to be organized in southern France. A year later he was arrested and sent to Dachau. After leaving the camp and recovering his health, he held public office continually until his death, representing the Catholic Popular Republican Party. A member of the French cabinet, he succeeded André Malraux as Minister of Culture; in this position he labored to alleviate the desperate situation of the Paris Opera.

A great French patriot, he will be remembered for the leaflet he distributed in June 1940, asking the French people to continue the war. One day later, Charles de Gaulle reached the same decision.

"Open mind, generous heart, faithful companion." These were the words Charles de Gaulle used to describe his steadfast supporter.[3]

In Malraux's *Anti-Memoirs*, I read that Charles de Gaulle waited at the station to welcome Michelet and the deportees returning from Dachau with him. What were Michelet's feelings?

"Are we the pensioners of Hell?" he asks. "When we came back, what we felt to begin with was that life was a bonus . . . we should have been dead; after that everything was a jumble."

The *Anti-Memoirs* conclude with a memorable passage in which Michelet, Malraux, and three other survivors assess the impact on themselves and the world of the organized brutalization and the degradation that characterized the Nazi prison camps. "The true barbarism," says Malraux, "is Dachau; the true civilization is first of all the element in man which the camps sought to destroy."[4]

In the offices of the International Tracing Service is a Master Index of thirty million cards, in which individuals' names are classified according to a phonetic-alphabetical system which allows for variations and modifications of Slavonic names and suffixes. There is a continuing demand for information from all over the world; in 1970, more than 169,000 reports and certificates, many of them relating to deaths, illnesses, and pension and indemnification proceedings, were dispatched from Arolsen.[5]

The Director of the International Tracing Service, Mr. A. de Cocatrix, has been generous in his efforts to answer my questions, but despite a search of the voluminous files has been unable to provide information about Leon Malczewski, the IPC secretary, Mr. Farnik, the warehouse supervisor, and some of the other internees. He wrote that the files pertaining to the Dachau concentration alone consisted of 177,447 *Schreibstubenkarten* (index cards), 45,729 envelopes with individual records, 275 files with lists of transports, work assignments, and similar material, as well as infirmary and death records and lists of liberated inmates.

A total of 31,951 *reported* deaths at the camp were confirmed by the Tracing Service. Others were unreported, hence could not be traced. These included persons sent by the Gestapo to the camp for execution, Soviet POWs executed under the "Commissar Order" of 1941, and prisoners who died in outgoing convoys and death marches.[6]

Had Stalin's son been in Dachau?

Svetlana Alliluyeva wrote about the events that led to the death of her stepbrother. Jacob, stubborn, unambitious, quiet, honest, and a great friend, had been a lieutenant in the Russian Army when taken prisoner by the Germans in 1941. Josef Stalin believed that his son's capture had dishonored Russia: "I have no son called Jacob." He told a foreign correspondent that "in Hitler's camps there are no Russian POWs, only Russian traitors, and we shall do away with them after the war is over." After hearing his father's statement, which had been broadcast, Jacob was disconsolate. "That day, he went in search of death, and perished by throwing himself on electrified barbed wire." [7]

A different account says that Jacob was shot to death by his German guards before the Americans liberated the camp in which he had been interned.[8] But the report of the suicide seems more tenable. Kurt von Schuschnigg wrote that Stalin's son had not been with the honorary prisoners of Dachau. From "reliable sources" he had learned of his suicide at the Sachsenhausen concentration camp.[9]

Other loose ends.

After the war, Kurt von Schuschnigg taught at St. Louis University. In his book, *Austrian Requiem*, he expressed his longing to return to his native land. In 1967, twenty-nine years after his imprisonment by the Fuehrer, he returned to Austria.

Prince Jean, who visited my office in Dachau early in May 1945, became the Grand Duke of Luxembourg in 1964.

Gertrude Stein never left France. In July 1946 she died in Paris, the city ablaze with fresh-cut flowers on every street, the radiant sunlight pouring over the busy boulevards, noisy markets, and colorful houses, and the streets teeming with the opinionated, stubborn, happy, vivacious people she loved so much. I was astonished to learn that she was 72—she seemed much younger.

The only member of the Team with whom I have been in contact is Theodore N. Ferris, Jr., in 1945 the clerk-typist, now an editor and writer living in Lakeview, Ohio. His poem describing the burial processions at Dachau is from *Cloudview*, his book of verse published in 1970.

Other letters were unanswered or returned with the ominous words, "ADDRESS UNKNOWN."

George Hathaway, the XVI Corps Surgeon, retired from the Army and moved to my home town. It was my pleasure to write a letter of recommendation for him when he applied for a position as medical administrator. We rarely talked of the past —for both of us it was a nightmare that we thought we had buried. In 1967, he died at the age of 72.

After I had begun this book, Mrs. Hathaway told me about the day she received a call from a reporter on the *Minneapolis Tribune*, May 6, 1945. Did she have any comment to make about her husband being in the Dachau concentration camp? This was the first she had heard of his whereabouts in many weeks, and she assumed he had been taken prisoner by the Nazis. She had no comment for the reporter. She fainted!

After the war, Harry Pires, the Red Cross representative, spent a year in Paris as director of supplies. Here he was "able to eradicate the smells and emotions experienced in Dachau." He now lives in North Hollywood, California.[10]

In 1966, Paul D. Adams retired from the United States Army with the rank of general after thirty-eight years of distinguished service as a commissioned officer. He lives in Tampa, Florida. In 1958 he wrote to Harry Pires about his return to Dachau: "The smell of death and human filth is still there and I suppose it always will be." In 1972, General Adams responded to my letter telling him about this book: "I am glad you have written it because I have found few people who did not see Dachau or similar camps can begin to comprehend the horror of them and the evilness they constituted and represented. . . . A whole flood of recollections comes back to me. Perhaps the most significant . . . is that we had an opportunity to see how shallow is the veneer of civilization on mankind."

After the hospitals closed and repatriation ended—the last known meeting of the IPC was in August 1945—American troops remained in the camp as part of the occupation force, and, as of this writing, are still quartered at the former SS barracks.

There have been a few changes since 1945, many of them related to the museum and memorials planned and arranged by the Comité International de Dachau with the help of the government of Bavaria. One row of prisoners' barracks has been rebuilt. Several churches were erected, a Catholic "Christ in Agony" Chapel in 1960, and a Jewish Memorial Temple and a Protestant Church of Atonement in 1960. The same year, the buildings in which the kitchen and storerooms were located, and the shower rooms where prisoners had been flogged and hanged, were converted into a museum open to the public between 9:00 A.M and 5:00 P.M.

In the museum, visitors first see commemorative posts symbolizing the many countries whose citizens were interned at Dachau, then the exhibits telling about the origin of the camp in 1933, the life of the prisoners, the importance of the camp to the SS as a training center, the persecution of the Jews, the medical experiments, the transports, the deaths, and the liberation of the camp.

Every thirty minutes, trains leave the Munich Hauptbahnhof for the town of Dachau, where they connect with Dachau ost buses to the camp grounds. In 1970, more than 350,000 visitors inspected the camp.

Dachau revisited? I have never gone back.

In 1968, the impressive International Monument located in front of the museum was unveiled, the culmination of many years of planning—the foundation stone for the Monument had been placed in 1956.

At the Hartheim Castle, where 3,166 prisoners of Dachau had been gassed between 1942 and 1944, a memorial plaque was installed.

"Remember us," it says.

The dead must be buried.

The cemetery of the town of Dachau served as a final resting place for the last 1,230 inmates to die in the camp hospitals. Between 1955 and 1958, the bodies of Italian prisoners were removed from the camp and reinterred in a Military Cemetery in Munich. The bodies of prisoners who had died on death marches were transferred from village churchyards to the empty graves in the camp, and covered with the good earth.

Only then was the last burial detail at Dachau dismissed.

REFERENCES AND NOTES

CHAPTER 1 Back to School

1. *Guide to Assembly Center Administration for Refugees and Displaced Persons*, Displaced Persons Branch, G-5 Division, SHAEF, July 1944.

2. My anxieties were without foundation. Many years later, I discovered that the Army had begun to make plans about DPs and refugees long before March 1945, shortly after the disastrous British experiences during the defeat of France and Belgium in 1940. The British believed that the Germans had deliberately terrorized civilians, causing them to flee in large numbers, block highways, and so prevent reinforcement of Allied armies. They also thought that the Germans used civilians to camouflage their own troop movements, so that the only way French and English soldiers could shoot at the Germans was by firing over the heads of the civilians—or through them. Allied tacticians wanted to be sure that this did not happen again. Furthermore, they hoped to use foreign workers in Germany as a disruptive force. This was attempted in 1944 when slave laborers were instructed by radio and air-dropped leaflets to flee from their factories and go into hiding. The effort was successful, and many of these DPS committed acts of sabotage helpful to the Allied cause.

The military analysts developed plans for two different situations. The first covered the possibility of a slow, difficult advance into Germany, during which only relatively few DPs would be encountered. The other, the plan that was used, took into account what might happen if Germany collapsed quickly, with great numbers of civilians being liberated. It is likely that if plan number one had been used, DP teams would never have been assembled.

The refugee movements in France and Belgium before 1945 reinforced the belief of the Allied command in the necessity for military control of civilians during the war—the DPs needed military protection for their own survival—and during the postliberation days in order to prevent vandalism and rioting, terror, chaos and revolution, all of which would constitute a danger to the DPs, refugees, and Allied troops.

Obviously the Army strategists did not share my apprehensions. I also learned that they were content to staff DP teams with company grade officers and enlisted men from combat units (Malcolm J. Proud-foot, *European Refugees: 1939-52* [Evanston, Ill.: Northwestern University Press, 1956], pp. 107-125).

They had confidence in the abilities of these men to repair houses and plumbing; maintain vehicles, public utilities, and all sorts of equipment; establish and operate facilities for mass housing and feeding; handle large-scale transportation; understand and administer curfews, detention centers, checkpoints, and roadblocks; guard restricted areas; maintain group discipline; exhibit an aggressive attitude toward procurement of supplies from the enemy; provide adequate and safe latrines; guarantee water purity; construct and manage group showers and dispensaries; supervise warehouses; and sympathize with people exposed to harsh treatment by the Germans.

'Such talents and attitudes, essential for the survival of large numbers of people under adverse conditions, were readily available in the infantrymen in the field, hence G-5 could afford to wait till the last minute to form its teams.

But in 1945, I did not realize that we possessed these endowments. Nobody told us we were special.

CHAPTER 2   The Dragon's Teeth

1. Years later I discovered the explanation. On November 9, 1918, a republic was established in Germany and World War I was considered lost (William L. Shirer, *The Rise and Fall of the Third Reich* [New York: Simon and Schuster, 1960], p. 29). This explained the discrepancy between the date we celebrated for our Armistice Day—Veteran's Day—and the German date. Furthermore, Germany had sustained a military defeat, her allies had collapsed, and mutiny and revolt were widespread; despite this, the German military caste could not accept the thought of being conquered by the force of arms and so began to disseminate the idea of the "stab in the back"—that the defeat resulted from treachery at home and on the battlefront, not from Allied military conquest. This explained the meaning of the slogan. Later, Hitler exploited the myth in his quest for power and then commemorated the date as the time of "the greatest villainy of the century" (Jacques Dela-rue, *The Gestapo* [New York: Wm. Morrow Co., Inc., 1964], p. xxii). I suppose that the object of the sloganeer of 1945 was to suggest that the same thing was happening in World War II, hoping that a future tyrant would appear to capitalize on a new mythology.

CHAPTER 5   The Journey

1. He is holding court in his underground bunker in Berlin, beneath the bombed-out Berlin Chancellery. Some of his staff are on hand: Goering, Goebbels, and Speer. They wish him well, but there is

no party. He congratulates a few members of the Hitler Youth organization for their bravery in combat—in the past, this had been the day for the ceremonious induction of 10-year-old boys into one of the young people's groups that would qualify them for membership in the Hitler Youth. Then, although Germany is almost split in two by the Allied armies, he predicts victory before retiring into his private apartment, a six-room suite that he shares with Eva Braun (Delarue, *The Gestapo*, p. 73; H. R. TREVOR-ROPER, *The Last Days of Hitler* [New York: Berkley Publishing Co., 1960], pp. 93–99; Roger MANVELL and Heinrich FRAENKEL, *Himmler* [New York: Paperback Library, Inc., 1968], p. 236; Albert SPEER, *Inside the Third Reich* [New York: Macmillan Co., 1970], p. 474).

CHAPTER 6 *The Indigenous Authority*

1. *Guide to Assembly Center Administration*, p. 29.

CHAPTER 9 *Population Changes*

1. Proudfoot, *European Refugees*, p. 175.

CHAPTER 10 *Dusty Days*

1. A diagnosis that was soon to be out of date. Epidemic jaundice had been known for centuries, but patients occasionally erupted with the same symptom pattern in the absence of an epidemic and were diagnosed as having the catarrhal form. More than the anticipated number of such cases began to appear in the troops, and so the Army Medical Corps started an investigation that led to the separation of catarrhal jaundice into two different, though similar, disorders—infectious hepatitis, spread by contaminated food and water, and homologous serum hepatitis, spread by infected blood and needles. Both are of viral origin (*Medical Department, United States Army, Preventive Medicine in World War II*, vol. 5, *Communicable Diseases*, Office of the Surgeon-General, Department of the Army, Washington, D.C., 1960, pp. 412, 432–33).
This was a significant contribution to medical science, and from this discovery arose a method of prevention, or modification, using a blood product, gamma globulin.

CHAPTER 11 *New Orders*

1. Helmut Krausnick, Hans Bucheim, Martin Broszat, and Hans-Adolf Jacobsen, *Anatomy of the SS State* (New York: Walker & Co., 1968), p. 531.

CHAPTER 13   Liberation

1. Slogans and aphorisms were popular with the Nazis. Over the entrance to the Buchenwald concentration camp were two signs reading "Right or Wrong—My Fatherland" and "To Each His Own" (John TOLAND, *The Last 100 Days* [New York: Bantam Books, Inc., 1966], p. 403).

CHAPTER 14   The Inspection

1. Several military units were involved in the battle (*History*, 157th Infantry [Rifle] Regiment, April 1945; *Extract*, 42d Infantry Division, April 1945; *Extract*, 222d Infantry Regiment, 42d Infantry Division, April 1945; *Dachau*, G-2, 7th Army, 1945, pp. 16–18, 28–30).

Early in the morning of April 29, an escapee from the camp reached an outpost of the 42d ("Rainbow") Infantry Division. He was frantic —the German guards had threatened to burn down the concentration camp and kill all the inmates, he said. If the prisoners were to be saved, immediate action was needed.

After a few more questions, the decision was made to attack. A fast-moving motorized assault force of the 222d Regiment led by Brigadier General Henning Linden set out on the rescue mission. Jeeps filled with infantrymen were followed by tanks, in the rear because roads were poor and bridges destroyed; they could not travel as rapidly as lightly armored vehicles.

Simultaneously, armored columns of the 157th Regiment of the 45th ("Thunderbird") Infantry Division were dispatched to approach the camp from the east. They sped through the highways and roared through the city of Dachau, meeting light opposition.

Units of both regiments converged on the camp, meeting in the railroad yard where the gruesome boxcars stood. From the putrid, bloody heaps of bodies, the advancing infantrymen pulled out a few still alive, then advanced cautiously to the camp. SS men began to march down from the watchtowers, their hands up. One of them held a gun in his hand; he was shot down. Small-arms sniper fire was encountered, and additional supporting troops were called for.

Many prisoners who resembled the bodies in the railroad yard had begun to run toward the front gate, calling to the Americans. Others, trying to escape from the camp, threw themselves at the barbed wire and were electrocuted. Some got through and turned on their former jailers, kicking, gouging, and beating them with their fists and with sticks and stones. The prisoners were given guns and joined the assault on the SS, shooting them or throwing them in the moat first and then shooting them. They discovered several SS men dressed as prisoners and killed them.

From one of the towers, an SS trooper who had not descended with the others fired into the crowd of prisoners in the compound. Enraged, the advancing soldiers poured through the outskirts of the camp, shot the guards, and machine-gunned the big dogs used by the SS sentries in their patrols.

The battle was over. About one hundred of the enemy surrendered. The excited inmates surrounded and embraced the soldiers, who found it necessary to shoot over their heads to regain control. They asked the inmates to turn in their arms, and to go back to the inner compound. The order was obeyed; the gate was closed.

This was the moment of liberation. Thousands of emaciated ragged prisoners had crowded up to the fence, the electrical circuits now out of commission. Those who couldn't run had walked, limped, crawled. They laughed and cried; they jumped up and down; they danced for joy; they sang native songs; they shouted "America! Americans! Hurrah for the United States!" Almost everyone waved—hands, hats, shirts, branches torn from trees, improvised flags. They pushed against the fence and waved; they climbed to the roofs of their low barracks and waved. A few seemed dazed, their faces vacant.

An astonishing sight. The soldiers began to throw everything they had to the prisoners: cigarettes, candy, chewing gum, food cartons, everything left in their packets, then their jackets and field coats; they wrote their addresses on little pieces of paper and gave them to the ecstatic inmates. Some of the GIs made the ultimate sacrifice. They reached into their musette bags, carefully removed well-wrapped bottles of bourbon and scotch whiskey intended for the celebration the day the war ended, passed them, without reservation, to the inmates.

A jeep appeared. One of its occupants, an Army chaplain, ran to the top of the nearest watchtower. His voice shook as he asked the prisoners to join him in the Lord's Prayer. The roaring of the crowd died. Everyone near the gate bowed their heads and, for a few minutes, prayed.

A few infantrymen toured the camp. Then for some of the soldiers it was time to go. A battalion of the 45th Division released two of its companies to guard the camp, to keep the unofficial quarantine so obviously needed. Two other battalions left for Munich, 18 kilometers away. They were to reach the outskirts that night and capture the city the next day. Some of the men of the 42d Division also headed toward Munich. Others drove south toward the Bavarian Alps.

See also Appendix A.

CHAPTER 15 *Priorities*

1. E. Z. Dimitman, *Horror of Dachau*, reprinted in *Report to America*, from a dispatch sent to the *Chicago Sun*, May 3, 1945.

2. Proudfoot, *European Refugees*, pp. 306, 314.

CHAPTER 16 The Famish'd People

1. *Nazi Conspiracy and Aggression*, vol. 5, United States Government Printing Office, Washington, D.C., 1946, pp. 953–54.

CHAPTER 17 Camp Fever

1. *Nazi Conspiracy and Aggression*, vol. 4, pp. 118–21.
2. Praezifix affidavit.
3. *Dachau*, G-2, 7th Army, 1945, pp. 5–15.
4. Proudfoot, *European Refugees*, p. 307; Krausnick et al., *Anatomy of the SS State*, p. 452.
5. Bettelheim, once an inmate at Dachau, wrote about the battle for survival which led to the emergence of a new class structure; even those dedicated to the concept of a classless society were quick to grasp the benefits of the new system. The ruling upper class consisted of the seniors and Capos. Prisoners selected by them for the coveted jobs essential to the operation of the camp constituted the middle class. To qualify for these positions, the prisoners designated themselves—or were designated by the seniors—as "doctors," "carpenters," "farm workers," or whatever was needed. These occupations had no relations to previous skills except by coincidence. The lower class consisted of the remainder of the internees, expendable because there were no jobs available for them. Perhaps these men had been skilled or unskilled workers in the past, or professors, or politicians, or professional men. Now they were of no importance. Despite their eminence, the members of the new middle class could not afford to be indolent. If their efforts were unsatisfactory, or one of their group resisted, others in their group suffered as well as their leaders, and this was not conducive to survival. Therefore, the second-line leaders, the Capos, were often more brutal toward the prisoners than the SS guards (Bruno BETTELHEIM, *The Informed Heart* [New York: Free Press of Glencoe, 1964], pp. 179–81).
6. *Dachau*, G-2, 7th Army, 1945, pp. 5–15.

CHAPTER 18 The IPC, the Visitors, and the "Pigs"

1. One was Melazarian, an Armenian, a former Russian Army officer, and at one time the camp senior. The other was Wernicke, the former German chief of the camp police. Both were severely beaten before they were turned over to the Americans (*Dachau*, G-2, 7th Army, 1945, pp. 5–15).
2. Nansen, the great Polar explorer, scientist, and statesman, was awarded the Nobel Peace Prize for his efforts in international relief work, which led to the international certificate for stateless people referred to as a "passport," and recognized as such by the League of Nations (*Encyclopaedia Britannica*, vol. 16 [Chicago: William Benton, Publisher, 1961], pp. 67–70).

3. Unfortunately, this is what eventually happened. The countries of the world were uncharitable and myopic in their attitudes, establishing conditions and quotas for immigration. The DPs who did not wish to return to their countries, and the Jews who did not wish to remain in Germany, could find very few nations to accept them. These people did not wish to go to the Communist areas; in fact, many fled from the eastern to the western zones of occupation. The inability of many Jews to migrate probably contributed to their determination to find a homeland. The country most generous in accepting DPs was the United States.

4. Bettelheim, *The Informed Heart*, pp. 132–34.

5. See Appendix A, p. 267.

CHAPTER 19 The Burial Detail

1. A. Philippe, personal communication.

CHAPTER 20 The Last Days of Dachau

1. The message was authentic. One of the captured Nazi documents introduced at the war crimes trial was a special order issued by the head of the Gestapo and Security (SD) Forces of the SS: "Should the situation develop suddenly in such a way that it is impossible to evacuate the prisoners . . . [they] are to be liquidated and their bodies disposed of as far as possible [burning, blowing up the buildings, etc.]. . . . The liberation of prisoners or Jews by the enemy . . . must be avoided under all circumstances. Nor must they fall into their hands alive" (Whitney R. HARRIS, *Tyranny on Trial* [Dallas: Southern Methodist University Press, 1958], p. 343).

2. G. Himsl, affidavit.

CHAPTER 22 Friction

1. "O'Leary" was an alias, used for security reasons by a Belgian doctor, Albert Guérisse. It was a common practice for those in the French Resistance movement to adopt cover names; they feared that if their true names became known to the Nazis, reprisals would be made against their families. Guérisse had actually been a lieutenant commander in the British Navy, which he joined after the military disaster at Dunkirk; through the Navy he became involved in the French underground in a plan to aid escaped Allied prisoners find their way from Paris to the Spanish border; a system of housing and guides was established, supervised by a British officer and French Resistance volunteers. After the British officer was captured, Guérisse took his place. With his resourcefulness and attention to detail, the "Pat" escape route became very effective, enabling some six hundred Allied flyers to thread their way through this secret path successfully.

Guérisse's organization grew. Its members became skilled at jailbreaks, bribing German guards, communicating with submarines and surface vessels for important supplies, and placing special "cargo" along the coast of the Mediterranean Sea. But no one lasted too long under the scrutiny of the Gestapo and the treachery of collaborators, and Guérisse was apprehended and sent to Dachau (Ruth JAKUSCH, personal communication; Blake EHRLICH, *Resistance: France 1940–1945* [New York: New American Library, Inc., 1966], p. 21).

2. Krausnick et al., *Anatomy of the SS State*, p. 425.

3. Rosenbloom was absent from this meeting of the IPC. Later, when he heard about the French claim, he became upset and announced at another IPC meeting that the food had been sent by the American Army. (This was my understanding.) Rosenbloom added that he was stating not an opinion but a fact that could be proved by documents. Then he asked for a committee of inmates to probe the matter. I was to hear more about this subject later.

4. International Prisoners' Committee, *Minutes*, May 8–10, 1945.

CHAPTER 24 Research

1. *Trials of War Criminals Before the Nuremberg Military Tribunals*, vol. 1, United States Government Printing Office, Washington, D.C., 1951, p. 12; *Dachau*, G-2, 7th Army, 1945, pp. 31–33, 61; *Nazi Conspiracy and Aggression*, vol. 5, p. 950.

2. Many other "research" projects were carried out at Dachau. A survival study for the Air Force attempted to assess the effects of drinking sea water and chemically treated sea water. Gypsies were chosen to be the subjects. Other test persons were forced to participate in experiments concerned with techniques of liver puncture, the value of homeopathic treatments, the efficacy of experimental blood coagulants, and the usefulness of new drugs for the treatment of typhus fever and tuberculosis. None of the tests performed at Dachau achieved anything of value. Many test persons died, some were driven insane, and others were permanently disabled or executed to prevent their telling tales (*Dachau*, G-2, 7th Army, 1945; Alexander MITSCHERLICH and Fred MIELKE, *Doctors of Infamy* [New York: Henry Schuman, 1949], pp. xxxii–xxxiii; Shirer, *Rise and Fall of the Third Reich*, pp. 984–91).

3. *Nazi Conspiracy and Aggression*, vol. 5, p. 952.

4. Manvell and Fraenkel, *Himmler*, pp. 113–18; Gerald REITLINGER, *The SS: Alibi of a Nation* (New York: Viking Press, 1968), pp. 259–61; Delarue, *The Gestapo*, pp. 280–84; Jakusch, personal communication.

5. Krausnick et al., *Anatomy of the SS State*, pp. 95–96, 99.

CHAPTER 25 The Warehouses

1. We knew that Pires and the other American Red Cross workers were indispensible, but I did not appreciate the extent of their contributions until many years later (*Field Report #2*, American Red Cross, Civilian War Relief, May 1945; see also Appendix A).

CHAPTER 26 *The Rabbits, the Plantage, the Chapel, and the Women*

1. Dietrich Bonhoeffer, *Letters and Papers from Prison* (New York: Macmillan Co., 1962), p. 57.
2. *Nazi Conspiracy and Aggression*, vol. 5, p. 1041; J. S. Conway, *The Nazi Persecution of the Churches, 1933–1945* (New York: Basic Books, Inc., 1968), pp. 298, 447–48; Gunter Lewy, *The Catholic Church and Nazi Germany* (New York: McGraw-Hill Book Co., 1965), p. 227; *Nazi Conspiracy and Aggression*, vol. 1, p. 286.
3. André Malraux, *Anti-Memoirs* (New York: Holt, Rinehart and Winston, 1968), p. 398.

CHAPTER 30 *Vacation*

1. American Red Cross, Release, July 28, 1945, by Ruth Y. White.
2. *Dachau*, G-2, 7th Army, 1945, pp. 64–66.
3. Ibid., pp. 35, 41, 45.
4. Krausnick et al., *Anatomy of the SS State*, p. 482.

Afterword

1. It was reputed to have belonged to the *Reichsfuehrer SS*. Eighteen convertible sedans were built by Mercedes-Benz for the Nazi leaders. Each weighed 7,500 pounds, measured 20 feet and 6 inches, and could achieve a speed of 180 miles per hour with its supercharger in operation; its engine was capable of 1,200 revolutions per minute. A toilet was supposed to have been installed in Hitler's car, but he deleted it from the plans. Workers at the automobile factory were amused by this and risked imprisonment by referring to the vehicle as "the Volkswagen." Ken W. Purdy, *The Kings of the Road* (New York: Bantam Books, 1963), pp. 66–68.

APPENDIX A *Loose Ends*

1. *Encyclopaedia Britannica*, vol. 19, pp. 61–62; Anthony T. Bouscaren, *International Migrations since 1945* (New York: Frederick A. Praeger, Publisher, 1963), pp. 12–13, 21.
2. Proudfoot, *European Refugees*, p. 213.
3. Burton C. Andrus, *I Was the Nuremberg Jailer* (New York: Coward-McCann, Inc., 1969), pp. 25–26, 39.
4. Edgar Kupfer, *The Last Years of Dachau*, part 2 (Chicago: University of Chicago, microfilm), pp. 541–42.
5. *Dachau*, G-2, 7th Army, 1945, pp. 29–30.
6. *XII-Report of a Representative of the International Committee*

of the Red Cross, on His Activities at Dachau from April 17 to May 2, 1945, pp. 149–52.

7. *New York Times*, May 22, 1945, p. 8.

8. *Report*. International Committee of the Red Cross, vol. 3, pp. 77–84; *Encyclopaedia Britannica*, vol. 19, pp. 19–21.

9. Ibid., p. 19.

10. *Medical Department, United States Army*, vol. 7, pp. 191–92, 246–48; *Encyclopaedia Britannica*, vol. 15, p. 916.

11. Mitscherlich and Mielke, *Doctors of Infamy*, pp. xxxi–xxxii.

12. George L. Mosse, *Nazi Culture* (New York: Universal Library, Grosset & Dunlap, Inc., 1968), p. 233.

13. *Nazi Conspiracy and Aggression*, vol. 2, p. 218.

14. Manvell and Fraenkel, *Himmler*, pp. 71–72.

15. Louis Lasagna, *The Doctors' Dilemmas* (New York: Harper and Bros., Publishers, 1962), pp. 197–99.

16. Martin Gross, *The Doctors* (New York: Dell Publishing Co., Inc., 1967), p. 364.

17. *Nazi Conspiracy and Aggression*, vol. 6, pp. 288–93.

18. William Manchester, *The Arms of Krupp* (Boston: Little, Brown and Co., 1964), p. 634.

19. *Nazi Conspiracy and Aggression*, vol. 6, pp. 288–93.

20. William G. Niederland, "Psychiatric Disorders among Persecution Victims," *Journal of Nervous and Mental Diseases* 139 (1964), pp. 458–74.

21. Gregory A. Kimble and Norman Germezy, *Principles of General Psychology*, 2d ed. (New York: Ronald Press Co., 1963), pp. 364, 370.

Appendix B   The Special Prisoners

1. Clarissa S. Davidson, *God's Man* (New York: Ives Washburn, Inc., 1959), pp. 94–95; Shirer, *Rise and Fall of the Third Reich*, pp. 238–39.

2. Dietmar Schmidt, *Pastor Niemoller* (Garden City, New York: Doubleday & Co., Inc., 1959), p. 125; Davidson, *God's Man*, pp. 97, 111, 126.

3. Kurt von Schuschnigg, *Austrian Requiem* (New York: G.P. Putnam's Sons, 1946), p. 283; Davidson, *God's Man*, pp. 97–98, 108; Shirer, *Rise and Fall of the Third Reich*, p. 655.

4. Hans Gisevius, *To the Bitter End* (Boston: Houghton Mifflin Co., 1947), p. 409; Schuschnigg, *Requiem*, pp. 282–83; Nerin E. Gun, *The Day of the Americans* (New York: Fleet Publishing Corp., 1966), pp. 147–53; Shirer, *Rise and Fall of the Third Reich*, pp. 644–46.

5. Schuschnigg, *Requiem*, pp. 280–81.

6. Ibid., pp. 263–84; Shirer, *Rise and Fall of the Third Reich*, pp. 352–53; Gun, *Day of the Americans*, pp. 158–67.

7. Ibid.

8. Charles de Gaulle, *War Memoirs: Unity* (New York: Simon and Schuster, 1959), p. 101.

9. Gun, *Day of the Americans*, pp. 111–12.

10. De Gaulle, *War Memoirs: The Call to Honor* (New York: Viking Press, 1955), pp. 50, 272; Gun, *Day of the Americans*, pp. 111–16; Ehrlich, *Resistance*, pp. 65–66, 122–23.

11. Schuschnigg, *Requiem*, pp. 285–89.

12. Gun, *Day of the Americans*, pp. 158–63.

13. Shirer, *Rise and Fall of the Third Reich*, p. 115.

14. *New York Times*. May 8, 1945, p. 12; Gun, *Day of the Americans*, pp. 157–58; Laura Fermi, *Mussolini* (Chicago: University of Chicago Press, 1961), p. 358; Louis P. Lochner, *The Goebbels Diaries* (Garden City, New York: Doubleday & Co., Inc., 1948), pp. 430, 480; Shirer, *Rise and Fall of the Third Reich*, pp. 352–53; Andrus, *Nuremburg Jailer*, p. 39.

15. *Newsweek*, August 30, 1971, p. 64.

Appendix C Postscript: 1972

1. A. de Cocatrix, personal communication.

2. Gun, *Day of the Americans*, p. 261.

3. *Newsweek*, October 19, 1970, p. 80; *New York Times*, October 10, 1970.

4. Malraux, *Anti-Memoirs*, pp. 405–6.

5. *Operations Report 1970*, Report No. 42, International Tracing Service, Arolsen, Germany.

6. A. de Cocatrix, personal communication.

7. Svetlana Alliluyeva, *Only One Year* (New York: Harper and Row, 1969), p. 370.

8. Ibid., pp. 201–2.

9. Kurt von Schuschnigg, personal communication.

10. Harry Pires, personal communication.